TIV SONG

Charles Keil

TIV SONG

THE UNIVERSITY OF CHICAGO PRESS

Chicago and London

The University of Chicago Press, Chicago 60637
The University of Chicago Press, Ltd., London

82 81 80 79   5 4 3 2 1

Library of Congress Cataloging in Publication Data
Keil, Charles.
  Tiv song.
  1. Songs, Tiv—History and criticism. 2.   Music—
Nigeria. 3. Ethnomusicology. I. Title.
ML3760.K38   784.7′6′963   78–3178
ISBN 0–226–42962–8

CHARLES KEIL, an anthropologist and
ethnomusicologist, is an associate professor in
the American Studies Program at the State
University of New York, Buffalo. He is the
author of *Urban Blues,* which is also published
by the University of Chicago Press.

in highest praise of the matriline
and patriline as represented by my parents,
Marcia Rudd and Carl Keil,
and with thanks to other elders who
have protected me along the way, especially
Lawrence W. Chisolm, Alan P. Merriam, and
David M. Schneider

Contents

List of Illustrations and Tables   ix

Acknowledgments   xi

Introduction   1

1   Tiv Music Terminology   25

2   Song in the Tiv Imagination   55

3   Tiv Composers   97

4   Technique and Style   159

5   Circles and Angles   181

Epilogue   259

Appendix A: Transcriptions   261

Appendix B: Questionnaire   281

Bibliography   285

Index of Tiv Terms   291

Subject Index   296

Illustrations and Tables

PLATES (following page 178)

1. A clay penis ready for tale-telling night
2. Everyday stances with elbows out
3. *Swange:* A dancer's salute to the mother drum
4. *Swange:* Orshio's *gida* leads the way
5. *Swange:* "Getting down" (*cagh*) with *genga* and *kwen*
6. Tuning up the mother drum
7. Mother and male drums played as a pair
8. Use of stone for changing pitch on mother drum
9. Anande Amende, also known as Ikpamkor London
10. Gari Kwaghbo sings of his sufferings (*ican*)
11. Kundam Agure with his assistant
12. Figure carved by Chiki (2 feet high)
13. *Atsuku* figure (7 inches high)
14. Common stool (8 inches high)
15. *Twel* figures
16. *Gbercul:* "Strike the forehead" dance
17. *Agatu:* Leader and circle counterpoint
18. *Agatu:* Witches must never touch
19. *Ingiogh:* Dancing their diseases
20. *Ingiogh:* Terror and paralysis
21. *Icough*
22. *Icough*

FIGURES

1. Social-structure model   15
2. Typical song pattern   177

x

3. Peace symbol   201
4. Yin-yang symbol   201
5. Tiv expressive grid   201
6. Kyagba's compound in MbaGor   208
7. Mounding of yam field   210
8. Land adjustment of a Hausa market   211
9. Pottery mat   213
10. Calabash decoration   217
11. Calabash decoration   217
12. Calabash decoration   218
13. Carved staffs   222
14. Body scarification   225
15. Body scarification   228
16. Body scarification   229
17. Women's belly scars   231
18. Woman's belly scar: Mudfish design   232
19. Drumming patterns   242

TABLES

1. Interval Percentages   263
2. Percentages of Each Interval in the Total Song Body   264
3. Percentages of Narrow, Medium, and Wide Intervals   264

Acknowledgments

The period of research in Nigeria that is reported here was supported by the Foreign Area Fellowship Program. The faculty and staff at the Institute of African Studies, University of Ibadan, were my gracious hosts during a difficult two years.

I hesitate to single out individuals in Tivland beyond those mentioned in the text, because there are so many, and their contributions have been so varied. But I must thank Joseph Werna for all his help and great patience during the two months in London when we first began to learn the Tiv language. Once we were in Tivland, Raymond Loho Ityo Ashibi quickly made himself indispensable as an interpreter and as a translator of texts and lyrics, and he continued that work with us during our stay in Ibadan. Richard Ordoon, Joseph Beba, Pius Ayila, Dennis Huma, Moses Jirgba Ahire, and Stephen Akoson performed a variety of data-collection and translation tasks with great competence and good humor, while Mough Adanyi kept us fed, clothed, and clean under trying circumstances.

I learned new things from different people every day of my stay in Tivland. It is a tribute to the Tiv people that one can visit any compound among thousands and not only be received cordially but have one's questions answered candidly. Ihundu and Ayila Nungwa, my elders and hosts at the compound where I lived, upheld these Tiv traditions of hospitality and honesty without exception. A visiting student can not ask for more.

Professor David Arnott, at the London School of Oriental and African Studies, introduced us systematically to the intricacies of Tiv grammar and intonation. If I still can not make my nouns and verbs agree, it is certainly not the fault of this most agreeable teacher.

I met Robert Tooner at the School of Oriental and African Studies. We traded notes and queries in the field, and he has been a trusted ethnomusicological correspondent ever since.

Fela Sowande took the trouble to provide Alan Merriam with the tape of eleven Tiv songs, which I transcribed in Professor Merriam's class fifteen years ago. Thanks to Professor Sowande for providing the songs, thanks to Professor Merriam for giving them to me and showing me how to analyze them, and thanks to Professor Sowande again for permitting my transcribed versions of them to appear here (Appendix A).

I am especially grateful to the late Professor Lloyd Fallers for specific criticisms in response to this manuscript, and to Professors David M. Schneider and Ella Zonis for their patience and wise counsel on the committee that read my work so long in progress. Professor Schneider's periodic impatience is also warmly appreciated. During our stay in the field, correspondence from Professors Schneider and Clifford Geertz picked up my spirits, and upon my return, letters to Professor Paul Bohannan with pleas for help always gained a swift and thorough response. Special thanks are due the Bohannans for permitting the use of so many figures from their various publications.

Richard Price's enthusiastic response to a first draft of the last chapter a few years ago was a timely boost, and his subsequent criticisms of the manuscript as a whole helped me to expand the introduction.

Robert P. Armstrong's book *The Affecting Presence* reached me at exactly the right moment, and our subsequent discussions have been most rewarding. '

Robert F. Thompson has been an alter ego in pursuit of African essences for so long that an adequate salute is impossible. The enthusiasms we exchanged so intensively in 1960 have had such lasting impact on me and suffuse this book in so many ways that I take our implicit collaboration for granted, and therefore the possible value to other scholars of making explicit the many thematic overlaps and interconnections between our studies was not obvious to me in the writing of these chapters. As more of Thompson's work is published (especially the results of his two-decade study of Latin music-dance and its roots), as more Thompson students (for example, John Chernoff) and kindred spirits (for example, John Storm Roberts and Robert Palmer) are heard from, and finally, as more Africans and Afro-Americans speak out from within the hundreds of black cultural experiences as yet unexplored in print, an exciting period of theoretical synthesis will be inevitable.

A number of technical problems in putting this book together were solved by very able people: Brian Clark clarified and condensed my song transcriptions; Diane Yawney retyped portions of the manuscript on a moment's notice; Dick Blau, Bill Staffeld, and Bonnie Fletcher were able to salvage useable prints from my variably exposed negatives; Tarwanger Jagusa, a Tiv student, suffered through a Buffalo winter and a chapter by chapter reading of the manuscript simultaneously and was able to make important additions to my understanding of Tiv terms, ideas, and customs while politely ignoring my excessive or irrelevant speculations; Sue Berger and Dolores Crapol put the figures and song lyrics into shape.

Throughout the writing of this book, my colleagues in the Program in American Studies, State University of New York at Buffalo—Lawrence Chisolm, Robert Dentan, Elizabeth Kennedy, Richard Blau, Michael Frisch, and Angeliki V. Keil especially—have all made innumerable contributions ranging from child care through the editorial to the theoretical.

When next in Tivland, I will commission a composer to sing the praises of all these friends, one who can curse our common enemies completely for good measure.

Introduction

This book is an introduction to future research on Tiv song and dance. It cannot be otherwise, for I have not done the fieldwork that an ethnographic treatment requires. This lack of fieldwork deserves some explanation.

When I arrived in Tiv Division, Benue State, Nigeria, with my wife and eight month old daughter in November 1965, we set up house in an old office building in the town of Makurdi, the town (population of about 10,000 then) that serves as the administrative center for Benue State. By January I had arranged to spend most of my time in a Tiv compound two miles outside Makurdi. For six months or so my efforts to learn Tiv progressed slowly but surely. I made no special efforts to contact composers and dance groups but employed a few elementary school graduates to collect names, locations, and a few facts about as many performers as possible so that, on that happy day when mastery of Tiv idioms would be complete, I would have a map of the general terrain and a select list of representative experts, and could plan a parsimonious course of study.

In retrospect it was a grave if understandable mistake to have taken my family along, at least during the initial months, for my language learning was slowed immeasurably by my returning home every few days and retreating into English. A less forgivable sin was to have assumed that one learns the language first and then does fieldwork. I wanted to work without interpreters, to surprise the prominent composers with my fluency, and so I bided my time in an easily accessible compound, observing everyday life, conversing as best I could, recording folktales when they were told, learning drum patterns from the more proficient young men of the family. But there was no composer in residence, no dance group in rehearsal, and I have yet to observe the day-to-day activities of a man who is rewarded for making new songs, and have yet to assess the complex problems that must be involved in forming a new dance ensemble.

Events quickly overtook my gradual approach to research. In January, just before I began to aportion my time between home and work, the first military coup in Nigeria took place, and in May the first pogroms against the Igbo occurred in the Northern Region. Though there were no attacks upon Igbo in Makurdi or Tivland at that time, the atmosphere was suddenly tense in a town shared by substantial numbers of Hausa, Igbo, Tiv, and many other peoples. By July, when the second coup by Northern troops occurred, I found myself increasingly preoccupied by Nigerian events rather than Tiv language learning. I began to spend more time assisting my wife's study of student and elementary-school–graduate TAT responses. Focused upon problems of ethnocentrism and projection, it seemed to matter more than studies of music and esthetics.

The second round of killings following the second coup was much worse than the first, but again bypassed Makurdi. During July and August a virulent hatred of the Igbo hung over the land like a harmattan cloud, and all eyes were on the battalion of troops stationed on the hill. The danger signals were obvious, but no one would acknowledge them; the same people that mouthed racist epithets would state in their next breath that a pogrom "can't happen here." On the latter point expatriates and the people were in absolute agreement. These were months of the deepest frustration I have ever known. People who are preparing themselves psychologically for a lynching, whether to enact it or to witness it, can not be persuaded to see it coming, much less prevent it. The only person who seemed to share our dread was a "madman," once a soldier in the Burma campaign in World War II and later an appointed chief for Ityoshin Division, who called himself Gypsy Fullstop or Lord Rawling Stone. He came to our house every few days with written statements, reflections of a crystalized mind gazing upon a universe about to implode.

In August we made plans to leave Makurdi in late September for Gboko, the town that serves as administrative center for Tiv Division. We would stay there through December, and I would work with the better known composers who visit Gboko periodically to disseminate their songs and praise the ambitious men who congregate at the center. Then we would move to Turan-Turan, a remote part of Tivland, in the hope of following the formation of a dance group and the day to day activities of one or two rurally situated composers.

In late September, however, units of the army that had participated in the July coup arrived in Makurdi, and within hours the killing and looting began. We spent two nightmare days trying to help Igbo and Efik acquaintances, storing possessions, negotiating with Northern administrators to permit their assistants and clerks to leave their posts and get on the last train to the Eastern Region. We watched the remains of the Igbo community board that overloaded train at gun point, and the urge to leave ourselves was irresistable. We left the next day in fear and disgust, counting the disemboweled and bloated corpses along the roadsides, crying from the smell and from the shame.

At some point in the near future I want to render those days vividly, dissect my continuing mortification into all its parts, decipher the Gypsy Fullstop word-salads for whatever they may reveal about the psychology of imperialism, tell the world why Biafra lost the war and what Africa and the world have lost in consequence. At the time, however, the experience was numbing and demoralizing.

We traveled to Ibadan where I spent eight months studying a Yoruba urban musical style called *juju* and trying to maintain my Tiv language proficiency with visits to the small Tiv community in the neighborhood where we were living. In May of 1967 I returned to Tivland for just six weeks of hasty work—taping songs, doing surveys at the secondary schools, interviewing a few composers—before Biafra declared its independence and my Foreign Area Fellowship time ran out.

The result of this particular pattern of study has been that I have a fair knowledge of the Tiv musical vocabulary (chapter 1), a few clues derived largely from folktales (chapter 2) as to the ways in which this terminology might be transposed into a conceptual framework, a quantity of superficial data on the lives of various composers (chapter 3), and a singular dearth of evidence concerning the actual creation and evaluation of song and dance in Tivland. Though I may know the vocabulary, I don't know who actually says what about a particular song in a specific social context. I have never watched a composer introduce a new song for the first time. A few times I visited compounds where dance groups were in the midst of rehearsals. I've never been to a Tiv funeral, an especially damning confession in the light of the Bohannan ethnographic works. In short, the most important data on song and dance in Tiv culture—the processual "how" of it—is extremely fragmentary where it exists at all. This lack of facts is particularly apparent in chapter 4, "Technique and Style," a discussion of errors made, oversights, and pressing questions as yet unanswered.

Without the solid fieldwork on which sound conclusions could be based, chapter 5 became a speculative reading of a variety of Tiv forms

4 in relation to Tiv song. It formulates a preliminary theory of Tiv expression that raises a few basic questions and manufactures still others that sympathetic and critical readers may wish to refine or reject.

This is an unfinished and uneven work not only in terms of the data gathered, but also in terms of establishing a scholarly context for the interpretation offered. These chapters were written over a period of seven years from 1966 through 1973. My anger in the opening pages of chapter 1 concerning the lack of attention to music terminologies in other cultures and the resultant ethnocentrism of much Western scholarship is an anger now more than twelve years old. I am still angry even though I am aware that much has probably been written in the past few years that challenges the universal applicability of concepts like "art" and "music." Similarly, the discussion of "taking-out-songs" in chapter 1 could be enhanced by discussing the work of Carpenter and others, but Carpenter's notions about Eskimo creation pop up in chapter 5, because that's when I discovered them, six years after chapter 1 was begun. There are numerous other gaps and inconsistencies, areas of ignorance, that scholars and specialists will notice. But I have left this somewhat unconventional, slightly dated, and essentially unrevised thesis the way it is in the hope that it will be read as something like an archeological record. As in many a "dig," the first layer of evidence is the most substantial; with each succeeding layer the evidence becomes skimpier, the digger more desperate, until (in chapter 4) he throws down his shovel and decides to make believe he knows all that the site can reveal (chapter 5).

This leap from ignorance and increasing frustration to synthesis and sweeping assertion is forced, I think, by a triple ambivalence or sense of contradiction that is built into the profession of anthropology: (1) I don't like the imperialist way of the world, the ever tightening exploitative grip of our greedy economy on the rest of humanity (Chinweizu 1975), but I enjoy the specialist's benefits from this system each day. (2) I don't like anthropology's role in this systematic oppression, but here I am making my second report on the poor to the powerful. (3) I don't like parading my inadequate fieldwork and even sloppier scholarship as a harbinger of better ways to understand human being, but I hope that it is. I hope there are ways of knowing and describing life that can facilitate social equality and cultural diversity rather than contribute to their destruction. Since it is this third source of ambivalence that probably bears most directly on why I am a slow writer, even slower to publish and slowest of all in taking a Ph.D. for this work, and since these same problems may be troubling others, this third contradiction and the leap it forces may be worth a closer look.

Put in negative and defensive terms, if imperialism is evil and anthropology serves it, then doing anthropology badly (thin data, weak scholarship) and boldly (following hunches, admitting errors) may be the best we can do. But this is to look at this book as though we are trapped within the anthropological profession. We are not trapped, unless we choose to be.

I believe we anthropologists can make ourselves human again by reversing and fusing the conventional priorities and processes. "Ethnography," "fieldwork," and "diary" are usually thought of as separate and in that descending order of importance. But if "diary" is the goal—the best possible record of what happens at the point of perception—and "fieldnotes" are incorporated into "diary" so that "ethnography" becomes the optional or residual category (what a field diary is now), then we are on our way not simply to rethinking and reinventing anthropology but to renouncing it. There is some theorizing on the shelf that points in this direction, but very little practice reported as yet. It is easier to talk about seeking truth intersubjectively and finding it in between cultures than it is to do it (Devereux 1967). "Confess more and profess less" has been good advice to intellectuals for at least two millennia, but few of us follow it. Still, the pressures on anthropologists (and others engaged in conventional or bourgeois social science) are going to increase and accelerate over the coming years as more people resist arrest and refuse to be packaged as "ethnographic presents" given from one anthropologist to the others in the endless kula ring of professional reciprocity. As the pressures increase, more of "them" may want to study "us," and a more interested anthropology will emerge—interested, both in the *inter* or exchange sense of intersubjective, intercultural, interpretive, or hermeneutic, and in the sense of partisan, critical, revolutionary.

Though fully aware of these pressures in a liberal sense for years, I only began to feel them and the full urgency of the question asked above—which methods can transform anthropology to defeat imperialism?—in the course of writing this thesis. So *Tiv Song* does not illustrate much in the way of confessional, intersubjective, or critical modes; it merely stumbles toward them, slowly. It takes time to unwrap the doubly falsified ethnographic present and pull out any sense of their

6   time and trajectory in relation to our own. It takes time to learn and unlearn the "analytically abstractable aspects" of reality taught in graduate school.

Let's go over the first four chapters again as archeological levels. They exemplify idealist scholarship. They proceed according to the standard social science models of static "action theory" (Parsons and Shils 1951), from culture to society to personality to lowly organism, models learned more directly from Alan Merriam's (1964) concepts-to-behavior-to-product version of reality and from Clifford Geertz' and David Schneider's visions of cultural systems floating symbolically above the events of everyday life. (You may have felt it as good old-fashioned sexual intercourse, but it was also, and perhaps more importantly, a symbol of diffuse enduring solidarity.) So the chapters, like the graduate study and fieldwork before them, try to move from concepts to behaviors to products, from cultural systems to social systems, from words (chap. 1) and fantasies (chap. 2) to lives (chap. 3) and actions (chap. 4), from determining thoughts and ideas to determined deeds, from roles defined to roles filled and acted out. Idealists should read this book as presented; materialists can finish this Introduction and go directly to the last chapter.

As noted above, the consequences of adopting an idealist or materialist perspective (consciously or unconsciously) can be very serious. I could have been observing the social relations of composers for months and watching dance groups rehearse week after week had I not been so confident that language learning and cultural expertise were somehow separable from daily life, prior to reality, and the one and only royal road to true understanding.

Even the most dedicated idealist infers roles from behaviors, and concepts are usually derived from words in a language spoken by people living together on the ground; but however empirical and inductive the fieldwork may be, the style of reporting it should be from the top down, culture shaping society shaping personality, and all of them bearing down on the organism, giving it ulcers, heartburn, high blood pressure, and piles (unless, of course, the organism belongs to a very positive thinker). On the other hand, it is just as much a parody to suggest that Marx's carbuncles generated *Das Kapital*. One can show the absurdity of idealist and materialist positions carried to their logical conclusions; one can meditate, mediate, and debate those positions or declare the whole issue increasingly sterile, but the why questions, the causality questions, refuse to go away. Why do Tiv make songs? And why do they come out sounding so very Tiv?

Over the past twenty years I have learned most of what I know about answering such questions from an "idealist" (or "culturological" or "superstructural" or "structural-functional") perspective. I continue to learn and to think within that perspective much of the time. I still believe that "styles" of expression have a life and logic of their own. But in the course of writing chapter 5 something snapped, and in the years since 1973 I find myself becoming more and more of a "materialist," a Marxist, someone who believes that cultural systems are organized, disorganized, and reorganized by socioeconomic forces. Asked to choose between superstructuralists and bassists, I am a bassist. As a bassist I know that harmony, a sense of tonic, makes the flights of melody possible and that rhythm energizes and actualizes them both. Melody attracts all the attention, is learned more easily, can be transcribed, translates well across cultures, but it is not the heart of the matter. Similarly, the cultural or superstructural mode lends itself to description, but is not as satisfying when it comes to explanation. What snapped into place during the writing of chapter 5 was a sense that in trying to describe how songs fit with "everything else" in a cultural pattern, I was also discovering that the "everything else" was as simple as roof structure and compound layout, as basic as everyday conversations and social interactions, as direct and urgent as the struggle for classless society.

The partial answers of chapter 5 seem to emerge then from a semi-conscious mixture of and conflict between top-down idealist description and bottom-up materialist explanation, a struggle in the book that reflects a struggle within me and within my society, within Tiv composers and within their society. This four-way struggle to build classless societies in America and to keep class society from emerging in Tivland has six aspects if we note the ways in which Western imperialism encourages the development of class society in Tivland and recognize also the small but tangible contribution Tiv resistance to this imposition can make to winning the next round of revolutions in the West. In all these struggles I feel a common cause with Tiv composers: to act as "a conscience for the lineage," to attack the "big men" who exploit us, to sing loudly and clearly of *ican*—pain, poverty, alienation, anxiety, in short, *oppression;* when it lands on us personally, we must identify its source and urge everyone to eliminate that source.

This may be a good point to introduce the Tiv as a people and the

8   literature about them, since in reading the chapters which follow, some knowledge of the geographic, linguistic, social, economic, and ideological context in which Tiv song makers work is certainly needed.

I wish I could assume a reader already familiar with the outstanding ethnographic work done in Tivland by Paul and Laura Bohannan in the period 1949–52. The brief sketch which follows is no substitute for a reading of Laura Bohannan's well-known fictional account of field-work in Tivland, *Return to Laughter* (1964), written under the pseudonym Elenore Smith Bowen, and of the concise report of Tiv institutions and beliefs to be found in the Bohannans' *The Tiv of Central Nigeria* (1953; 2d ed., 1969). The former gives an experiential account of customs and conflicts in Tivland and the feeling of everyday life in rich detail, including many instances of song, dance, and tale telling. As an account of how fieldwork is actually done, how an anthropologist is drawn into power struggles, forced to take sides, forced to retreat, forced to return to laughter after a smallpox epidemic has wrought havoc in the social life of the people, it is one of the few human and honest books to have escaped the disciplinary clutches of anthropology. We are extremely fortunate that this revelation happens to have been inspired by the Tiv. *The Tiv of Central Nigeria* is just one-hundred pages long, including the comprehensive bibliography of the second edition, and every page represents a subtle condensation of complex ethnographic facts. The chapter headings remain tied to the Western conceptual system of how life should be organized—"Nomenclature and Demography," "Language," "History and Traditions of Origin," "Social Organization and Political Structure," "Main Features of Economy," and so on—but under each heading, the Bohannans take pains to distinguish the various ways in which Tiv conceptions and actions differ from our own, as well as the ways in which Tiv theory and Tiv practice are or are not consistent in general, and in specific instances, through time and from place to place. Cultural variations as well as observed discrepancies between society and culture are not sacrificed to the goals of factual summary and handy generalization.

The entire series of books, monographs, articles, and sourcebooks published by the Bohannans over the past twenty years—notably *Tiv Farm and Settlement* (1952), *Justice and Judgement among the Tiv* (1957), *Tiv Economy* (1968), the seven sourcebooks on life cycle, technology, religion, and so forth, in the Human Relations Area Files —is exceptional both in quantity and in uniformly high quality. Not only did two gifted anthropologists spend twice as much time in the field (four times the usual amount of study), but they did it in three separate trips, interspersed with valuable interludes for reflection, over a four year period. There is also no way to measure or apply a multiple of value to the process wherein two very different intellects make and compare perceptions and analyses and are able to put so much of what they learned into print.

Finally, the Bohannans and all subsequent students of Tiv society are much indebted to R. C. Abraham's excellent dictionary (1940a), his detailed, if colonially biased, ethnography, *The Tiv People* (1940b), and most important, *Akiga's Story: The Tiv Tribe as Seen by One of Its Members* translated, annotated, and edited by Rupert East (1939; 2d ed., 1965). Akiga was the very first Tiv to have worked for the Europeans. When he was 13 his father, Sai, a prominent elder, sent his favorite son, blind in one eye, with a deformed foot, and deserted by his mother, to replace the servants who had run away from the first missionary. (Akiga had been his father's "assistant" for some years.) The year was 1911 and most of Tivland was far from being under British control. Akiga was probably the first Tiv to write in his own language and perhaps the first to perceive that European penetration and control of Tivland would create great and irreversible changes in Tiv life. It was out of this awareness that he wrote hundreds of pages describing Tiv customs, skills, beliefs, only a portion of which appear in East's four-hundred page translation. To my knowledge, no African has written so much and so well about his own people in his own language during the first generation of imperialist impact.

In short, the Tiv shelf in our libraries is unique in at least three aspects: we have an outsider's candid version of Tiv reality, *Return to Laughter;* an insider's equally forthright version of Tiv traditions and their transformation under British colonial rule, *Akiga's Story;* and an extraordinary range of well-organized ethnographic reporting in between.[1]

Why does all this literature about the Tiv exist? Why all this interest from missionaries, administrators, ethnographers, and even ethnomusicologists? Because the Tiv people are especially aggressive and creative,

---

1. In addition to these books about the Tiv, I would like to recommend three more that define, for me at least, a broader context within which *Tiv Song* can best be read: Stanley Diamond, *In Search of the Primitive: A Critique of Civilization* (New Brunswick, N.J.: Transaction Books, 1974), Gary Snyder, *Earth House Hold* (New York: New Directions, 1969), and Philip Slater, *Earthwalk* (New York: Doubleday, 1974).

because they are also a typical "tribe without rulers" and because on both counts they have presented a long series of special and typical problems to their would be manipulators and exploiters as well as to themselves.

The Tiv have gained some reputation in the wider world both as warriors and as song-and-dance men. Tiv soldiers fought well for the British in Burma during World War II, and though they are less than 2 percent of the Nigerian population today, a quarter to a third of the gun-carrying soldiers in the Nigerian army are Tiv. Tiv dance groups have won top prizes at African arts festivals, and if anyone were to organize the diverse song-and-dance resources in Tivland, the variety and quality of the Tiv troupe would put the multicultural "ballets" of most African nation-states in the shade. Killing capacities on the one hand, a great song-and-dance tradition on the other, and these hands belong to the same body politic.

I have chosen to describe this body politic as classless and competitively egalitarian despite the facts that men clearly have more power and influence than women, and some men clearly have more power and influence than other men, because both social facts contain a strong element of paradox or contradiction and because both of these power differentials are foci of Tiv concern and action aimed at restoring equality. In traditional Tiv theory, men ought to control women's reproduction and much of their agricultural production too, but in practice women shape their own destinies, increasingly so as Western influence weakens the old marital ties and production norms. Conversely, in traditional Tiv theory all men are created equal and should remain so, but in practice some rise above their brothers, and this tendency has also been exacerbated by Western imperialism. The British policy of indirect rule encouraged elders and men of influence and prestige to assume tighter control of Tiv affairs, but policies modifying Tiv marriage customs and opening schools encouraged young women and men to actions independent of kinship and custom. "Big men" were given more power and, simultaneously, less ability to exercise it. Basic Tiv contradictions have been intensified and are not yet resolved. While not as classless as most hunter-gatherers and many settled "cooperative egalitarian" peoples, such as the Semai (Dentan 1968) and the Waunan (Kennedy 1972), in any division of the world's peoples into class and classless categories, the Tiv belong with the latter.

The Tiv number approximately one million people, and during past centuries this growing population has moved down from the mountainous Nigeria-Cameroons border area northward into the sparsely forested savannah lands on either side of the Benue River. Tiv speak a Bantu language, and it is from the Nigeria-Cameroons area that other Bantu-speakers expanded south throughout the rest of Africa in the more distant past. These geographic and linguistic facts are very important for the interpretation they suggest of Bantu history and social dynamics. Put simply, the Tiv went down one side of the mountain and remained classless and egalitarian, while the Bantu who went down the other side of the mountain and expanded over two millennia to fill large portions of central, southern, and eastern Africa, developed a variety of hierarchical social structures, including kingdoms, Bantu bureaucracies (Fallers 1956), and militaristic conquest states, for example, Shaka's nascent Zulu empire of the early nineteenth century. From a broad southern perspective, from the other side of the mountain as it were, one might infer that the Tiv have been poised on the brink of class society for many centuries.

Traditionally, all Tiv have been subsistence farmers; recently, cash crops and education for jobs have been claiming increasing energy. Yams, bullrush millet, guinea corn, and cassava are the staple food crops, but almost all men grow some combination of beniseed (sesame), soy beans, ground nuts, rice, or cotton for cash to pay taxes and bride prices and to buy imported goods like cloth and hardware. Women control the produce from their kitchen gardens and from specified plots of cropland, giving them an important measure of economic and personal autonomy. Men often form reciprocal teams to clear and plant each other's basic crops and may be called upon by the compound head to work his fields periodically.

The Bohannans describe traditional Tiv economy as follows:

Three spheres of exchange could be recognized in the early 1950's. With the introduction of money and European goods, an incipient fourth sphere was created, but the general-purpose money contained within it is contradictory to the system and is destroying it.

The first sphere is that marked by the commodities Tiv call *yiagh*. Allocation within this sphere is carried out either through gift-giving or by marketing and ultimately by trade. The commodities are all locally produced foodstuffs . . . craft products . . . some tools . . . raw materials. . . . Within this sphere those goods that are exchanged go through a free market, and the bargain is the dominant value.

The second sphere of exchange is a matter of prestige (*shagba*) and is in no way associated with the markets. Whenever one of its component items enters a market situation, special explanation is required. The goods within this sphere include[d] slaves, cattle, horses, ritual offices purchased from the Jukun, that type of large white cloth known as *tugudu,* medicines and magic, and brass rods.

The third sphere is the supreme and unique sphere of exchangeable values. It contains a single item: rights in human beings other than slaves, especially dependent women and children. Even twenty-five years after official abolition of exchange marriage, it was the category of exchange in which Tiv were emotionally most entangled. Its values are expressed in terms of kinship and marriage. [Paul and Laura Bohannan, 1968, pp. 229, 231]

The abolition of exchange marriage in 1927 at one end of the continuum and the introduction of taxes and money at the other end during the same period collapsed the three spheres of exchange. The multicentric economy was largely a memory by the 1960s, but for many Tiv a very vivid one.

Tiv live in small (20 to 30 people on the average) autonomous patrilocal and patrilineal compounds scattered over the land. Each compound is occupied by an *or ya* or "person of the compound," his brothers and sons, with some of their wives and children, plus any daughters of the compound or their children who have returned home, and often a few "guests" or "strangers" who have chosen to live there.

This is a concise way to describe a Tiv compound, but it disguises a maze of kinship complexities. It is easy for Westerners to ignore or forget that classless societies are always, so far at least, intensely familial societies, simple in form or basic structure perhaps, but subtle and flexible in their actual functioning. The term *ityɔ,* roughly translatable as "agnates," can refer to one person or thousands on the father's side of the family. "The meaning of *ityɔ* is always personal, that is, one must always speak of someone's *ityɔ.* 'My *ityɔ*' can mean: my agnatic lineage segment as opposed to my mother's agnatic lineage (*igba*), my jural place in the lineage system; the vantage point from which I see the lineage system when I am concerned with my citizenship rights" to land for farming, to moral, financial and diplomatic assistance in obtaining a wife, to allies and support in any social conflict involving other lineages (Laura and Paul Bohannan 1969, p. 23). Though Tiv are essentially patrilineal and patrilocal in organization, patriarchal tendencies are held in check by an array of lineages reckoned on maternal lines.

In one of its usages, *ityɔ* is complementary to *igba*; the two words serve to define each other. Thus a rough and preliminary definition of *igba* is the *ityɔ* of a female ascendant . . . there are five lineages to which any one man may refer as *igba*: (1) the *ityɔ* of his mother (*igba ngɔ* or just *igba*); (2) the *ityɔ* of his father's mother (*igba ter*); (3) the *ityɔ* of his father's father's mother (*igba ter u tamen*); (4) ·the *ityɔ* of his mother's mother (*igba ngɔ u tamen* . . .); (5) the *ityɔ* of the mother's secondary marriage guardian (*tien, or sughel*) through three generations (*igba tien*)—the strength of this tie varies greatly both regionally and individually. I may address any member of any of these lineages as *igba* and any one of them may call me *igba* (or *wan igba*). [Laura and Paul Bohannan 1969, p. 24]

This range of *ityɔ* and *igba* lineage segments (ideally, you marry someone from a distant "clan" to broaden this range and to insure a minimum of *ityɔ* overlap with any of your *igba*) gives Tiv individuals a wide choice of living arrangements, and they exercise it. Lateral social mobility within Tivland is astounding to an outsider. A son unhappy with his position or prospects or afraid of an uncle, leaves his father's compound for a more hospitable *igba* lineage. A daughter unhappy with her marriage returns home, with a few children, but may go back to her husband again a few weeks, months, or years later when the dispute is resolved. A compound head quarrels with his younger brother, who leaves, taking half or a portion of the compound's population with him to form a new settlement.

It is difficult to estimate the frequency of departures and arrivals in an average compound, but during the eight months or so that I lived in a compound, two daughters returned home with children; one left again, but not to return to her husband; the male child of a daughter came to live with his grandfather; the oldest son of the compound head went off gambling or hunting for weeks at a time; two different older male "guests" came and stayed a few weeks; one elder took a young wife, but she left after a month or so. I never did find out precisely who the previous occupant of the hut I lived in was, but a return was not expected.

In short, the description of a compound as composed of an *or ya,* his brothers and sons with their wives and children, is good enough for the ethnographic present, but falsifies the ethnographic continuous.

The compound itself consists of a circle of round buildings for living and cooking; in large compounds there is also an inner circle of a few reception huts and an outer circle of storage buildings and kitchen

14   gardens surrounded by farmland. The immediate, tangible, architecturally defined grounds for being in Tivland are concentric circular; a young infant focuses his eyes upon a conical roof of layered circles, later looks out the door into a circular compound of round houses, listens to 360 degrees of social life, and takes his first steps and utters his first words within these spheres of influence.[2]

Even though fields and lineage areas are laid out in straight lines, Tiv conceptualize their wider social space as an ever widening series of concentric circles, each circle representing a broader and more tenuous lineage and clan affiliation, the last circle representing the very extended family of Tiv himself. These concentric circles are spoken of by Tiv in terms of *tar, ipaven,* and *nongo.*

> The *tar* refers to territorial segments with political relevance and a fixed relative position to each other in space; it also refers to the land in a sense of political activity.
>
> The segment (*ipaven*) refers to a lineage segment in a genealogical system giving the order of segmentation and determining the social distance between *utar.*
>
> *Nongo* impersonally refers to the span of any lineage and to the lineage group, or living members of any lineage segment. [Laura and Paul Bohannan 1969, p. 25]

What I have suggested may be the logogram or "logo," an "expressive grid" for Tiv culture in chapter 5 (fig. 5) might also serve as a reasonably accurate visual model for Tiv social structure.

In the idiom of socially defined land, *tar,* a Tiv places himself in the center of the circles and traces his affiliation outward circle by circle (see fig. 1).

Nongo literally means "line." "The commonest *nongo* identification terms are the names of leaders, men of influence, prominent elders" (Bohannan, Laura and Paul, 1969, p. 23), so it may be that a Tiv at the circumference uses a prominent living elder as a coordinate to establish a line between himself and the ultimate ancestor, Tiv, at the center.

Ipaven, from the verb to divide or segment, might be thought of as "the slices of the pie," though it is not immediately clear how the slices

---

2. "In psychiatric terms, architecture is a frozen expression of interpersonal relations; in social terms, it is a symbol of the institution; and in cultural terms, it is a long-duration communication" (Hall 1973).

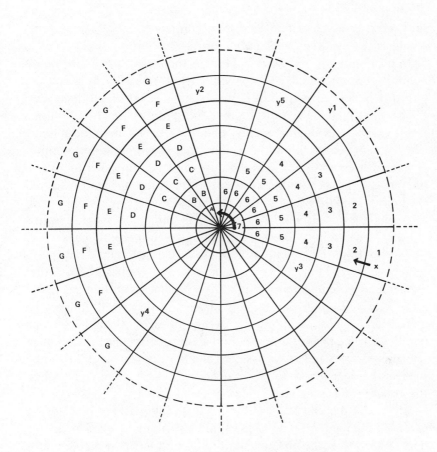

Fig. 1. Social-structure model

should be "read" on the diagram, inward from the contemporary individual on the circumference, *1*, in his small *ipaven ken iyou* (literally,
"segment in house"), back through 7 to Tiv the ancestor in the center,
or the other way around from *A,* the individual in his smallest lineage
segment, to *G,* his broadest clan affiliation.

Similarly, if we place an individual in his *ityɔ* at a square on the circumference, *x,* then his various *igba, y's,* would be scattered around in
other boxes of various depth and distance. Or *x* could be a center segment, with *y's* dispersed accordingly. The inward/outward problem
with the diagram is both an insider/outsider problem and a synchronic/
diachronic one; from a historical and outside perspective, Tiv the ancestor belongs at the center and his children on the periphery, but the
contemporary perspective of any individual Tiv is self-centered, with

16   *utar* and *ipaven* calculations and claims on land (via the *ityɔ*) or sustenance (via the *igba*) radiating outward.

In relation to this diagram, the Tiv see themselves expanding on all points of the circumference. "Tiv subdivide internally in a cell-like growth which necessarily pushes Tiv boundaries out in all directions" (Bohannan, Paul and Laura, 1968, p. 8). The Bohannans offer three reasons why individuals, families, and entire small lineages migrate, (1) the same complex mix of motives that drove nineteenth-century Americans westward; (2) land shortage; and (3), the desire to "escape the range of political influence of a man or group of men considered tyrannical"; and they suggest that these reasons combine variously with three modes of migration, (1) "steamroller" migration, when a related cluster of land-hungry lineages expand together at the circumference; (2) "leap frog" migration, usually associated with an escape-from-tyranny motive, in which a segment moves through and past other segments to settle next to similar "refugee" segments at the border; and (3), "lone-wolf" migration by individuals and very small groups who go to live as "guests" with other unrelated lineages (Bohannan, Laura and Paul, 1969, p. 54). If one adds to all this movement the aforementioned departures and arrivals of sons and daughters with children and the fact that Western pressures have been accelerating all these trends, the visual model seems static indeed.

All of this movement "solves" very basic internal Tiv problems; it constantly limits the power of potential patriarchs by evasion and reduces by invasion the pressures toward class society and property relations. "Land is not property among the Tiv. It cannot be sold—that would be tantamount to selling a genealogical position. It cannot be rented, for one's right to it depends on kinship status and residence." (Bohannan, Paul and Laura, 1968, p. 8) But this propertyless society is purchased at the expense of its neighbors, especially to the north, east, and west, where the old colonial boundaries are less firm than in the south, and Tiv lineages steadily encroach upon a variety of peoples. The statement "Civilization originates in conquest abroad and repression at home" (Diamond 1974, p. 1) might be inverted to fit the Tiv case: civilization is postponed by fleeing oppression at home and encroaching abroad.

How does Tiv culture reflect this society? How do myth and religion charter this social organization? What values guide action? Although the Tiv have been carefully studied by administrators, missionaries, and anthropologists, answers to these questions are not as clear and unequivocal as one would like. It is only a slight exaggeration to say that, as we know these terms or cultural categories, the Tiv have no pan-Tiv polity, no laws, no myths, no religion, no art.

Politically, the Tiv have been described as an egalitarian or acephalous society, a "tribe without rulers." To the extent that political power exists it is polycentric: the influence of elders and others rises and falls, expands or contracts, depending upon how wisely they exercise it; a prominent man today may be ostracized tomorrow; the older, wiser, and more powerful a person becomes, the more likely he is to be accused or attacked in time of crisis. But can we speak of politics when there is no *polis,* no city, no center?

Legally, every case in Tivland is assumed to be unique, and "the law" is whatever an assembly of those concerned can agree upon in a particular instance. The only precedents which apply are those which have involved the families of the litigants. Any miscarriage of justice perceived in retrospect will lead to another case or be taken into consideration when the next case involving the same lineages emerges.

Aside from the story about Tiv and his family coming down from the mountain, some subsequent migration legends, and the metaphor of world as stooping man (never given narrative form to my knowledge), the Tiv have no myths. There are numerous tales, often acted out with much energy and great relevance to everyday life, but they usually do not address the cosmological questions.

"Art," "beauty," "symbol," "esthetics," "creation," "music" are not concepts that translate easily into Tiv. A rich vocabulary of technical perfection is applied to songs, dances, and other forms of expression; these terms subtly subdivide the categories "good" and "bad." Though they are not considered artists by the Tiv, there are more expert songsters and dancers per capita in Tivland than in any society known to me.[3] In more consistently classless and cooperative-egalitarian societies,

3. Greater Buffalo, N.Y., has roughly the same population as Tivland, but we have only four or five struggling dance troupes (most of them in the black community) compared to the hundreds of dance organizations in Tivland. There may be a composer of songs in Buffalo who has achieved an original and easily recognized style, but I don't know of one, and I keep my ears open. Again, Tivland boasts dozens of original song stylists. Are Tiv really a hundred times more musical than Americans? Probably the multiple is only ten or twenty, given a closer comparison. But were it not for Buffalo's Afro-American churches, Polish-American polka dances, and some big events in the small Puerto Rican and Serbian communities, there wouldn't be anything worth comparing at all. See John Blacking, *How Musical Is Man?* (Seattle: University of Washington Press, 1973), for further discussion of these issues.

everyone is a "music expert" or no one is. But again, it is perhaps this very position of the Tiv on the brink of class society that encourages the proliferation of part-time specialists—every compound needs a few good drummers, and every large compound should have a dance group, if they are to stay in the thick of the competition among elders, compounds, and lineages. An esthetic may be implicit in all this activity; it is not explicit.

Religion is the most difficult category of all. Missionaries sometimes describe the Tiv as animists; certainly the Tiv live "in the midst of the personified impersonal," for on this stooping man of a world, every sizeable tree, every water hole, and some of the spaces in between, including the cooking hearth, may be inhabited by many different kinds of sprites or *adzov* who must be propitiated if their domains and resources are to be utilized. "Fetishists" is another outsider's label often applied to the Tiv for there are a bewildering variety of major and minor rituals (*akombo*) performed in Tivland which rise and fall in popularity according to their effectiveness in "repairing" whatever has gone wrong with individuals, families, lineages, and lands. Some evidence exists to support the attribution of ancestor worship. The bible has been translated into Tiv for the 10–15 percent of the population who are nominal Christians. But when all has been said and done—the sprites propitiated, the appropriate *akombo* repairing-rites performed, the dead libationed, visits made to mission church and hospital perhaps—and a disease still persists or a death occurs or the crops fail, then the problem is one of *tsav*.

The people of *tsav*, the *mbatsav*, are alledged to leave their sleeping bodies for nighttime cabals, during which they exhume corpses, revive them, and then slaughter, divide, and consume them, in a never-ending round of acquiring and paying flesh debts to each other. Some deaths are necessary: a parent expects to lose one child sooner or later, for the *mbatsav* in their benign aspect must sacrifice to repair the land and increase general fertility. Some deaths are expected: an elder cannot last forever. But the *mbatsav* are known to be prone to greed; they are all too likely to desire an increase in their powers at the expense of others. *Tsav* grows with age, and all elders, all survivors, possess it. Its potency, and your protection, is greatest in the *ityɔ* or near patriline. But your father, and especially his elder brothers, may sacrifice you at any time, either actively or by refusing to protect you from the *tsav* of others. The *tsav* of your mother's people (*igba*) can only protect you, and it is to them that you flee if you feel that your "fathers" are out to get you. The potency of *tsav* decreases with distance from the patrilineal homeland, hence the propensity of Tiv, individually or in family groups, to split from a troubled compound and move to the farthest circumference of Tivland; hence also the fine record of Tiv soldiers in faraway Burma.

Tsav is imaginary, "the Tiv myth," but no less real for all that. As Akiga puts it in the first sentences of his long chapter on *tsav* (1965, pp. 235–95): "That which is not in Tiv as *tsav*, is not. There is no reality in it whatever, nor in any of the ideas associated with it; yet it is of all things the one in which every Tiv places the most implicit belief." No corpses are ever exhumed at night for ghoulish feasts, but virtually all Tiv believe that such events may be occurring anywhere in Tivland on any night when the owls are out and the moon is not bright.

Call it vile superstition if you will, but as a belief system it is a tighter, more realistic, perhaps even a more humanistic version of our own Christian Science, Christian Science taken here as both an appropriate label for the prevailing American ideology and the name of the church I went to as a child. "Divine Mind," the power of positive thinking, enables us to gloss over error, sin, war, disease, old age, and death in America; the *Tsav* Heart may manifest evil at any moment in Tivland. Tiv are always ready to unmask god the father; we are not. Tiv ostracize or punish a greedy elder swiftly and efficiently; it took us a long time to retire LBJ, longer to impeach our mad Quaker captain, even longer to put his Christian Scientist assistants—Haldeman and Erlichman—in prison. Having viewed one of the most popular American films of all time, we come away from three hours of bloody manslaughter deeply satisfied, despite ourselves, with the young godfather's growing ability to survive. We identify with the survivor; Tiv do not.[4] Tiv try not to blame the victim; we search for new victims to blame.

I do not want to romanticize the Tiv. If we attempt to avoid the problems of evil and "the Survivor" (Canetti 1963), the Tiv are sometimes obsessed by them. When an epidemic or famine strikes—extreme conditions we no longer face—life can become a war of all against all in

4. Portions of the foregoing and following description were first presented in a symposium, "The Nature of Cultural Space," at an American Studies Association meeting. In preparation for this event, Richard Blau and I spent many long hours together trying to connect our respective analyses of "personal and cultural space" in the novels of Herman Melville and the dances of the Tiv, but in keeping with our analysis of the American "imperial self," I'll simply claim any winning ideas expressed here as my own!

20 Tivland. If body and body politic are mere figures of speech here, they are taken too literally there, where every diseased body becomes a political battleground.

> It had to be one of these two, Amara's husband had cleared himself. Lam was too weak a character to be seriously suspected. Yabo or Yilabo, which? We were utterly absorbed in the duel between these two. Only Amara lay unconscious of the fight for her life.
>
> Amara could yet live, if they could force a confession from the witch. Each knew himself innocent. Each therefore knew the other guilty. I knew them both innocent. I watched while each strove to break the other, to force his confession, to save Amara. I knew they could not. Their battle was the more terrible to me because it was in vain and fought against shadows. [Bohannan, Laura, 1964, p. 193]

Having described, in brief, the broader geographical, social, and ideological grounds for being Tiv, let us return to the question of the ways in which these values shape Tiv cultural space and guide behavior within it.

Under normal circumstances the *tsav* ideology gives Tiv a great inner confidence. On good terms with the patriline, every Tiv, in theory at least, stands to live in good health forever. Everyday life is full of chatter and bustle; Tiv are cheerful, active, exceptionally candid, conveying the strong impression that they have nothing to hide and little to fear. Some Tiv are quiet, more circumspect about treading on the toes of others, much less likely to shout out or elbow in; but in general, activities are characterized by a more or less genial struggle for the center of the concentric circles. Five people begin to offer testimony in court at once, but only one will continue to speak. Before the first story is quite finished, three tale-tellers jump to the center, but two will quickly give up or be shouted down.

The force of personality is culturally prized up to a point; Tiv delight in spotting hubris in a child: "look, he has *tsav* already!" When Tiv speak in the idiom of personality—*a ta urum,* "he shoots brightness"; *a wa ime,* "he puts us in the dark"; *a wanger yum,* "she certainly glows"—one can sense pride in and resentment of the person so described and the space they are able to appropriate. But Tiv space can become finite, inner and outer space identical, under adverse circumstances. Between confident core and outer cheerfulness lies a thin paranoid layer that can expand infinitely as an individual contracts, lies down, refuses to eat, waits for the death of the bewitched.

It is the underlying argument of the chapters which follow that song, tale telling, and especially the dance represent the most positive, life-affirming forces and values in Tivland, a powerful collective antidote to the negative or individualistic aspect of *tsav*. Tiv composers and their helpers offer a constant corrective for whatever is going wrong and loud praises for those who do right. The tales, as told and enacted, not only return the Tiv to laughter but create a parallel world in which the powerful, the "big men," are always undone and "the people" are made wiser in the undoing. The circles of men's and women's dances, in which virtually all young people take part, are the best organized and most enjoyable events in Tiv life. The unifying pulse of the drummers at the center and the encircling audience define a middle ground in which individual actions compliment each other perfectly. Here at last every individual angle can find its proper place within the circle. The dance perfectly summarizes the Tiv pattern, the best grounds for being in Tivland. Yet the intense focus on song, tales, and dance is a reciprocal function of the worst forces in Tiv life, a middle ground that can suspend, only temporarily, the middle layer of paranoia that always threatens to fill Tiv space.

When the songs and tales and dances are over—and the Tiv too wish that they would never end—the struggles for the center and the expansions at the circumference continue. In crisis, the Tiv turn on their elders; uneasy at home and land-hungry, they appropriate the space of their neighbors; they will kill with some pride and for pay outside their own circle.

One can suppose that more planned parenthood, less land hunger, lowered infant mortality, an end to famines and epidemics, and the dissolution of empires and nation states, would allow the Tiv to become the classless, just, and cooperative community of artists that we in the West would call Utopia. But this is not the world the Tiv live in, nor do we.

On a smaller scale, with greater clarity, grounded Tiv being is quite similar, though not nearly so deadly, as the ungrounded American "higher standard of living." We both play the competitive zero-sum game—my success is your failure; A's loss is B's gain; our pleasure the world's pain. Broadly speaking, Tiv selves are subject to the same explosions and implosions, aggressions and suicides, as their American counterparts, with the basic difference that in Tivland these processes are acknowledged, expressed in the idiom of *tsav* and known to be evil, while in America the language is one of "free enterprise," "positive thinking," "success," and climbing to the top over a pile of corpses is thought to be natural and good. Tiv play the zero-sum game to keep classes from forming and are relatively successful, while we play it more or less unwittingly to help the ruling class become richer and more secure. Finally, of course, the respected survivors of the American way have immense financial and technological power in their hands, the distrusted survivors of Tivland do not. So, while I hope that some of what I have been able to learn about Tiv song will assist both Tiv and ourselves in finding ways out of our worst competitive practices, the necessity of transforming this society is immeasurably greater and more urgent.

Tiv Music
Terminology

ONE PLACE to begin is where I began about fifteen years ago, with a book entitled *Muntu: An Outline of the New African Culture* by Janheinz Jahn (1961). Jahn's work has sometimes been ignored or abused as unscholarly, but I still find it a source of inspiration despite or perhaps because of its basic weaknesses—German romanticism, Hegelian idealism and dialectic gone wild, sweeping generalizations, utter neglect of the most basic political and economic realities, and so forth. In some strange way Jahn's weaknesses fit Africa's strengths, but however one assesses the compatibility of author and continent, Jahn was the first person, so far as I know, to attempt an analysis of African expression on and in African terms. Upon closer inspection the terms he uses as chapter headings turn out to be nothing more nor less than variations of the verb "to be"— some copulas from any Bantu grammar book might serve equally well —and these verb forms are made to carry the burden of Jahn's Western imagination. His grand synthesis of previous systematizations of Bantu thought by Tempels (1959) and Kagame (1956) with three other African systems (Griaule 1965; Dietherlen 1950; Deren 1953) centers upon the essential idea of dynamic forces and their transformational role in any medium of expression. While all of this adds layer upon layer of significance to each poem or piece of sculpture, the composite effect is of an ideal Africa that never existed, and Jahn's system of systems is a distortion of any particular African culture.

Still, Jahn tried to take an African view; any reading in the earlier African art books or in the fields of African music, dance, architecture, and so on, reveals what an important step forward Jahn's intent to use African names for African energies represents. We have known about the problem of ethnocentrism for most of this century; the danger of not attempting to examine and counter our own cultural biases when doing any work with alien cultures has long been acknowledged. Yet art historians and musicologists venturing outside the Western stream still persist in carrying all their Western interpretive baggage along with them. The assumptions are, I suppose, that art and music are universal languages that transcend cultural boundaries and that it would be ethnocentric of us *not* to discover and praise art and music among the primitives. Despite Jahn's breakthrough over fifteen years ago, there are only a few analyses to date that attempt to frame a study of an African art in African terms. Were it not for Thompson's work (1971, 1974), some of the contributions in a recent collection (d'Azevedo 1973), John Blacking's pages of Venda music terminology (1967, pp. 17–19), and a *Glossary of Hausa Music and It's Social Contexts* by Ames and King (1971), the scandal would be worse.

Avoiding the sort of tangled net that Jahn spreads over all Africa, I would like to demonstrate what I take to be his general thesis, that the equivalent of an esthetic or an "ideology of expression" is embedded in an African language, implicit in any language for that matter, if we choose to interpret it as such. This thesis might seem to oppose the one offered by Roy Sieber (1959), who feels that an "unvoiced esthetic . . . lies at the center of a hard core of beliefs" in African cultures and that the aims of African expression are "known, understood, assumed, shared," hence "taken for granted" (quoted in Merriam 1964, p. 271). Yet it does no great violence to Sieber's interpretation or to McAllester's concept of a "functional esthetic" (1960, p. 471) to state that the aims that are "taken for granted" are explicitly present and constantly "voiced" in normal everyday speech.

And so, in this chapter, I will work along from word to word, spending more time on the verbs of creation and singing with their connotational ranges and associated nouns, then move through a more lexicon-like presentation of adverbs, concluding with a consideration of the vocabulary of the dance. Because I am not nearly fluent enough in Tiv language or at home enough in Tiv culture to know when a word or set of words really defines a cultural "concept," "unit," "domain," "force," "pattern," or whatever, this chapter should be taken as a partial listing of pieces at the language level to be put in place only after further fieldwork and thought have clarified the parameters of the larger puzzle.

There are at least two very obvious reasons for studying the musical terminology of another culture. First, the exercise serves to remove some of the blinders, biases, and distortions inherent in our own vocabulary. Coming to terms with (or with terms to) another system of musical thought, we are forced to question the axioms of our own musicology. Secondly, advanced students of musical terminology in another culture can begin to phrase intelligent questions; one can discuss the conceptual issues which the terminology invariably raises with the people who use the terms daily, those who, in some sense, invented them.

The problem of our biases hit me rather forcefully when it became clear that a word corresponding to our term "music" could not be found in one African language after another—Tiv, Yoruba, Igbo, Efik, Birom, Hausa, assorted Jarawa dialects, Idoma, Eggon, and a dozen other languages from the Nigeria-Cameroons area do not yield a word for "music" gracefully. It is easy to talk about song and dance, singers and drummers, blowing a flute, beating a bell, but the general terms "music" and "musician" require long and awkward circumlocutions that still fall short, usually for lack of abstraction, for example, "the voices of the tools of the dance," a way of bringing together instruments blown and beaten which when supplemented by "plus singing" almost adds up to "music." So what seems to us a very basic, useful, and rather concrete term is apparently a useless abstraction from a Tiv, Yoruba, perhaps even a pan-African or non-Western point of view. If it should turn out that West African cultures are typical and that the vast majority of the world's peoples do not bother with a word for "music," it's conceivable that we may eventually think it silly, ethnocentric, even pompous to be designating disciplines with names like "musicology" or "ethnomusicology." On the other hand, "music" may continue to define quite precisely the somewhat ambiguous range of patterned sound phenomena we are interested in exploring across all cultural borders. We may eventually coin a still more ambiguous term that includes both music and dance, something more elegant than "musico-choreographic," I hope, since song/dance/musical-accompaniment are virtually inseparable in many cultures.

Lest we assume from this absence of a word for "music" in African languages that abstract terms are the privilege of the civilized West while concrete designations give more satisfaction to the so-called primitives, we should first consider the Tiv term *inja* in all its abstract and mysterious breadth and depth. A large number of important Western abstractions can be subsumed under the heading of or translated into Tiv as *inja,* for example, character, custom, culture, color, habit, nature, behavior, reason, meaning, sort, type, kind, method, style, utility, correctness. The closest English equivalent might be "immediate essence" or "contextually relevant aspect," perhaps even "primary force."

28   It is an indispensable word for the student of Tiv culture, providing the pivot point of innumerable leading questions, for example, *inja i kwagh la, ka nyi?* (literally, *"inja* of thing that, it is what?"), and one can substitute freely for *kwagh* ("thing") with "person," "event," "song," or whatever. In response, one is given the salient feature or features of the subject under discussion. Conversely, the anthropologist responding to the frequent question "What are you doing in Tivland?" can reply, *"M ngu timen ken andza a Tiv"* ("I am investigating the *andza* [plural of *inja*] of Tiv"), that is, their customs, habits, culture, characters, meaning, methods, styles, modes of being, and so forth—a very essential word indeed.

The second reason for worrying about musical terminology is that it opens the door to communication and plunges one into the problematic worlds of translation, semantics, concept-definition, esthetics. Without a minimal working knowledge of the language and a good grip on musical terms in particular it is easy to return from the field with findings that are fuzzy or irrelevant. If we look at Alan Merriam's work with the Basongye of the Congo as a possible case in point, please note that criticism is the sincerest form of flattery. Taking a few small lumps from latecomers is a price sometimes paid for pioneering. Prof. Merriam writes (1964):

> Distinctions of an acoustic nature are not, of course, commonly made in most societies; rather, the differentiation is achieved along other lines. Among the Congo Basongye, for example, there is a broad concept of what music is, although it is not expressed directly. In speaking of this question, the Basongye tend to respond with aphorismic statements such as the following:
>
> > When you are content, you sing; when you are angry,
> > you make noise.
> > When one shouts, he is not thinking; when he sings,
> > he is thinking.
> > A song is tranquil; a noise is not.
> > When one shouts, his voice is forced; when he sings, it is not.
>
> Using statements such as these, as well as detailed questioning and observation, it is possible for the outside observor to construct a three-part "theory" of noise and music as held by the Basongye. [p. 64]

Merriam, after a few paragraphs of exposition, concludes:

By these three criteria—music is produced exclusively by human beings, it must be organized, it must have continuity in time—the Basongye do define the boundaries between music and non-music. Not surprisingly, however, there is an intermediate area between the two in which some disunity of concept is expressed, and in which the context of the sound determines its acceptance or rejection as music. [p. 66]

This concern with differentiating music from nonmusic or defining the concepts "music," "sound," and "noise" is certainly understandable: it is an interesting, if not crucial, problem in the esthetics of Western music today. But are the Basongye really interested in these issues at all? I doubt it. A "broad concept of what music is" is held by the Basongye but it is "not expressed directly"; the outside observer constructs a "theory" (Merriam's quotation marks) of noise and music for them to hold, presumably by questing assiduously after distinctions not ordinarily made. Some "disunity of concept" results. While recognizing that a cultural "concept" need not always be tied to a linguistic unit or term, it seems sensible to map, however provisionally, the cultural terrain that a language delineates. It is not at all clear from Merriam's discussion that the broad Basongye concept "music" is tied to anything more than some solicited aphorisms about angry shouting and the existential value that only humans sing. Ultimately, the three Basongye criteria for music as reported by Merriam are not very convincing or exciting to me, simply because I do not know how the initial questions were asked. Do they have a word for "music" or don't they? Assuming that terms of even rough equivalence exist, how do the Basongye terms for "music," "sound," and "noise" match up with our own? Nothing in Merriam's account hints at the answers.

In Tivland the matching effort is as awkward as it is instructive. Where we would use the word "noise," Tiv use a more specific word, for example, *iov* for rustling, tinkling noises; *ihuran* for rushing or buzzing sounds; *an* as a verb of cackling and some other animal cries; *ayɔɔso* indicates the chattering and giggling of children. Where we might refer to the sound of something, they speak of its *imo* or "voice," and *imo* is the word most often used for our word "song" as well. The more denotatively restricted but less commonly used noun for "song" is *icam*. It has no meanings other than "song," and the sense of group singing—call-response pattern or leader-chorus—is usually implicit if not explicit in normal usage. It may well be the root of *icam* that is used in expressions like *ve de eren cám càm cám ga!*[1] ("Let them stop their noise!"). As noted above, long circumlocutions must be resorted to in any gloss of "music." The specificity or concreteness of the Tiv terminology makes gibberish of "our best questions." Is "music" different from "noise"? Is "the voices of the tools of the dance plus singing" different from "the chatter of small children" and "rustling of grasses"? Although I never attempted such a question, it might be possible to use *imo* in all three senses of "sound," "music," and "noise," in a sentence something like, "How is the voice of the train whistle different from the voices of dance tools and the voices of angry disputants in court?" But even the most rational effort to frame our Western question in Tiv terms is thwarted. Certain questions can't be asked, much less answered, intelligently.

So what are the first questions to ask in Tiv? What are the right questions, the ones that interest Tiv? How are they to be phrased? With these questions in mind, I would like to suggest here a simple method, one that helps to define terms and delineate concepts. So far as I know, the linguistics literature doesn't tell us yet how to pin down a sememe or unit of meaning. The semantic side of language is usually left for last in analysis because it is messy, always in flux, unstable from time to time and place to place and person to person. It is difficult to restrict the dennotation and map the connotations of a word with any precision. A new idiom, a new inflection for irony, a new metaphorical context for the word always postpones exact definition of the word itself. Still, the linguist's best tool, the frame, gives us a way to chase down the possibilities of a word to near exhaustion.

First, select the word or short phrase that is of interest. Second, contextualize it by seeing (a) what can fill a blank placed in front of the word; (b) what can fill a blank placed after it; and (c) what words can replace it in various contexts. After exhausting the possibilities of a particular blank (or exhausting oneself in the attempt), the real work begins: one must evaluate, essentialize, try to measure degrees of abstraction, expansiveness, connotational range, and conversely, try to estimate density of denotational focus, concreteness, compactness. If the word seems to have many meanings, is it possible to establish some

---

[1] While every Tiv word has tones that could be indicated for each syllable, I have used tone markings only when necessary to avoid ambiguity. The acute accent mark is used for a high tone, the grave for a low tone, and the macron for a down step, a tone slightly lower than the preceding high tone.

priorities or a hierarchy for them? How does this word fit with the rest of the musical terminology?

To illustrate, let's begin with *dugh,* apparently the Tiv equivalent of our verb "compose." Names and pronouns typically come before it, but an interesting assortment of nouns other than song can come after it:

a dugh imo—he composed a song
a dugh icam—he composed a song
a dugh ishu—he caught fish (in a trap)
a dugh íyòúv kera—he dug up yams
a dugh iyóu—he collects honey
i dugh un tor kera—he's been deposed as chief
a dugh ishol—he coined a proverb, spoke figuratively
a dugh anyi—he filed down teeth to a point
a dugh bank—he withdrew funds from the bank
a dugh iyav—she miscarried
a dugh ijor—he dug a well, cleaned out a well
a dugh kwase—he married a wife from another people

What is the common denominator? Can this very broad connotational range be reduced to reveal the essence or *inja* of the verb *dugh?* Not really, for the usages above far from exhaust the frame "*a dugh _____,*" and each instance is more complex than the single or double gloss offered above would suggest.[2] But provisionally we might evaluate *dugh* as meaning "to take out" or, more precisely, "to subtract quickly after slow addition," "to effect the quick emergence of something after a steady preparation." More ponderously, and perhaps still more precisely: "something that already exists is taken from a prepared context so that a new effect is suddenly achieved."

The pregnancy follows conception, develops slowly, regularly, but aborts quickly. One must usually make a few deposits in the bank before making a withdrawal. Old teeth of many years become new teeth

---

[2] Somehow it escaped my attention that the Bohannans had added five volumes of source material on Tiv Religion (Bohannan, Paul and Laura, 1969) to the Human Relations Area Files. In perusing this material just prior to publication, I found two more very important usages for *dugh:*

a. *a dugh akombo,* "he removed an *akombo*"; in this case *akombo* means the dangerous aspects of a ritual performed to protect farmland and crops.

b. *a dugh or u kpwen,* "he exhumed a corpse by magical means," said of a specialist among the sorcerors (*mbatsav*) who can remove dead bodies from the grave without disturbing the soil.

with a few deft strokes of the chisel or file. One weaves a trap, places it strategically in a stream, and with luck a fish may be retrieved from it in time. Yams must be planted and grown before they can be harvested. A chief must be installed and display his ineptitude for a considerable period before he can be deposed. A well can not only be dug but cleaned as well with *dugh*. Each analogy illuminates and complicates the idea we have of "composing" a song in Tiv. The verb *dugh* insists that making a song is like trapping a fish, harvesting a yam, digging a well, collecting honey, and so forth. These suggestions can and should be followed up with Tiv composers: "Is trapping a fish or taking it from the trap *really* like 'trapping' a song?" "Why say *dugh* for these two operations?" "*Is* a composed song like a tooth filed down to a point?" Discussions of this sort might move beyond the verb, the term, *dugh*, toward a Tiv concept of *dugh*.

Sharper assessment of the term *dugh* rests upon comparisons with other languages as well, starting with one's mother tongue: "He composes songs." "He composes sonnets." "He composes type." "He composes himself." "For headaches aspirin; for nervous tension—Compose!" The *inja* or essence of our term would seem to be "to put in order," with connotations of arranging things in lines, adding things up, almost the very opposite of "to take out" or "to pull out quickly after slow preparation." The American Heritage Dictionary gives us "to make up the constituent parts of; constitute or form" and follows this with nine other meanings and some likely etymologies for the word. Working with a language like Tiv, etymological work is nearly impossible, but the relative frequency of various usages could be estimated by asking a sample of schoolboys to fill in the blanks. If thirty out of fifty cite *a dugh ishu*, catching fish, and only two in fifty use *dugh* in connection with a woman's miscarriage, we at least have a clue to the verb's denotative center. It would be a mistake to rely too heavily on usage frequencies of this sort, however, for the use of *dugh* as a verb for "composing" may be an extended, peripheral, connotational usage and far removed from the central meaning.

Composers seem to think of their work, *dugh*, as more intimately related to the basic "taking out" and "harvesting" notions and only distantly related to the miscarriage meaning. Responding to questioning, they say that they pull out songs "from the chest" or, less often, "from the heart." This is conventionally accomplished while lying quietly in bed. (See chapter 4.) The heart and chest are habitual metaphors, standard idioms, for the centers of emotion and power. Sorcerers are alleged to have a special substance, *tsav,* growing on their hearts that gives them power. People seemingly without this power of witchcraft are commonly referred to as "the empty chested." To savor the full implications of a Tiv composer's statement that "I take out songs from my chest," we will have to explore more of the range of phrases used to encompass emotional states. In any attempt to analyze a single word in depth, one drifts inevitably into a variety of cultural domains.

I have given only a dozen contexts for the verb *dugh* to simplify the essentializing process somewhat, but as many more usages could be found that would have to be considered in a more definitive analysis. Yet the connotational matrix for *dugh* is complicated enough already. Certainly the notion that whatever is "pulled out" was there before, preexistent in some sense, should give us a moment's pause for a quick check of philosophical first principles. How much violence are we doing to *a dugh imo* if we gloss it as "he creates a new song"? Isn't this an even worse translation than "he composes"? Given the fish-from-trap, yam-from-heap, money-from-bank analogies, slow preparation and building a context for taking out is the more important part of the process; the actual subtraction or removal itself is almost automatic, inevitable. The yam is there to be harvested, not spontaneously created. Is any given song somehow preexistent as well, waiting there to be actualized? From a Tiv ontological perspective, would "he actualized a song" or "he manifested a song" or "he took out a song" (with the big question—from where?—left implicit) be preferable translations? Rather than burden the reader with a phrase like "song-taker-outer" or "song-manifestor," let me simply substitute *or u dughun amo* occasionally or keep the quotation marks of ambiguity around "composer" to remind readers of an unresolved problem.

The compatability of our "creation" idea with *dugh* is further compromised by the more negative usages of the Tiv verb—"to miscarry," "to depose a chief," even "he stuck out the tongue rudely" (*a dugh nombor*) and "he took the last piece of food from the pot" (*a dugh luam*), though the latter two usages are only singly attested and are probably fresh metaphors. These few examples make it clear that *dugh* as a process is morally neutral and not freighted with connotations of goodness like our "create" and "compose."

Having set out a familiar method and an exemplary verb of "creation," an even more complicated verb falls immediately into mind: *gba.* R. C. Abraham, in two pages of entries for the verb, divides usage into seven categories, A through G, and a number of additional idioms

(1940a, pp. 47, 48). Under A the primary meaning is given as "to fall down," for example, *a gba nya* (earth), "he fell down"; *a gba jime* (back), "he went backwards, retreated"; *a gba toho* (grass), "he fled to the bush"; *a gba sha tindi* (lit., "on rules"), "he transgressed the law" or, in a similar idiom of our own, "he fell afoul of the law"; *a gba a mo*, "he attacked me." The diverse sense of these examples and the others listed under A would seem to be of "falling into, through, on, across, under, etc.," not simply "down."

Abraham's entry B reads as follows: "B. to carpenter. (a) *m gba kon* I did carpentry: *ikon ii gban* act of carpentry. (b) *Aondo gba tar* God created the world. (c) *mbatsav gba tar* the *mbatsav* by sorcery, caused the crops to fail: *or u gban tar* a destroyer of the land by sorcery: *tar gba* the land has been destroyed by sorcery or hunger" (p. 47). Adding that sculpting figures from wood is also a *gba* process, we are faced again with the problem of translating "creation" into Tiv. Something like *dugh,* the process itself is neutral; here it becomes a destructive or creative force, negative or positive, according to the subject—sorcerer or God—rather than in reference to the predicate as in *dugh* above.

Abraham's third category begins "C. to proceed to do. (a) *a gba tom* he began work. . . . (b) *kwagh gba* something occurred: *ku gba* a death occurred: *tugh gba* night fell" and continues with gba usages that include becoming thin and becoming fat, as if one falls into these corporeal states. The opening formula of many folktales, *kwagh hil wam gba nahan ga,* literally, "thing marvelous mine falls thus not" (see chapter 2), fits into this category.

The fourth category is "D. (impersonal) (a) to want, e.g., *kwagh gbam*" literally, "thing falls on me," but meaning either "I want to do" or "I am in needy circumstances," according to context. D includes a few other reflexive usages. In category E are all the *gba* usages meaning to die of wounds or poisons, for example, *a gba 'ivaan,* "he died of an arrow wound"; and to fall sick, for example, *a gba hough,* "he got a cold." The sixth category is "F. *gba* . . . *tsɔ* (*tsɔ* here implies that no good purpose can be or has been served) e.g., *se gba van tsɔ* we've come in vain . . . *m gba ungwan tsɔ* I happened to smell it." The seventh Abraham category lists a few noun-like usages, for example, the missionaries' invention, *Gba aondo,* "God the Creator," and the Tiv phrase *ka gba aondo wase,* "such is our temperament" or literally "it fall sky ours."

Merely summarizing the Abraham treatment of *gba* gives a sense of mystery, of too many things falling into and out of place, but what can we *dugh* with it, what *inja* can be pulled out of such a semantic mix? Considering the diversity of meaning for our own word "fall" ("the Fall," "fall of Rome," "fall in love," "to fall ill," "fall by sometime"), we might be disturbed if some outside speculator were to ascribe a particular "cultural dynamic" or "mode of being" to us on the basis of a dozen diverse idioms that employ the word "fall." Is *gba* really so different a verb? An immediate answer would be affirmative, for while *gba* and "fall" match up in many ways, especially the more negative idioms, "fall" is not a verb of creation in any sense whatever. Is *gba* any better a gloss for "to create" than *dugh*? The central creative usages seem to be carpentry and sculpting, since *Aɔndo gba tar* might have been translated "sky fell to earth" or "earth fell from sky" before the missionaries came and gave *aɔndo* a capital letter, changing Tix expressions like "heaven only knows" to "God only knows." Given all the other usages and the central notion of falling down, on, in, and so on, the carpentering meaning probably stems from the descending motions used in handling the traditional Tiv adze. There are other verbs for sawing, hammering, building particular kinds of structures. It is hard to make *gba* very "creative," so to speak. There is an interesting sense in which *gba* indicates the sudden beginning (with connotations of inevitability) of a larger process, just as *dugh* indicates the sudden end of a slow preparation. It is as if we have labels for the start or finish of creative processes, but no word for the process itself. "It" is down there somewhere, to have things pulled out from, or to be descended into.

We might summarize by stating that the two best possible translations of "to create" in Tiv differ from our verb in being (1) morally neutral and (2) based on motion. The third and perhaps crucial difference is more difficult to define: the motions of initial "falling in" or final "pulling out" seem to catalyze or tap larger processes, processes that seem to be natural from a Tiv point of view, whereas our verbs "create" and "compose" imply culturally approved and individually synthesized efforts of construction.

Asking what other verbs can replace *dugh* in the frame "*a* _____ *imo*" immediately raises the question of Tiv equivalents for our verb "sing." Two verbs are most frequently used, and they seem to be completely interchangeable: *a wa imo* and *a gber imo*.

Wa is a very common and versatile verb meaning variously "to put a thing into," "to fix in place," "to make." Some examples, almost all of them from R. C. Abraham (1940a: 309, 310): *a wa un ken gaadi*, "they put him in prison"; *wa ishe na*, "fix its price!"; *a wa tsar*, "he made a bridge"; *a wa asange*, "it produced grains (crop is beginning to mature)"; *a wa icul*, "he tied a knot"; *a wa agba*, "she put on a bracelet, anklet"; *a wa akov*, "he put on shoes"; *a wa aie*, "he's a liar (lit., he puts forth lies habitually)"; *a wa ishima*, "he plucked up his courage (lit., he put heart)"; *m wa kaven*, "I understood slightly"; *a wa un kwagh er . . .* , "she incited him to . . ."; *aondo wa ime* or *ime wa*, "it has got dark"; *or la wa ime*, "he is of strong personality (lit., person that put forth darkness)"; *a wa ifan*, "he placed a curse"; *a wa usu*, "he placed kindling for a fire." Another fifty contexts for *wa* could be given, but the denotative center reduces to "place," "fix," or "put forth," without much fuss, and one gets the feeling that singing in Tiv is possibly equivalent to arranging a song's position, putting it into public space, fixing it in place.

The other basic verb for singing, *gber*, is somewhat more specific in its applications, meaning generally "to make a slash in, slash off," "to incise, cut into," for example, *a gber amine*, "he reaped millet"; *a gber un ivav*, "he wounded him"; *a gber un abaji*, "he incised face marks on him"; *igber un akar*, "body cicatrices have been cut on him"; *a gber luam*, "he dipped out food from one container into another"; *a gber un ivambe*, "he vaccinated or innoculated him"; *a gber ihwa*, "he drew a line on the ground with a hoe"; *a gber logu*, "he cut in cassava [a way of planting]"; *ikegh ngi gberen*, "the chicken is pecking the ground for food"; *a gber ifan*, "he cut the curse" or *a gber mgerem*, "he agreed to let bygones be bygones"; *a gber hunda*, "he cut a doorway space from a wall"; *a gber takerada*, "he typed a letter"; *a gber kon*, "he chopped down a tree"; *a gber usu*, "he struck a match, lit a fire"; *a gber akor*, "he removed sprouting yam ends from the ground to serve as seedlings."

Add this last usage to the use of *dugh* in the context of harvesting yams, and we have an extended metaphor of yam cultivation for the "composing-singing" process. "Composition" is pulling out the big yam buried deep; "singing" is the snipping of yam tips suitable for transplanting.

When *gber* and *wa* are compared as verbs for singing, *gber* clearly has a more dynamic emphasis. Two explicit contrasts emerge from the usages just cited: *wa ifan*, "to put or place a curse," as opposed to *gber ifan*, "to cut a curse"; and *wa usu*, "to place kindling for a fire," versus *gber usu*, to actually "light a fire" (*gberusu* is the expression used for matches).

In the course of arguing that a particular rite, *kenda mku*, is not a manifestation of ancestor worship, the Bohannans (Laura and Paul

1969) provide a neat contrast of *wa* and *gber* in connection with *ifan,* "curse."

> while the parent was alive he "placed a curse" (*wa ifan*) on the man. The curse may not have "caught" (*kor*) until after the death of the person who placed it. If it did catch before the death of the man who placed it, first amends are made and the reason for which the curse was originally placed is removed; the curse itself is then removed by "cutting the curse" (*gber ifan*) or "spitting out the curse" (*hamber ifan*); both parties take water into their mouths and blow it out in a spray. If the man who placed the curse is dead, practical amends are made to the dead man's closest agnates and heirs; then, since it is impossible to "spit out the curse" (*hamber ifan*) with a man who is dead, the rite known as *kende mku* is performed by the living party with identical results. The original curse must have been uttered or placed (*wa*) while the parent was alive; he can do nothing after his death. [p. 83]

It is easy enough to grasp the connection between *wa*, "to place a curse," and *wa*, "to sing"; it suggests both that song and curse are heightened forms of speech and that they are almost physically put on or in someone else. It may be that *wa* is the appropriate verb to use if the content of a song is negative, spreading gossip, abusive. Conversely, *gber* for "cutting" or "lifting" curses may be somewhat more appropriate for positive songs, praise-singing that builds a relationship between composer and patron; the former lifts his voice in song and the latter empties his purse. Not infrequently a composer will spit out abuses on one man, place the blame for his destitute condition on him, in order to magnify his praises of another—X refuses to pay the shilling he owes me, and it has caused me unspeakable sufferings, but Y has given me a fine shirt.

The contrasting uses of *wa* and *gber,* to prepare a fire and ignite it, respectively, suggest a possible connection between the two aspects of *dugh*—slow preparation and quick subtraction—and two modes of singing: placing a song versus igniting or striking it into existence. Speculating a step further, are there echoes here of both "verbs of creation": *dugh,* "to pull out," is like *wa,* "to put in place," while *gba,* "to fall into," is like *gber,* "to incise"? If these echoes are audible (and the possibly phonesthemic bilabial explosive "*gb*" helps me to hear them), then we are brought again to these parallel questions: Where precisely is the song being put or placed? What does a song cut into?

Though I have yet to press these specific questions upon the wisest

Tiv elders, most Tiv state, when asked to differentiate *wa* and *gber* as verbs for singing, that the two verbs may be used interchangeably at any time, any place, whatever the context. The two common nouns for "song" are *icam*, plural *atsam*, literally "song" or "call and response song" ("part-song" in the Abraham dictionary [1940a, p. 12]) and *imo*, plural *amo*, literally "voice." (Abraham also gives *mliam*, literally "crying" as in "a dirge," but this no longer seems to be in common usage.) The two basic nouns are also said to be interchangeable so that the straightforward, unconnotated, and even redundant English sentence "He sings a song" can be translated at least four different ways: *a gber imo, a wa imo, a gber icam, a wa icam.* Although contemporary Tiv will not admit to shades of meaning among the four that would make each expression more or less appropriate in particular situations, I feel sure that favored usages in special contexts once existed and that even today extended analysis of tape recorded Tiv conversations about singing would reveal some patterning and predispositions, if not rules, for these four terms in combination. In terms of frequency, at least, *gber* is more commonly used than *wa*, and *imo* is even more clearly favored over *icam*, so that a "singer" is almost invariably referred to as *or u gberen imo*, literally "person of incising voice."

There are a number of other verbs that indicate what can be done to or with a song in Tivland. Other verbs that can fill the blank between *a* ———— *imo* or *a* ———— *icam* can be sorted into four general categories: (1) verbs of starting, (2) verbs of responding, (3) special verbs, and (4) obvious verbs. To dispose of the fourth category first, it includes all the easy and more obvious Tiv-English translations, for example, he likes the song, he listens to the song, he remembers the song, he finishes the song, he practices the song, and so forth.

While it seems that Tiv and English have roughly the same verbs for finishing, ending, concluding, stopping a song, starting a song in Tivland is a process that can be described in a variety of vivid ways. I have encountered over a dozen beginning verbs, and there are probably many more localized and colloquial usages that have escaped my attention: *a baver imo*, "he explodes or crackles (like a fire) into song"; *a gengese imo*, "he starts the song abruptly, loudly"; *ger* and *genger*, both meaning "to shout the song"; *gever*, "to start loudly, abruptly, especially in sorrow, to begin in the throat with a sob or a roar"; *hii*, "to start first and alone" (this verb also has the sense of attacking, provoking a quarrel); *kende*, "to start, raise, lift, promote, to hit a high note" (also to set a dog on the scent of an animal); *nande*, "to break out in song," also "to scold," "to set fire to something"; *ngol,* "to start with violence, suddenly, to scream, to strive joyfully"; *ta,* "to begin," but the primary meaning is "to aim, shoot at, and hit" something; *yɔhɔr,* "to release" the song (usually used with triggers and springs); *yuwa,* "to pick up, clutch, raise with force"; *ndera,* a verb used only in connection with the initial phase of five processes in addition to singing, that is, (1) beginning beer brewing, (2) and (3) making the framework for a basket or a piece of cloth, (4) setting out on a journey or task whose end is not known, (5) starting a house framework or roof; *tɔɔ,* "to take up, carry, lead," "to put the roof frame on a house prior to thatching."

The last two verbs are cited by Abraham in his description of praise-singing:

> The most important type of song is that called *icam;* this is composed and sung by professional bards on public occasions, such as a wedding-dance, and one example has already been given. The bard sings the theme to the accompaniment of drums and flutes and the spectators join in the chorus, the bard going from man to man, encouraging them to sing up. It is particularly employed to commemorate the achievements of the spectators and their relations, and to mention one (*ter*) in an *icam* is highly prized and correspondingly rewarded by its subject. To the Tiv mind the composition of such a eulogy suggests a roof built over the head of the one eulogized and this simile is kept up in the phraseology, for he speaks of intoning the first words of the *icam* in the same way as he speaks of beginning (*ndera*) the roof-frame and the eulogy is raised up (*tɔɔ*) as it gets into its stride, just as the finished frame is raised on to the walls and benefits the house-owner. [1940b, p. 82]

Recalling that *gber* can be used "to cut a door from the wall of a house," we can add another small piece to this architectural metaphor.

As one might suppose from the list of "starting verbs" above, Tiv begin their songs with a great deal of energy, and the first call or phrase frames and launches the rest of the performance. One might learn this simply from listening to Tiv songs, but I think it important to note that the Tiv do not take this stylistic feature for granted and have a wealth of expressive verbs to describe this practice in all its many variants.

Verbs of response are fewer in number but equally interesting: *rumun,* a familiar verb meaning, basically, "to agree, to answer" but also "to sing after, to join in" or, as one Tiv put it, "to welcome the song"; *kever,* "to catch a thing thrown to one," also "to snap across"; *tɔɔ,* listed above under beginning verbs, can also be used for choral responses in the sense of "to pick up"; *hambe*, "to assist, to second" the composer, also "to hang something across something else" (the verb's basic meaning is "to wound or finish off an animal already hit by another hunter, thereby laying claim to a specific portion of the meat"); *yese*, literally "to act as nurse to a child," used primarily in the phrase *or u yesen imo* for the composer's assistant, who "nurses the song along"; and finally *tsorogh*, a key musical term in Tiv which can be interpreted variously to mean "to respond, or sing the chorus," "to interrupt," "to blend" or "to counterpoint," "to help or accompany," conceivably even "to harmonize." The man who plays the two smaller "male" drums in the usual percussion ensemble, supporting and elaborating the basic beats of the "mother" drum, is called *or u tsorogh gbande*, literally "person who plays *tsorogh* drum." The bongo player in an Afro-Cuban band would be called *or u tsorogh* by Tiv. A singer who deviates occasionally from the main chorus to sing an obligato or shout some encouraging exclamations is said to *tsorogh*. The term can also be used to compliment an excellent dancer who is moving different parts of his or her body in different meters simultaneously. *A vinen a tsorogh* might be translated "she is dancing polymetrically."

The third category, "special" verbs used in connection with singing, includes those for inviting singers, brewing beer for a song-fest, commissioning a song; for example, *a mil imo*, literally "he brewed song," actually means "he is preparing beer and an animal for slaughter in preparation for the arrival of a composer and his assistants whom he has invited especially for the occasion." (In some contexts *a wa imo* can mean the same preparation of a song fest.) Although I haven't investigated the matter systematically, there is probably a very important distinction to be made between those composers who work largely "on invitation" and those who sing uninvited at bars and markets. The verb *ma*, "to drink," is used in the expressions *a ma imo* and *a ma icam* to mean "he is taking up composing" or "he is a composer," a reference to the medicine or potion that many Tiv purchase from a composer in order to become composers themselves (see chapter 4). The verb *tér* is highly specific, meaning only "to mention" or "to mention or eulogize in song," as in the instance described by Abraham above. It seems plausible that the verb is linked etymologically to the noun *tér*, "father" or "ancestor." That there exists such a discrete verb for "to praise in song" indicates the importance of praise-singing in Tiv culture.

When Tiv begin to talk about how songs are sung, they can draw upon an infinite array of what might be called "adverbial doubles" and "stretched adverbs," infinite in the sense that from area to area and even from individual to individual, different morphemes, stems, onomato-poetic sounds can be doubled or stretched to describe and evaluate a singer's performance. Many items can be doubled or stretched at the whim of the speaker, for example, "slowly" can be *tegh tegh* or *teghelee;* "very slowly" becomes *tegheleeeee.* A few can be doubled or tripled and stretched, for example, *kusu kusu,* "timidly, tightly, fee-bly," can become *kusuuu* or *kusususuuu* or *kusususu kusususu.* And in theory, at least, it seems that any common noun or verb can be dou-bled or stretched to fit a particular descriptive problem of the moment. In a sample of eighty-five schoolboys filling in the blanks for the frame "*a gber imo* _____ _____," every other respondent offers a unique "adverbial double" that I haven't heard before or a new and daring spelling for an old standby.

A number of adverbs indicating dynamics are fairly standardized throughout Tivland. Singing which is slow, soft, smooth, low in pitch can be described as *kure kure, lugh lugh, legh legh, tegh tegh, dough dough, leghem leghem, hiin hiin, shoon shoon,* and so forth. Each ad-verb has its own distinct if subtle connotational stress—"slowly" is the main message of *tegh tegh;* "softness" is probably the defining feature of *lugh, legh,* and *leghem*—but all of them tend to muddle up the Western variables of slow tempo, low pitch, low volume, and smooth delivery.

Similarly, loud volume, high pitch, and strong delivery overlap each other in adverbs like *zever zever, gbang gbang, geng geng, gengese gengese, taver taver, agee agee.* While fast tempo is implied in these adverbs, it can also be described separately—*fele fe fele, fefa fefa, ayem ayem.* Slow tempo can be indicated by adding the negative particle *ga* to these "quickly" expressions; otherwise low volume, low pitch, and slow tempo are never discrete. There are also a half dozen or so adverbs for voice qualities, for example, *kande kande,* "thinly, lightly," with "high" connotations; *jande jande,* "scratchily, broken," with "low" con-notations; but these seem to be infrequently used. In short, the Tiv dynamics vocabulary can be reduced to degrees and kinds of high-loud-fast-strong and low-soft-slow-smooth. These are, of course, the "natu-ral" correlations that Western orchestra conductors are forever battling against in pursuit of various special effects. When one tape records Tiv singers, it becomes obvious after a while that every high note will be attacked with maximum lung power and that passages in the lowest part of a singer's range can be virtually inaudible. Honest recognition of these factors does not, unfortunately, enable the engineer to predict and set the proper recording level; invariably a few high notes hit un-expectedly are distorted, or a few low notes are lost along the way.

Another cluster of adverbial doubles can be grouped under the heading "Tiv perfectionism." Certainly a mere list of adverbs does not define the essence or *inja* of Tiv expression, but it points us in that direction. The Tiv language has no words for "art," "beauty," "esthet-ics," but the following vocabulary demonstrates a strong and pervasive concern with quality that renders any lack of these correlated Western abstractions irrelevant.

Songs and singing can be described as "good" and "bad": *a gber imo doo doo,* "he sings well, correctly, very nicely"; *a gber imo dang dang,* "he sings badly, carelessly, roughly, foolishly." But the Tiv do not stop there: *a gber imo tsember tsember,* "perfectly, completely, clearly"; *a gber imo tsee tsee,* "distinctly, clearly"; *a gber imo sha mi sha mi,* "ex-actly, perfectly, convincingly"; *a gber imo kpen kpen,* "very accurately, reasonably, precisely"; *a gber imo sha inja sha inja,* "carefully, according to the essentials, thoroughly, perfectly"; *a gber imo sha alo sha alo,* "pur-posefully, clearly, slowly"; *a gber imo gbar gbar,* "clearly, openly, flu-ently, fearlessly"; *a gber imo sha itseghen sha itseghen,* "proudly, with dignity"; *a gber imo tondo tondo,* "perfectly, carefully, crisply"; *a gber imo war war,* "precisely, clearly"; *a gber imo kile kile,* "bit by bit, skill-fully, exactly"; *a gber imo vighe vighe,* "step by step, in detail, dis-tinctly"; *a gber imo jighilii,* "steadily, straight ahead, faultlessly"; *a gber imo pera pera,* "vividly, clearly"; *a gber imo pav pav,* "clearly."

And of course this preoccupation has its negative dimension as well: *a gber imo nzughur nzughur,* "he sings mixed up, over-complicated, confusedly, messily"; *a gber imo gben gben,* "unsteadily, crookedly, clumsily"; *a gber imo cov cov,* "sloppily, roughly, dirtily"; *a gber imo atoon atoon,* "haphazardly, without connections."

Longer glosses like "with exquisite attention to detail" or "consistent ennunciation without undue strain" might be added to many of the positive adverbs above. The very wide variety of translations given by Tiv students for any one of the adverbs illustrates more than their lack of fluency in English. Some of the adverbs will never be rendered con-cisely into our idiom. And, as with the dynamics doubles, the semantic overlapping is formidable. If one looks over the list, the basic criteria for quality in song are obvious: precision and accuracy, a sense of de-tailed completion or perfection, and above all, clarity. We might reduce this to a single criterion of perfect-complete-clarity, and the adverb *tsember tsember* or *tsembereee,* perhaps the most frequently heard compliment to a singer or composer in Tivland, encompasses this concept better than any other adverb.

The concept is further illumined by consideration of another frequently used expression not listed above, *a gber imo wang wang* (or *wanger wanger* or *wangeraaa*), "he sings clearly, brightly, explicitly, cheerfully, and so forth." This adverb can be applied to most sources of light—the dawn, freshly cleared land, clean clothes, a thoroughly scrubbed and well-oiled body, a job well done (*tom wanger vo!,* "the work is complete"). In his article "Beauty and Scarification amongst the Tiv" (1956), Paul Bohannan describes at some length the ways in which "glowing" suffuses the Tiv world and provides the first principle upon which subsequent decoration, scarification, and adornment techniques rely.

> Tiv oil their bodies with palm oil, castor oil, vaseline, or, occasionally, groundnut oil. The resultant shining quality is highly prized: it is said of a person with a glistening skin, "he glows" (*a wanger yum*). The same word is used of the sun or the headlights of an automobile. The impersonal form of the same expression, *i wanger,* means to be light and can be said of the day, of a kerosene lamp or of an idea.
> One of the most effective ways of glowing is to rub the skin with camwood, a red wood which Tiv import from the forests to their south. Camwood is ground and made into a paste with either water or oil, and is used as a cosmetic. It is also involved in ritual: the notion of lightening or causing to glow joins the profane and sacred worlds. The bride and groom, especially if it be the first marriage for both, are smeared with camwood so that they glow; they may wear it for several weeks. A newborn child has camwood smeared on his head. Corpses are smeared with camwood; this "lightens" them, but also (Tiv are practical people) absorbs the liquids from the corpse and keeps down odour. Whenever a person is put into special contact with a fetish force or *akombo,* camwood is necessary to the ceremony. The greatest protecting force in Tivland, *swem,* has camwood as one of its ingredients. Yet many people smear camwood on themselves merely because they think it attractive. Occassionally, if camwood is unavailable, yellow ochre may be substituted for cosmetic purposes. Today talcum powder is a cosmetic, and the same phrase is heard—"he glows." The whole notion of lightening by making oneself smooth, attractive and sacred is important to Tiv in their religious and personal lives.

44   Tiv say that it is possible to make oneself very light by means
which are horrible and nefarious: if one smears one's body with human fat, one becomes irresistible. There are said to be men who
deal in human fat: they come, with sacks across their shoulders, and
sit menacingly at the side of the market; their mark is a piece of a
certain grass hanging from their lips. A prospective buyer approaches
circumspectly; the haggling does not take place in the market, but
arrangements are made to meet for a special "market held at night"
(*kasua tugh*). We can see that Tiv are expressing metaphorically
their belief that if one man achieves too much worldly success—
including too much beauty—he must have got it at the expense of
another.

The are other, less drastic, magical or medicinal means of "glowing." Tiv wear charms sewn into small leather bags or bracelets, some
of which make one invisible or turn bullets to one side, but many
more of which protect one against witches or make one attractive in
general and sexually attractive in particular.

The first notion of physical beauty, then, is that the body must
"glow" or *wanger*. It is also the point of much ritual. The word
means to be beautiful, to be clear, and to be in a satisfactory ritual
state.

I am not sure that "to be beautiful" and "to be in a satisfactory ritual
state" are really Tiv states of mind, but clarity, "glow," if not brilliance,
are clearly of the essence or *inja* in any Tiv "esthetic system" we care
to posit.

Still another adverb, *engem engem,* may be a variation on this theme;
it is applied to singing and dancing, though much less frequently than
wanger, and refers to reflected light, glittering, shining brilliance.

The brilliance factor or "glow" enters into descriptions of personality in ways not described by Bohannan. *A wa ime,* literally "he puts
forth darkness," can be said of a singer, storyteller, dancer, orator, or
any person who carries the day by sheer presence or force of personality, irrespective of his or her skills and actual appearance. A little old
elder coming along the path somehow urges you to take not one step
to the side but two, and you breathe a sigh of relief when he has passed
—*a wa ime.* Similarly, *a ta urum,* literally "he shoots (at and hits with)
brightness," can be said of a "flashy dresser" or of a poor boy, simply
dressed, who is particularly neat and, as Afro-Americans would say,
"together." Some Tiv state that it is possible to "put forth darkness"
and "shoot brightness" simultaneously, usually on the grounds that

these phrases are metaphors, figures of speech, and not to be taken that literally.

Speaking of Afro-Americans, I am reminded of a statement by Don Cherry, the jazz trumpeter and a leading exponent of what is called "energy playing" among the jazz avant-garde: "when everybody's got their mind and feelings in tune, it's separate from the presence of the audience. Everybody carries their brightness . . . Be at the instant, absolute. The music will have a quality at the instant absolute. And that will be brilliant" (Jones, Le Roi, 1970, p. 167). It is a theme we will return to in conclusion (chapter 5).

In addition to "bright-darkness," another synesthetic paradox can be seen-heard-felt in the application of hot and cold adverbs to song and dance. *Baver baver* (compare "starting" verbs above) usually applies to a crackling fire but can be used to describe performances that are loud, clear, energetic, very hot. Good dancing is commonly said to "heat up the land." On the other hand, one can sing or dance *kundu kundu,* "in a cool fashion, sweetly, softly, slowly, nicely," or *ndohor iyol,* literally "to cool the body," "cool and satisfying, slow and steady." While these adverbs usually apply to different styles, *baver* more appropriate for strong singing and energetic men's dances and *kundu* and *ndohor iyol* more applicable to women's dances and moderated singing, it is important to note that "hot" and "cold" are both positive qualities and in this sense analogous to Afro-American descriptions of hot and cool jazz. There is also a contrast to be noted (see chapter 4) between the "dry" or fluid-free throat and chest desirable for composing and the "wet," lubricated, durable throat desired for singing.

Perhaps we can summarize this discussion of how songs are sung and evaluated by describing some of the things that are left out of the Tiv lexicon relative to our own. The esthetic topography offered by Tiv terminology is, in an ethnographic sense, self-sufficient: the mountains there to be climbed—*dugh, gba, gber, wanger,* and so on—define their own valleys, I suppose, and my main concern in fieldwork has been to understand the Tiv terms rather than generate glosses for our own. But the discovery that the word for "music" was missing raised important issues, and I hope to spend more time probing the discrepancies between our words and theirs in the future.

It is especially striking that Tiv modifiers describing emotions in relation to songs are so few and far between. The Tiv emphasis, when it isn't glowingly mystical, is almost entirely technical, firmly focused

46

upon skills or the lack of them. One might almost speak of "technique raised to the level of mystique." A sample of eighty-five students filling in the blanks for the frame *a gber imo* _____ _____ cites the adverbs of perfection, clarity, completeness, and their opposites over and over again, whereas the adverbs for "happily," "sorrowfully," "peacefully," "crazily" appear only once or twice. Basic emotions like love, hate, anger don't appear at all. This may have something to do with the way in which the basic emotions are "phrased" in Tiv, which is, usually, by employing a "compound verb" made up of the nouns "body" or "heart" and a verb: for example, "to anger" or "to be angry" is *vihi shima*, literally "spoil heart," and the same phrase is most often used for "to be sad"; "to be happy" can bring together *doo* (good) and *shima* (heart) in various combinations or can be expressed in phrases like *i saan un iyol*, "he is happy" (literally "it is happy regarding him in the body") (Abraham 1940a, p. 229). Perhaps such constructions are not readily adverbialized by Tiv, but that is such a lame explanation that it is not worth a second thought. Anything can be adverbialized in Tiv! We are left with a problem, then, for songs do have great affective force; composers wouldn't be sued in court, imprisoned for their songs, rewarded handsomely by politicians, and so forth, if they didn't.

Two other frames used in this research, which were designed to elicit descriptive phrases, metaphors, and similes, confirm the impression of a technical preoccupation. *A gber imo er* _____, "he sings like _____" or "he sings as _____," produces many character referents and analogies to voices from the animal kingdom: "like a madman," "like a drunkard," "like a bird," "like a fool," "like frog," "like an absent-minded person," "like thunder," "as if he has no lungs," "as if crying," "as a monkey laughs," "like a dove," "like an old man," and so forth. The frame *a gber imo sha* _____, "he sings with, in, at _____," elicits largely technical observations once again. He sings "in the right manner," "with much force," "through the nose," "correctly," "at the tips of his teeth," "with dignity," "without experience," "in a lazy way," "with tiredness," and so forth. Obviously, these frames do not yield much in the way of catharsis and cathexis. The question of the affective force behind Tiv songs and their affective correlates remains.

What else, in our terms, is missing? What of our big three—harmony, melody, and rhythm? *Tsorogh* (see above), in the sense of "support" or "blending," could serve as a gloss for our concept of "harmony" in a very tight pinch. *Ikenge* or *ikyenge* can serve more easily as a translation of "melody," for a composer speaks frequently of his *ikenge* in the sense of his characteristic melodic line. But the word can also mean "tone," "pronunciation," "intonation," "shout," or "raised voice" in various contexts. Strangely enough, "rhythm" really has no single equivalent in Tiv either. One can use *kwagh kuhan*, "thing drummed," but it is just as ambiguous as that; the phrase can be a substitute for a specific drum, for example, *gbande* (one skin head, open bottom) or *indyer* (slit-log), as well as a reference to the sounds that come from a drum. And the notion of patterning or rhythmic sounds is only implicit in the latter usage. To say "he plays the drum in rhythm" or "rhythmically," one might use any number of expressions on the order of a *a kuhan gbande sha atsam atsam*, "he beats the drum on songs" or "according to the song (patterns)"; or one could use one of the adverbs that communicates accuracy, bit-by-bit-clarity, and so forth. *Ikenge* can even be used as a gloss for "rhythm" in some contexts.

As one moves further into the more esoteric aspects of English musical vocabulary, Tiv equivalents become, I suspect, harder and harder to find. The idea of "scale" or "mode," for example, is completely alien to Tiv. On numerous occasions, I spent long hours trying to persuade various fully professional *gida* players (the *gida* is a double reed or shawm used in *swange* bands and elsewhere; see plate 4) to play from the lowest note to the highest "by steps," "like stairs or a ladder." But my analogies and explanations were futile. They could understand what I wanted, but were forever lapsing into melody or "feeling around" for notes that might have been missed earlier in the ascent or descent—and finding them! This experience, among many others, confirmed my belief that Tiv "music" should be analyzed on its own terms, but that is easier said than done (see chapter 4).

While Tiv dance is not the central form of expression examined in this book, it certainly ought to be, since it is the central form of expression for Tiv. One can make a case for dance as the primary focus of attention in any analysis of the arts in any culture, certainly any African culture (see chapter 5), for it exists dynamically in both space and time and can bring together many of the other expressive elements in a culture—song, instrumental music, costume, elements of drama. And, in Africa, sculpture (see Thompson 1971, secs. 12 and 13; and Thompson 1974) and architectural context must sometimes be considered elements of the dance as well. Partially as a consequence of these multiple accretions, but largely because of what dance is itself, it is much more difficult to talk about dance than song (Keil 1966b, App. B). Some of those few secrets that dance may yield to rational inquiry will be revealed through the application of various sound-synchronized film techniques (Keil 1969) that permit repeated and careful observation. Other keys to understanding may come from scrupulous field studies that follow a dance from its inception through rehearsals to initial performances. In the meantime, a swift glance at the Tiv dance terminology adds to our semantic topography and presents some important problems.

There are again two nouns to consider that parallel the nouns for song in some respects. *Amar* is probably the more traditional and very specific term (like *icam,* for "call-and-response song") meaning "dance" or by extension "ceremony." Today it is also used for the drills of soldiers and policemen. The general term more often used (like *imo,* for "voice" or "song"), however, is *ishol,* which can mean in addition to "dance," "drawing lots," "gambling, playing cards, playing ball and other games," "jesting, talking figuratively or proverbially." The sentence *a dugh ishol* could mean either "he coined a proverb" or "he composed a dance." It is interesting that Tiv and English share this pair of homonyms: *ìshòl,* "to gamble," and *ìshòl,* "to gambol," that is, dance, frolic, and skip around for joy. Perhaps in old England gambling and gamboling may have had the common denominator of play or sport.

Both *ìshòl* and *ámár* invite dangerous etymological speculation, dangerous in that my knowledge of historical linguistics in general, and of the ways in which tonemic principles may or may not operate in spawning new words in an African language, is virtually nonexistent. The word *ìshól,* with a high tone on the second syllable, means "divining chain," as in the phrase *ìshól kor un,* literally "the divining chain siezed him or her" or "the divining chain has picked him/her as the guilty person." Both nouns, *ìshòl* and *ìshól,* belong to the same noun classes in both singular and plural—further evidence, perhaps, that one word may have derived from the other. Does the theme of fate, luck, games of chance, or the notion of playing with objects tie these two distinct words together in any way? And if they are linked etymologically, does that do anything to strengthen the notion, already implicit in the various uses of *ìshòl* alone, that to dance is somehow to tempt fate, to gambol with your body, to gamble with your life?

If only one could give in to the Western bias that sees the tone of a syllable as secondary, tacked on, not as vital to meaning as vowels and consonants, the hypothetical stem *mar* could then form the foundation of a very pleasing theory about dance as a life force (especially when conjoined with a positive answer to the timidly rhetorical question just addressed to *ishol*). Consider the following *mar* words: (1) *màr*, "to give birth (with female subject)," "to beget a child (with male subject)," with the additional meaning of "to recover" (be reborn?) in connection with wounds or snake bite; (2) *m̀màr̃*, "act of giving birth"; (3) *m̃ār̃*, "off-spring"; (4) *ìmàr̃*, plural *ámár̃*, any "flute"; (5) *ámár*, any "dance." Dances are an intimate part of courtship and marriage, indeed *ámár* is the preferred noun when referring to dance as part of a marriage ceremony. Tiv themselves view the flute as a phallic symbol (see chapter 2). A clay, wooden, or makeshift phallus (plate 1) is often erected in the very middle of the drummer's circle (only men drum) as women do their dance in a circle around them. Is it far fetched to assume that fertility, birth, rebirth, the life force is the root of *ámár*, the hub of the dance?

By far the most common verb form is *vine*, "to dance" and also "to spin," as in *a vine aco,* "he spins the top." I think that "to dance" is the primary referent, so we might more accurately say "he dances the top" or "he makes the top dance." Figuratively one can say *a vine ishom,* literally "he spins machete," meaning that he slashed at something with a stylized motion.

In my research to date I have encountered only six other verbs of motion that can replace *vine* in the frame *a vine ishol. A cagh ishol:* "he presses down the dance" might be a translation, or "he tramples the dance." There is a strong connotation of "dancing seriously" or "really digging into it." Additional meanings for *cagh* in other contexts are "to tread down," "to render level," "to crush underfoot," "to define a path," "to grind up (meat or bones)." The verb is appropriate to heavier, down-to-earth dancing, especially the style known as *ibiamegh,* the traditionally penultimate prestige ceremony for elders which involves extensive praise-singing and dancing. *Cagh* can also be used for most sections of any women's dance style in which the feet take small steps close to the ground and most of the movement is in the rest of the body. *A telegh ishol:* "she dances with the back bent forward, straightening it, and bending forward again" or, from another informant, "to dance by twisting your body slowly"; it is primarily a feminine motion. *A tsue ishol:* "he jumps the dance" or "to jump for joy in dancing," and *a shav amar,* "he dances with power, enthusiasm"; both are primarily masculine, the former probably exclusively so. *A ngurum ishol:* "he or she bends in dancing"; the verb used here can also mean "to bow to a person." *A dzomon ishol:* "she (probably less frequently 'he') twists the dance." This verb is usually used for winding a watch, plaiting rope, wringing out the wash.

There are scores of adverbs to describe dancing in Tiv, but I see no point in listing them all until I have had a chance to record more Tiv observations of and judgments on actual dancing and particular dancers. At various times, however, I did ask people to suggest those adverbs and descriptive phrases most appropriate to men's and women's dance movements; the contrasting modifiers most often chosen further illustrate the significant and potentially crucial dichotomy in Tiv modes of expression already apparent in the seven verbs for dancing and the contrast between "hot" and "cool" adverbs above.

For feminine motion the most frequently applied adverbs are from the set used for low-soft-slow-smooth singing, namely, *lugh* (softly, gracefully, gently) and *legh* (smoothly, calmly). *Kule kule* has approximately the same meanings, with "steadily" a frequently added gloss, and is only slightly less popular. After this "liquid L" trio, two adverbs of "perfection" are most frequently cited: *tsember tsember* and *sha inja sha inja*. Slow speed does not seem to be the pivotal factor one would expect, for Tiv students filling in the blanks are as prone to put in the adverbs for "quickly"—*fefa fefa* or *fele fe fele*—as they are to use *tegh tegh,* the nearest equivalent to "slowly." Taking away "slow" and "low" from the liquid trio, we are left with soft-smooth-steady-graceful perfection as criteria for women's dancing. On the negative side of the ledger, *jimba jimba* is the most frequently used adverb, with the usual gloss being "loosely"; "immodestly, roughly, immorally," are sometimes added, and the connotation of lascivious conduct is strong. A friend translated the adverb as "in an attractive harlotic manner." Other negative adverbs suggest that there is a point at which soft-smooth dancing becomes sluggish and sloppy, for example, *gbedaa gbedaa* or *gbedoo gbedoo* or *gbegheleee.* And an adverb for "stiffly, ungracefully," *gende gende,* is occasionally heard. Perhaps the highest compliment that can be paid to a woman dancing is, "She dances as if there were no bones in her body." Very rarely the verbs of twisting and bending— *dzomon, ngurum, telegh* (see above)—are turned into adverbs to communicate this idea, and every so often one hears phrases like *kelen mon,* "stretching the neck," or *sombon iwenge,* "as if to break her waist."

The primary adverbs for men's dancing are *taver taver,* "strongly," and *agee agee* (or *ager ager* or *sha agee sha agee*), "forcefully, energeticly." In the responses of eighty-five Tiv students, these two adverbs are linked with men's dancing five times more frequently than are any of the other adverbs (with the exception of *dang dang,* "badly," which is as frequently used in connection with poor dancing by women, and which is not very informative in either case). Interestingly enough, in this same sample at least, the adverbs of "perfection" are rarely applied to men's movement, while, as we have seen, they are liberally applied to women by the same respondents. Two secondary characteristics of men's dancing are "speed" and what might be called "pride of place." Not only is *fefa fefa* often heard, but *ayem ayem*, 'runningly," and a variety of other adverbs that carry strong connotations of swiftness and agility. No one adverb stands out for "proudly," but *sha iceen sha iceen* is fairly common, and *gbar gbar*, "openly, publicly, fearlessly," "as if speaking to many people without obscuring important points," can stand for a number of adverbs, each infrequently used, that make roughly the same impact—this dancer is happy to express himself, not afraid to take up public space. A few idiosyncratic negative adverbs, rarely used, make the same point in describing "cramped" or "pinched" movement—this dancer looks as if he needs room to move. If women err on the side of sluggishness, a few expressions like *kpoo kpoo, geen geen, gbue gbe gbue, kung ge kung* indicate that men can be too wild, abrupt, and over energetic.

Though much work remains to be done on the Tiv conceptualization of song and dance (gathering data from a female sample, devising and testing new frames, and, most important, spending many more hours talking with composers, singers, dancers, and their immediate audiences), the outlines of contrasting masculine and feminine modes of choreographic expression are already reasonably clear, not only in the ways they are talked about but in the dances themselves (see chapter 5). Less clear in my mind are the ways in which these masculine and feminine styles interpenetrate in the description of, and criteria for, "perfect" songs. The dynamics vocabulary—low-soft-slow-smooth-(cool) versus high-loud-fast-strong-(hot)—is equally contrastive and certainly complimentary, for I have no evidence that one singing dynamic is preferred to, better than, more "perfect" than, the other. Perhaps the simple fact of complimentarity, of interpenetrating masculine and feminine principles, brings us closer to the *inja* of Tiv song.

Many of the essential semantic themes in this chapter can be linked, however tentatively, to the idea of a male/female dialectic whose higher synthesis is the celebration of fertility or life. The hypothetical etymologies offered for *ishol* and *amar* fit this theme perfectly, but they were tailored to fit and they are hypothetical.[3] Perhaps the energies tapped

3. At least one Tiv reader, Tarwanger Jagusa, found the *ishol* etymologies

52

by *dugh* and *gba,* those morally neutral, motion-based "verbs of creation," are primarily sexual. It is no bold Freudian stroke to suggest this, yet it is harder to explain precisely in what sense it may be so. Are the many explosive verbs of "starting" masculine? Given the parallel adverbs of "high" dynamics and descriptions of men's dance movement, a positive conclusion is hardly escapable. But aside from *yese,* "to nurse" the song, there is nothing very feminine about the other verbs of response. *Tsorogh* seems to muddy the metaphorical waters, for it can mean to sing responsorily, to dance polymetrically, or to play the high-pitched male drums in "counterpoint" to the low mother drum. Perhaps *tsorogh* is neither masculine nor feminine in its connotations but rather a key concept of interpenetration and blending; that would help to keep the yin-yang feeling alive and the drum family playing happily together. The yam-cultivation metaphor that grew from the uses of *dugh* and *gber* could be transplanted in this fertile field somewhere. To be followed by a planting of cassava, *a gber logu,* or a harvest of millet, *a gber amine.* Other usages of *gber* have to do with rejuvenation, and some of the contexts for *dugh* could be united around the theme of fertility, a rich yield—collecting honey, catching fish, gaining a wife, digging or cleaning a well. But evidence of this sort seems somewhat circumstantial, the theory a possible imposition.

While the "singing" verbs *wa* and *gber* denote physical action—"fixing in place," "cutting into"—one hesitates before giving them phallic powers. What sexual slant dare we give to their parallel usages in placing and cutting curses or building (*wa*) and igniting (*gber*) fires? And the heavy emphasis on praise-singing in almost all Tiv songs, as expressed in the extended architectural metaphor, must give us pause. Possibly this psychocultural theory of "fertile song" receives its social verification in the analogy between a song of praise and the roof constructed and raised to cap a new dwelling, presumably for a new wife with children of her own.

Before presuming any further, however, it might be wiser to turn from single words and their enticing connotations in order to explore verbal narratives for further clues to the nature of Tiv song.

---

and connections very persuasive. The posited fertility relationships between *mar* words were greeted with some skepticism, though he noted that *amar* can mean a lot more than dance: festival, ceremony, eating, drinking, many people talking, enjoyment, as well as dance, are all implicit in a phrase like *mba wan amar,* literally "they are putting or making *amar.*"

Song in the Tiv Imagination

T HE PRECEDING survey of the vocabulary used in talking about song and related phenomena gives us many clues to the ways in which Tiv conceptualize song. Seeking to enrich these concepts, to fill the terms with energy and feeling, Tiv tales seem a likely source of illumination since most stories contain a song and in most instances the song is clearly central to the action. The usual questions—Who sings? When? Where? How? What? Why?— ought to serve well enough, but one can hardly embark upon such a straightforward path without frequent nervous glances over the shoulder at Freud, Jung, Propp, Lévi-Strauss, Jakobson, Stith Thompson and a number of other theorists.

In an often told Tiv tale that may be a model of and for my own predicament, a small boy returning home with his parents from a distant farm suddenly remembers the flute he léft behind. Against his parents' wishes he goes back to fetch it. They caution him to stay on the "dirty and thorny road" and avoid the clear wide path of the supernaturals, but flute safely in hand, he takes the neat path home and is soon confronted consecutively by the Hand, Head, Thigh, Chest, and Intestines, who view him as meat for their stew. He postpones his capture by fluting a song so that each body part dances to exhaustion. Eventually they recuperate and give chase until finally the Head (or in some versions a finger of the Hand) descends upon him as he enters the compound, gouging his back, hence the hollow of the back or the backline (in one version the backbone) all humans have today. Some versions end with the moral that "advice is second mother to a child."

It is a cautionary tale. But like the boy, all I want is my flute, the *inja* or essence of song, and I would prefer to ignore parental advice for whatever appears to be the easiest path. Surely versions of many of these tales can be found in other Bantu cultures and beyond; but pointing in a footnote to the variations of a Tiv tale in other cultures can

56 only raise important issues, not resolve them. Just as certainly, careful syntagmatic (Propp 1968; Dundes 1964) and paradigmatic (Lévi-Strauss 1969) structural analyses would reveal the significance of songs within narrative contexts more precisely. Kenneth Burke's work (1969) seems to have been designed with Tiv tales specifically in mind. And any thorough discussion should at least attempt to introduce the full panoply of psychoanalytic principles and mechanisms if only to assess the ways in which they can or cannot be modified to fit Tiv collective fantasies.

While the various theorists lurk along the analytic path we will be following and make their presence felt in more or less unpleasant ways, this "meat" would like to escape the grasp of any one of them and, if he can't avoid them altogether, make them all dance to the tune of his flute. I would like to be able to state what song does, what it mediates in the Tiv symbolic universe, and to speculate now and then upon the immediacy or immanent qualities of song in the Tiv affective universe —what song *is*. I am not at all certain that this distinction between symbolic and affecting universes is either plausible or useful, for there are so many easy ways of saying that a song is what it does, and somewhat more mysterious ways of indicating that a song does what it is. The Greeks may have had a word for it, "ethos," the power of music to "express and even generate qualities of good and evil" (Anderson 1966: 2). Whatever definition and kinds of power we eventually give to "Tiv song," the varying contexts for songs provided by the tales must be full of clues as to their nature.

Quantitatively, I have examined almost 150 tales that contain songs; over a third are "as told in situ" tales (taped, transcribed, and translated); another fifth come from three Tiv storytellers in Ibadan who were asked to narrate concisely only those stories that included songs; about a fifth of the remaining stories were culled from a large sample of tales written out by secondary-school students; the rest come from miscellaneous sources, including those published by Abraham (1940b, pp. 65ff.) and Frobenius (1924, pp. 266–352).

Songs are conspicuous by their absence in the Frobenius collection of forty-three tales, but versions of six stories that do have songs in my collection are found in the Frobenius set, and other tales there have implicit "song situations," events that might be punctuated with song if they were being told today. This absence of songs is mysterious; given Frobenius's enthusiastic response to integrated Tiv performances, one suspects that he would have made much of any songs the storytellers included, or at least would have noted them in passing. In the Abraham set of sixteen tales (pp. 64ff.) a song is explicitly part of the plot in one story and strongly implicit in at least two others (the chief sets up a drumming contest for suitors in one; the hare enters a dance riding a lion, and his retainers "set up a loud drumming" in another). Today certainly more than half the stories, as told, feature songs, but assuming the accuracy of previous collectors, this may be a comparatively recent emphasis.

Qualitatively, all visitors to Tivland agree that storytelling can be a very impressive dramatic event and that it is a focal point of Tiv culture. Frobenius seems to have been overwhelmed during his visit in 1912 and prefaces his opinion that the Tiv are the best storytellers he has encountered in Africa with the following:

> Und wie sie erzählten! Das war ein Leben, eine Mimik, eine Bewegung mit Armen und Augen und mit dem Korper! Mit dem sterbenden Tiere, von dem sie erzählten, warfen sie sich auf die Erde; mit dem entrüsteten Konig sprangen sie auf; mit dem Erschreckten prallten sie zurück und mit dem Weinenden weinten sie. Dichtkunst und Mimik waren eins, frisch, lebendig, effektvoll. [p. 243]

A storytelling event provides a fitting basis for the final chapter of Laura Bohannan's autobiographical novel, *Return to Laughter* (Bowen 1964). In the tales she finds many rich metaphors not only for Tiv situations but for her own absurd and disturbing situation as a socially scientific participant-observer deeply enmeshed in the lives and deaths of the people she came to study. Even a long excerpt can only serve to point the reader to the chapter itself:

> As the evening wore on, other men also rose to tell their stories, pressing brothers and cousins into service in the charades and commandeering props from the women of the homestead. A pot tied snoutlike over the face made a hippopotamus. Sheepskins, leaves and cloth-covered stools created strange monsters and sprites. There was not a single dull story. The audience wouldn't allow it. They were as loud in their criticism as in their praise, and people shouted down any fable teller who failed to hold their attention: "That's too long." "Your song's no good." "You've got the story wrong." "Learn to dance." Sometimes it needed only the momentary inattention of part of the audience to embolden one of the other storytellers to jump into the center even while another fable was being told. Then for a few moments we heard two tales, two songs at once. Soon peo-

58   ple would take up only the one chorus and the other fable teller
would sit down.

Mainly it was a contest between Gbodi and Ikpoom who were
the two great storytellers of the country. Gbodi, a short stocky little
man with a huge voice, excelled as a dancer and tumbler. In the tale
of the cricket and the praying mantis, he danced holding a heavy
mahogany mortar in his hands. First, as the praying mantis, he held
it over his head; then, placing the mortar on the ground, he continued to dance on it upside down, his hands grasping the edge of the
mortar, his feet in the air—and singing all the while.

Ikpoom excelled in mime. His ugly face was extraordinarily expressive, and he was at his best when he could himself act out all
parts of the story at once. Now he was telling the tale of the chief's
daughter who refused to marry any man, for she knew she was far
too good for any suitor who came to court her. Ikpoom's voice was
shrilly angry when, as the girl, he warned lovers off the farm and
threatened to shoot them with bow and arrow. His voice was eerie
and his song uncanny as he portrayed the chief of the underworld
sprites, Agundu, who is a head with wild, red eyes and with gouts
of blood on the raw cut neck that terminates the creature. He showed
us how Agundu borrowed the radiance of the sun and moon and
with them dazzled the girl, how she followed this bright illusion
away from her own people whom she had scorned, and how at the
very gates of the underworld Agundu gave back to the sun his glory
and to the moon her beauty. Only then, when it was too late, did
the girl see what monster she had chosen, and then, too late and in
vain, she longed for a human mate.

I had no need to hear the shouted proverb that marks the end of
each story. I knew the moral of this tale. Especially now, in this situation in which our common humanity and pleasure in amusement
was so evident, the dangers of parting from one's own to follow beck-
oning strangeness loomed perilous and sad. [pp. 287–88]

My own experience with a major tale-telling event was neither so
pleasant nor so profound, though the facts of that evening bear out
most of Laura Bohannan's fictions. Eager to hear the best raconteurs
in the area, I sponsored a contest, and word was sent out accordingly.
On the appointed evening, over a hundred people came to the compound where I was staying. Since I had anticipated the arrival of twenty
or thirty people at most, the millet beer I had commissioned vanished
quickly, and after much shuffling of inadequate seating arrangements
for the elders, the stories began to flow. As one story ended—more often
than not without a shouted moral or proverb—several people would

start other stories simultaneously, the narrator with the strongest personality, the most explosive opening formula, and the best crowd response carrying the day. Every tale was dramatized; the narrator at the very least seemed obligated to suggest the movements of an animal character, dance to his song, or highlight the narrative with action of some kind. A few days before the event, the eldest son of the head of the compound fashioned a clay penis for possible use as a prop (see plate 1). Occasionally, performers were recruited in advance and even hurriedly costumed; more often a narrator would enlist participants from the crowd to enact a particular episode, or more precisely, to demonstrate it, for the narrator always keeps control of the story, and the roles of extras are as brief as they are dynamic.

Everyone seemed to be having a good time, but soon the stories dwindled and thunder was heard rolling in the distance, and when the departing guests discovered that the anthropologist had provided only a duck for a prize, the scene became chaotic. Everyone had expected at least a goat or a beast of sufficient size to give at least a piece of meat to all participants and a bigger portion to the best. Under the circumstances, local elders whom I had counted on to assist in the judging were reluctant to appear connected to the fiasco, much less offer an opinion. It began to rain, and I found myself in a reception hut, surrounded by a chorus of eloquently angry Tiv. Expert storytellers had become equally proud of their skills at invective, and no one was eager to walk home in the rain carrying a duck or part of a duck. Finally, some hours later, I was left holding the duck, a mercifully quiet Muscovy.

Usually, however, storytelling is not a major dramatic event but a simple gathering of some children and adults eager to postpone going to bed on a moonlit night. In my experience the setting is almost always in the open air, next to a hut or beneath a tree. The adults trade stories —"Kwam is full of lies, let me tell you a true thing!"—and the children wait eagerly for a chance to laugh or sing the responses to songs. The stern Tiv elder or compound head, who is normally respected, if not feared, is often the best source of *akaa ahil*, literally "things strange or wonderful," and there is really no comparable event in Tiv life wherein so much sheer fun can be shared between the generations. While men are as a rule the outstanding performers and dominate any evening, the wives of the compound, who come from other areas, often have stories that the children haven't heard before. While there is no code of etiquette that prohibits women from trading tales with the men,

60   women usually tell their tales to children when men are not present. Children sometimes tell stories to each other, and I have recorded versions of tales by seven- and eight-year-old boys and girls. Often a visiting in-law or stranger provides a good excuse for a storytelling session, for he is bound to have stories that no one has heard before or interesting versions of familiar favorites.

Perhaps the most outstanding feature of Tiv narrative style is what might be called "the opening shot." The conventional opening formula is '*Kwagh hil wam gba ding!*' which R. C. Abraham translates as "my story fell plop!" But *gba,* we recall, is more than a mere "fall," and *ding* is also the sound of a gun firing. Just as the terminology suggests that a strong opening for a song is singularly important to Tiv, the variety of "opening shots" available to a narrator suggests a cultural preoccupation with force, not so much of impetus or momentum, but of inclusion, definitiveness, even, ironically, a sense of finality—This is it! All of it at once! For example, "My story touches the sky and the ground!" or "My story did not fall so, it occurred and killed six dogs." One can be sure the next man's story will kill twelve dogs. If it does, a bystander may jump in with, "Are you sure it didn't kill fifteen?" or "Is it only dogs your stories kill?" and be answered, "Yes! Let it kill them." In a story that includes a dance-celebration, the narrator begins, "Be ready to shoot your guns [onomatopoetically] when the time comes!" When a story begins with an account of famine, the hunger falls with terrific force—*jine gba kpeng! kpeng!* Even when there is no opening formula, the last words of the first sentence are likely to be shouted at a high pitch: *mimi je!* "true for certain!" or *shima i mom!* "with one heart!"

Another narrator opened his story in the following way: "Once the chief invited people to farm for him. In my story the toad fled and the rustling was yooooh! He put a tooth in a tree, twisted it, and it broke, kpooogh! The thing turned very quickly like the horns of an antelope!" These three flourishes after the statement of theme seem to advertise rhetorical potency, like quick sprints before a race, for the story which follows, as we shall see, has nothing to do with noisy toads, antelope horns, or broken teeth. In another version of this story, the narrator begins: "The tale! The tale of Gbogboachia! My tale never went so!" Starting with a bit of irrelevant but fine-sounding nonsense may be a way of framing effectively the coherent story which follows. Even when no one has preceded the storyteller, his opening line may insist upon the unique qualities and power of the coming story, "My thing did not say so!" "It's another thing I had seen and was startled!" "I never tell lies like the others."

In keeping with this explosive opening style, the problem of the story is almost always stated clearly in the first sentence or two following the initial formula.

Endings, conversely, are often matter-of-fact and sometimes mumbled: "The hare tricked them and he escaped again; so this is the end of mine." "That is why it is good that one should do something by himself and not go take another's by force. What is gotten by force is not good; God doesn't allow it, that is all." "But for only the strong people to stay together in one compound is very difficult; so that is how it is." A storyteller may have a favorite phrase for ending, for example, *m kule m kule ngu la jo!* "I have certainly finished that one!" which is clipped and precise, but it is said with the feeling of "so much for that." Occasionally a bystander will add a punchline: "And so that is how some women picked up big vaginas and others got small ones." "Imagine! Botwer's wife took a huge one!" Although almost every story has a moral, the moral often has a tacked-on or obligatory quality. Sometimes the teller will rephrase the point of the story in different ways, as if savoring the implications, or as if it were a commentary on the tale rather than part of the tale itself.

In the body of the story a great many stylistic devices may be used to intensify dramatic action: shifts of voice quality to identify characters, changes of pace, pregnant pauses, sotto voce asides, exclamations, pleasant alliterative conversations that are repeated more for sound than content, and so forth. But a full exposition of Tiv storytelling devices would be a long story in itself. The expressive range of technique is very broad. Indeed it occasions some difficulty in identifying songs within stories, for often a repeated conversation between characters, the intensity of a repeated exclamation, the onomatopoetics of a particular activity, will verge on song form. I have chosen rather strict criteria in selecting tales that include songs for the sample: a definite call-and-response pattern or an easily transcribed melodic shape.

The basic or normative structure of Tiv narratives seems clear enough; as in most folktales the world over, I suppose, there is a problem or situation, and a strategy for that situation is enacted (and the same action may be repeated with variations) which leads to a solution. Most Tiv tales would lend themselves to a fairly simple motifemic analysis, but not all would give in gracefully. While norms are clear, pressure toward enforcement of them seems very slight. When I asked three storytellers for abbreviated versions of all the stories they knew that had songs in them, compliance was swift and easy. The transcribed texts average a few hundred words in length, and only a few show obvious signs of truncation. If asked for folktale songs alone, with just the briefest description of the story itself, storytellers are equally adept at capsule summaries. Very short tales or abbreviated versions can also occur, though rarely, under normal circumstances.

More interesting is the apparent ease with which tales and episodes can be combined or embedded within each other. One young man of considerable talent (discovered at the otherwise disastrous evening I sponsored), when asked to write out copies of his best tales, gave me one text in which six stories were expertly woven together in a manner somewhat akin to Amos Tutuola's style (1952, 1954). I have recorded a few instances where a storyteller combines two or sometimes three versions of stories collected in isolation elsewhere; the presence of more than one song in a story may point to this kind of synthesis. Occasionally a set of situated characters introduced at the beginning of a story are simply abandoned, never to be heard from again; one character may simply leave the rest for another compound where a different plot is thickening. One suspects that the narrator has started something he can't finish, but rather than admit it, he has shifted swiftly to a plot he can remember.

There is also a rather involved and interesting "tar baby" sequence to consider: the hare tricks the tortoise into the boiling pot, eats him, but eventually gets stuck to the fat in his shell limb by limb, is hauled by the revived tortoise to the top of a mountain, where he is condemned to death by the animals assembled but escapes death by staging a bizarre death ceremony. This sequence forms the concluding section of three very long and quite different stories, but it does not occur by itself in my collection of tales.

A few tales seem to be deliberately "shaggy dog," with one strange sequence of events linked to another by a very tenuous thread. In one such story the hare's new daughter-in-law demands a slaughtered cow from her husband, one that no fly has touched. The hare undertakes the task for his son, climbs many mountains in search of a fly-free area, and runs afoul of a giant; giants battle each other; the hare and his family escape various traps; different taboos are broken and consequences paid; a tar-baby sequence occurs, and so on and so on; the story concludes with an episode that explains why the ant has a seg-mented body.

It is noteworthy, I think, that the vast majority of tales told at large gatherings, tales written by school boys, and tales tape recorded by in-dividuals in an "office" setting are unified and simple in plot structure, while almost half the tales taped at small, informal gatherings on moon-lit nights are complex in one or more of the ways suggested above. A number of experiments could be designed to test the hypothesis that, given the time and opportunity, Tiv narrators enjoy "stretching out" and improvising with their lore.

There are a few obvious generalizations to make, or recurrent pat-terns to note, concerning content before considering specific tales and the possible motives for, meanings of, and powers inherent in, song.

Most Tiv tales could be listed under the very general headings "food" or "sex," and a number of stories pivot upon the tension between these two basic needs. Most of the stories under the "food" heading posit famine as the situation, and strategic responses include cooperation in hunting or fishing (usually temporary), cannibalism, greed, hoarding, theft, and so forth. We might also include here those tales that begin with a farming competition and a few stories where a name must be guessed in order to eat.

Most of the stories under "sex" begin with the chief's unmarried daughter (or daughters), and winning her hand usually entails a con-test or completion of a difficult task. Stories about a widow seeking a penis, an envious co-wife, the distribution of different sized genitalia, and the problem of adultery could all be grouped here.

"Famine" and "chief's daughter" stories make up almost 30 percent of the tales; adding other sexual and food acquisition themes, one can account for more than half of them. The remaining 40 percent or so might be reduced to 10 percent by establishing a few residual cate-gories derived largely from the conclusions of tales rather than their beginnings: explicitly educational stories about stubborn, disobedient children or naive mimesis that fails; stories about suffering; stories that explain emnity between two animals; stories that explain the origin of a tool or technique—weapons or fire, for example. Most stories end with an explanation of a custom or a fact of nature; others provide a moral or recommend a rule of behavior. Consideration of endings alone, therefore, might well lead to a more convenient classification, but a number of singular cases would remain—for example, the "flute for-

64

gotten at farm" story summarized at the outset of this chapter. Another version of the latter exists, this one involving a "ring left at home," and these, with two stories about lost knives might add up to a category. But others seem to be unique: a story about a son avenging his father; a nearly plotless "story" about a blind man (an elephantiasis victim in another version) who tries to join the dance; a woman who kills her sister, burns her, and is rebuked in song by the ashes; and others could be cited that resist categorization.

A careful analysis by a trained folklorist might produce a very different overview of Tiv tale structure and content. Fable and fairytale genres are surely discernible, yet they seem to exist as poles of a spectrum: humans-and-supernaturals at one end, tales with exclusively animal characters at the other. But in most tales the hare and other animals spend more time, so to speak, with humans or supernaturals than they do with each other. In some exclusively animal fables a sprite pops up for an instant to offer the hare a piece of advice, or to shout a magical word or two, and then disappears. A human compound may appear in the conclusion of an animal story, if one of the animals takes refuge there. It would be interesting to distribute, say, a hundred stories into various categories according to the cast of characters: (1) humans, (2) naturals (animals and the occasional stone, plant, or object that acts), and (3) supernaturals (*adzov*, "sprites"; *mbakuv*, "the dead"; *mbakur*, "those other people"; or discrete body parts). Some patterns of association might emerge.

In any case, the cast of primary characters is easily summarized:

Tor, the chief, is a stock character whose motivation is invariably simple, for example, finding a husband for his daughter, providing food for a guest, seeking out a guilty party, trying to win a bet made with an animal, attempting to rule in a tribe without rulers. Although he often defines the initial situation or sets up the bet, contest, or task, he *never* wins. He never sings either. Lacking intelligence, he loses his precious dignity; he marries off a daughter but is tricked and humiliated in the process. It is clear that in real life the Tiv are ambivalent about authority, to phrase the problem politely. In the projected world of the folktale, the chief's role is clearly that of a pompous fool, a symbol of conscious control overthrown by unconscious forces.

Wantor, the princess (literally "daughter of chief"), is as stereotyped as her father, always an object or counter to be won or lost. Whenever Wantor or her general equivalent, any single girl, shows some character, it is usually fickleness, a silly fixation, an ability to cry for help with

fervor while being carried off by a monster or a loathsome beast. Al- 65
most none of the tougher qualities characteristic of many Tiv young
women are reflected in the tales.

When an older woman appears in a tale, however, she is invariably
a strong character and is likely to have various occult powers under her
control. Other human characters, "the husband," "the orphan," and so
on, appear in the stories but are usually undeveloped when contrasted
to the animals.

· Alɔm, the hare, is the hero or protagonist of most Tiv tales. To desig-
nate him "a trickster figure" may miss the mark slightly, though he is
certainly full of tricks. As he maneuvers through tale after tale, one is
impressed with his cunning, stubbornness, greed, cruelty, pride, fecun-
dity. He is a creature of pure will or id, a heightened version of Tiv
everyman acting out impulses that others hold in check, accepting any
challenge. He is anything but a timid little rabbit, though his ears hear
everything and he's ellusive. His family is large, and most adult Tiv
know the names of many of his six to fifteen children. Though the chief
always loses, the hare does not always win. Greed, mismanaged mim-
ickry, an overplayed hand may lead to humiliation or a violent death.
But Alɔm always bounces back.

Anjieke, the hare's wife, is as complicated as the female humans are
simple. Exceedingly practical, adaptable, and often more shrewd than
the hare, she usually has the last word when the hare outsmarts himself. Her sanity can be relied upon.

While Alɔm and Anjieke are superhuman, in the sense that their
virtues, vices, and actions are magnified, the other animal characters
seem to be more exact equivalents of Tiv personality types, but only a
very large collection of tales, much detective work, and a folk taxonomy
of personality types for comparison could verify this hypothesis. Im-
pressionistically, Nor, the elephant, is very much like Tor, the chief—
a clumsy, high-handed rival to Alɔm for the title king of the beasts.
Huer, the iguana, and, to a lesser extent, Kulugh, the tortoise, cooperate
occasionally with Alɔm, usually to their detriment; they are steady, per-
sistent characters (like Hum, the chameleon, hero of two stories in the
sample) who evoke Tiv sympathies. Yar, the buffalo or wildebeest, is
tough, angry, proud. Ihinga, the ground squirrel, substitutes for Alɔm
in a few stories. Representatives of the monkey family are appropriately
mischievous when they appear. The antelopes do not distinguish themselves in any way but are active as "extras." Gbev, the nightjar, a bird
with long double tail feathers, is said to be the only animal that can

outsmart Alɔm, but he makes only a few appearances in these tales. The other night birds that stand for the *mbatsav* (sorcerers) in Tiv belief are even more conspicuous by their absence. Sometimes the animals act in concert as a chorus to Alɔm's tragic or comic heroism.

Supernatural characters are not so easily classified. Presumably *Jongur,* the giant with the flaming anus and insatiable appetite, *Adembelia,* the half-man (one hair, one eye, one tooth, one arm, and so forth), and a host of other monsters with proper names are all members in good standing of one subdivision or another of the *adzov,* loosely translated as "sprites." *Adzov* of various sizes, shapes, and functions can be found living or resting in trees, in wells, and in streams; carved images of domestic *adzov* are found near the hearth of most Tiv cooking houses. The Bohannans report (Laura and Paul 1969, p. 83) that the *mbakuv,* or "spirits of the dead," are really but shades transformed into a kind of *adzov,* but I haven't heard this confirmed or denied by Tiv. Though the *mbakuv* are said to be the hare's *igba,* or "mother's family," they figure in very few of the tales I collected. The individual monsters in the tales seem to have individual natures, and I suspect that their relationships with each other are not nearly as important as the singular effect each has on mere mortals.

Personified body parts and genitalia seem to be separate casts of characters. The former are sometimes referred to as the *mbakur,* or "foreigners," "a tribe other than one's own" (Abraham 1940a, p. 143), and parts are played by Head, Hand, Thigh, Chest, and Intestines. In other stories *Mtswan,* the fierce clitoris (lightning usually flashes when she appears), *Ijua,* the potent penis, and somewhat less frequently, *Ikur,* the vagina, have roles to play, often but not always in conflict with each other. In one story, Vagina's family of four daughters (Clitoris, Labiaminora, Labia-majora, and Short-hairs) do battle with Penis and his sons (Testicles, Scrotum, and a part of the anatomy I haven't identified) and every subpart has a role to play! A whole genre of tales explaining the differential distribution of genitalia exists. This Tiv concern with fragmentation or dismemberment of the body, or to phrase it more positively, the autonomy of individual parts, seems to be unique in African folklore collected and indexed to date (Klipple 1938; Clarke 1958; Lambrecht 1967) and may prove to be a Tiv special emphasis within a worldwide frame as well. Certainly it is a theme in Tiv lore and life that we will return to in conclusion.

The farm-work wager between the chief and Alɔm, the hare, appears in every storyteller's repertoire. I have collected more versions of it than any other story. Since it does not appear in either the Frobenius collection (1924) or in Abraham's (1940b), the story's popularity may be a comparatively recent development.

Once the chief invited people to farm for him: in this my story the toad went and the rustling was yoooooh! He put a tooth in a tree, twisted it, and it broke, kpoooogh! The thing turned very quickly like the horns of an antelope!

The chief made an invitation for a farming festival, so the hare got up and told the chief that no one would dig the chief's farm on the appointed day. "How would you boast with me, saying that you will excel me? Well, let's see those who would attend your farm festival," the hare threatened the chief.

While the chief's workers were about to go to the farm, the hare got up with his own group. He went and hid on the way. He climbed to the top of a tree and stood out very clearly on the top. While the chief's workers were advancing, the hare got up and he took his flute and started to blow:

Igbieke, igbieke, igbieke kur igbieke
Screwing, screwing igbieke
I will use the civet cat's anus
Also the buffalo's
Cobra is his name
I the hare, king of the animals
I used to screw like this: ifiu-ifiu
Lian liaaa! The elephant has made a bet with me
The buffalo has made a bet with me
I say: iniuu! iniuu!

The chief's people threw away their hoes. "Who is that blowing such a sweet flute on the tree top?" they asked among themselves. Thus they turned to the music and started dancing. After a period, the chief sent his wives with food to take to the workers who were in the farm, so that they might eat, for he said that it was time enough for eating. As the women were going, they heard the flute, and the hare, upon seeing them, put a feather in the flute and started pumping it: "Hi fiong! Hi fiong! Hi fiong! TUNG! The chief's wives are now coming," the hare said. Then he began to blow his flute:

(song as above)

The chief's wives turned and started dancing. After a very long time, when the chief didn't see his wives returning, he said, "Eh, I'll go there myself!" He climbed on his horse and began to go to the

68 farm. He held javelins in both his hands. On getting there, he never knew the hare was in the treetop. The hare again pumped his flute with the feather and began to blow:

(song as above)

On his arrival the chief drove the horse away in order to dance. He said that the flute is such a one that he must dance to its tune. He pushed the horse aside, turned, and started to dance. The hare jumped down and asked the chief to give him the bet. "I told you before that no one is going to dig your farm today, but you said that it must be dug—so give me the bet." That is why they don't make bets nowadays, for very often it would result in trouble. My story has ended.

The tale begins with the chief asserting a big man's prerogative, asking people to farm for him. The hare immediately and gratuitously redefines the chief's claim to labor as a boast and transforms a cooperative work day into an individual status competition, though each rival is supported by his own group.

Phallic flute in hand, the hare climbs to the top of a phallic tree and seduces the chief's workers with a phallic song. Aside from the basic verb *kpa*, "to have intercourse," and a more colloquial expression for screwing, *a nul a nul*, onomatopoetics for intercourse abound: *igbieke, igbieke, igbieke kur igbieke* (*kur* has the only high tone in the otherwise monotonal melodic phrase and is probably a shortened version of *ikúr*, "vagina"), *ifiu ifiu, iniu iniu, ishiu ishiu, lian liaaa*. The hare boasts of screwing the anus of his bigger enemies, the buffalo, the civet cat, and by implication, the elephant, as well as the chief. "Cobra [*abuku*] is his name," may be his phallus as snake or one of the more powerful animals being mocked. Probably the hare is boasting of having seduced the wives of these notables, since the common complaint of a cuckholded husband is *a kpaam tswar* "he committed adultery with my wife" (literally "he had coitus with my anus"). In any case, the melody of the flute becomes a song about general phallic potency supported by the rich onomatopoetics of sex.

The workers dance and food production is abandoned. When the chief sends his wives to reciprocate the workers with food for consumption, they are seduced by the flute/song/sex as well, and we note that as the hare cleans his flute it becomes symbolically vaginal when pumped by a phallic feather—*hi fiong! hi fiong! hi fiong! tung!* Finally, fully vested in authority, mounted on horseback (the most prestigious mode of travel in Tivland) with "javelins in both hands," the chief is compelled to abandon high status and armed might for the dance. The narrator insists twice that the chief is oblivious to the source of his downfall.

A few basic equations seem obvious enough even if the units equated and related are not quite under control:

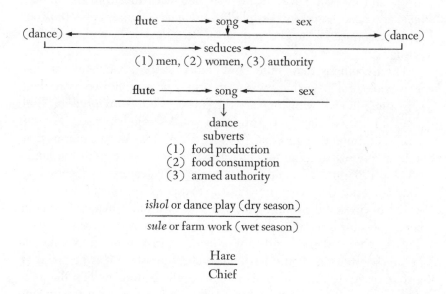

The arrows indicate that song mediates between abstract flute melody and concrete sexual lyric and that dance mediates between the preceding affective complex and its negative effects—no production, no consumption, no "war." If the United States were Tivland, the hare might stop the ecocatastrophe single-handed—that is, single penised. But Tivland is far from affluent, perhaps because from a Western point of view the Tiv spend too much time on beer, song, and dance. Indeed, the story's basic dialectic is probably not so much the status competition between Everyman hare and the chief, as the broader conflict between dry-season dance and wet-season work. Famine is almost always a yearly occurrence in one part or throughout large areas of Tivland, and famine is second only to unmarried women as an initial context for stories and the songs therein.

One might advance some strong propositions about the power or ethos of song in Tiv culture on the basis of this story were it not for the fact that it is bracketed by flute and sex in a metaphorical sandwich or

70 squeeze. Clearly the characters are responding to sweet flute melody, and the sexual lyric is an aside to the audience. Similarly the onomatopoeia accompanying the cleaning of the flute is something of a soliloquy. In the world of this narrative the sexual messages do not count. But the flute certainly does, for it is much more than a phallic symbol, though it is certainly that, both implicitly in the story and explicitly in the culture. We have already conjured with the word for "flute," *ìmàr̀* (pl. *ámā̄r*), and its possible link to *ámár,* "dance," plus the conceivable connection to the verb *màr,* "to give birth," and *m̀ār,* "offspring."

The hypothesis that "flute" and "birth" share a common root that is psychological as well as etymological may be complicated more than it is strengthened by a summary account of the *imborivungu,* or "owl pipe," in Tiv culture. R. C. Abraham entitles his chapter on Tiv sorcery "The Imborivungu Pipe" (1940b, pp. 35ff.); Akiga confirms that it "is a very big thing to the Tiv; it is used for setting right the land" (Akiga, 1965, p. 225), and a list of some of its features as reported by Abraham and Akiga certainly adds up to a powerful force (or the very model of an overdetermined symbol): it is usually made of human bone (possibly ancestral, perhaps representative of *Poor,* the original Tiv's brother) adorned with a wax head, or cast in metal as a figure, and most often this figure has female characteristics; it is designed as a voice disguiser (bat's wing membrane at the bottom, hole in the middle) but is nevertheless considered a flute; it is called *tar wase,* or "our land," in the secret language of the *mbatsav* and symbolizes the unity of a kindred; it is allegedly consecrated with the fetal blood of an induced abortion, with blood and water from this sacrifice put in wells and farms to increase fertility of women and land; catching sight of it obligates the viewer to supply a human victim and the sound of it indicates that a life has been given; it is extremely difficult to blow—the player puts his heel to his anus so as not to blow out his intestines, delivering a blast in one place and then running to a distant point before delivering another.

This last point suggests that the player is imitating the owl *ivungu* for whom the pipe is named, but there are other voice-disguisers pictured in Abraham's ethnography (1940b, plates 10, 11, 12, 13) that are intended specifically for this purpose, including one for *ivungu* as well as *akiki, mtsaan, kpire* (all night birds), *"boon"* or *hwa* the wild cat, and *alɔm,* our friend the hare! The night birds are thought to be the embodiments of the *mbatsav* (see *Return to Laughter* and below), and *hwa* is a night animal; but one wonders why the hare is a suitable animal-vehicle for a nocturnal sorcerer's spirit and what his "voice" is like.

Abraham describes these instruments and their use:

> The procedure is as follows: when a man who has previously provided another with the flesh of a human victim considers that the time is ripe to claim repayment of the debt, or when he is urged by the other members of the *mbatsav* to do so, he waits until one of the above birds settles on the roof of the debtor and utters its cry; he is secreted in the bush near by, and when he hears the cry he imitates the note of the real bird inside a small calabash or other vessel covered with the feathers of the bird in question, and often adorned with the dried head of such a bird. These instruments bear the name of the bird which they symbolize and there are likewise implements made of the skin and sometimes the tail also of the wild cat and hare.

> The calabashes represent the human head; the feathers represent the hair, the orifice the mouth, and the place of the eyes is taken by two cowries and sometimes by two small holes covered with spiders' web; the sagittal suture is marked out by a line of love-beads affixed with wax. . . .

> The orifice of the instruments is studded with a line of these brilliant scarlet beads (Abrus precatorius) and when the *mbatsav* set out at night to claim a flesh-debt, resin (*inyondo*) is smeared over the calabash and set alight, with the result that when the calabash is held near the face, the scarlet glow from the beads lights up the visage of the holder with a scarlet iridescence which lends him a truly terrifying aspect and ensures him a free field for his operations.

> When the real bird utters its first call on the roof, the man inside, who is the flesh-debtor, comes out and asks the bird, "Why have you come?" The bird, without replying, flies away in fear, and the man approaches his debtor with his instrument in his hand, saying "Pay me today what you owe me." The debtor endeavours to put him off with the reply "Go back; I shall search for what you want and tell you when I have got it." The *mbatsav* creditor or his representative as the case may be, refuses to be put off and is finally offered a goat which he accepts. [1940b, pp. 43, 44]

For the time being, at least: Tiv believe that a human sacrifice will have to be made eventually. Many of the remaining pages in the Abraham chapter are devoted to the exhaustive researches undertaken by the British administrators in an effort to substantiate the grislier parts of the Tiv belief pattern by submitting much evidence to the laboratories of Scotland Yard. It all came to nought; not a shred of evidence linking a single Tiv to a single case of magical cannibalism.

We enjoy a chuckle at the expense of the British imperial empiricists and then begin to wonder how much of the preceding account is pieced together hearsay, how much is Abraham hypothesis, and what to make of this pattern of belief and alleged behavior if one or both are "true" in some sense or another. Though the reflected glow of the sorcerer's apprentice as he blows his decorated calabash fits very neatly with the terminology, are we to believe that he burns up his instrument as he plays it, or that he holds the instrument (charred?) in his hot hand as he approaches the flesh debtor? Clearly Abraham is full of hot air, but just as clearly the air could have had but one source and been pumped in only by Tiv agents; so as cultural anthropologists, believers in Belief, we must press on to an interpretation.

The general fusion of nature and culture in this account, the fact that each instrument is iconic for "human head" and an "animal" simultaneously and that its "voice" could be the voice of either or the voice of a witch incorporating both, is striking and raises many questions. Are we to assume a Platonic "form" for "voice" or "song" with human, animal, and supernatural (or superhuman?), both discrete and mixed, manifestations? What is this Tiv quest for perfect mimesis, claiming the voices of the night, all about? Since *imo* can be "voice" or "song" or "sound," by what criteria are we to choose a translation each time? Do notions of "disguise" and "transformation" really fit these phenomena? Or should we speak rather of "intensification"? Or can one evade the issue of *what it is* that is being disguised and/or intensified by using the language of "overdetermined symbolism," intentional "ambiguities," and cultural "ambivalence"? I would like to postpone possible answers to these questions, at least until the final chapter, if not indefinitely, and in the meantime struggle along with what-stands-for-what symbolically, which forces take precedence over others ontologically. Still, I wonder what goes through the mind of a wise Tiv elder when he hears a "voice" in the night? Do Tiv assume a human or superhuman agency for *every* hoot of an owl?

Getting back to the chief's farm, is a song or message implicit in every flute melody? To the audience the song substitutes for the flute, but is there a sense in which the flute disguises the song for the workers within the world of the narrative? What can we infer about Tiv

"voice" or "song" from the fact that the hare's profane-day-flute stops
food production, food consumption, and the chief's progress while the
sacred-night-flute is alleged to promote crops, provide "meat," and enhance authority?

In another version of this story both the chief and the hare have
farms to prepare. They bet on who will be the first to finish; "the chief
then staked a cow, and the hare said he should die if he fails to win."
(Though the hare's life is not explicitly at stake in the other versions
of this story, in one he is described as lean, thin, and so obviously too
weak to farm that the chief challenges him.) Most people go to the
chief's farm; only five to the hare's. But the hare recruits his friend
Ikpienger ("a type of bird," according to the storyteller, but a new-
comer to the Tiv aviary whose name might be variously interpreted:
ikpi, "featherless," or *ikpi*, "sides [of farm or bush]"; *enger*, "[some-
thing] is loose," or *enger*, "to wait all agog") and sends him to the top
of a roadside tree while he hides under it. The workers are not initially
distracted in this story; the slaves who come with food are the first to
be seduced. *Ikpienger* feathers his flute as in the previous story, but the
cleaning of the instrument becomes the introduction to the song—*u
vinga, vinga tu, vinga tu*—and the storyteller instructs his listeners to
answer his calls with the response *Hmmmm*, as if they are teasing
or tickling with the feather: Leader, *"Uladoru uladaa"*; Chorus,
"Hmmm"; and so forth. The wives are sent by the chief and join the
dance; the workers join in, and finally the chief comes and dances till
dusk while the hare's five laborers finish his field. The chief hands over
the cow, and a listener comments in conclusion, "When you are dancing by yourself, you have really been defeated."

Feather-into-flute as metaphor for sexual intercourse is doubled and
reinforced by the call and response pattern. Song is sex, coitus, and just
as the flute is both penis and vagina in action and not merely a static
phallic symbol in the first version, it would seem that here we are not
necessarily witnessing phallic calls and vaginal responses (in this song
connections appear to be the reverse) but rather the dynamic union
itself.

It may be of interest that this third version of the "Chief's Farm Bet"
was told first in a long series of tales by one storyteller, whereas the first
version was next to last in a series of eighteen stories; further evidence,
perhaps, for the tale's centrality in Tiv consciousness, if we assume that
the latter narrator was saving his best for last, and the former wanted
to start "with a bang."

The tale! The tale of Gbogboachia! My tale never went so! Once upon a time the chief had a bet with the hare that he would be the first to dig his farm before the hare's. But the hare assured the chief that no one would attend his farming festival on the appointed date.

So on the day of the farming festival, the hare came there with his drum and sat at the bottom of the field. Then he began to play his drum. (While singing, you should be saying, "Chief, you have made a dancing festival but not a farming festival.") So as the people were cultivating, the hare slung his drum, went and sat at the bottom of the field, and started playing: Kpum! Kpu kpu kpum, kpuum!!

> Chorus: Chief, you've made a dancing festival,
>   But you haven't made a farming festival.
>   The Lion, you have made a dancing festival,
>   But you've not made a farming festival.

All the people broke away from their work and surrounded the hare's drum. They couldn't continue with their farming. The chief came and gave the hare a cow and said that the hare had beaten him.

In this simpler and much shorter version, the hare is less aggressive at the outset, and work stoppage alone wins the wager. The hare situates himself at the "base" or "bottom" of the farm (*ityósule*) to play a drum rather than at the top of a tree to play a flute, and the onomatopoetics are straightforwardly drum-like rather than sexual. Whereas the flute song was a solo, this song is essentially a chorus with drum interlude, and the lyric explicitly summarizes the story. In the chorus the audience seems to be taking on the roles of the workers in the fields, just as the storyteller becomes the hare.

An opposition may be implied by the hare's position at the "base" or "bottom" (*ityɔ* probably not to be confused with *ityɔ*, "patrilineage," unless a tone pun is intended), since the workers usually begin at the "head" or "top" (*ityough*) of the farm. If an *akombo* is set up on a farm to protect it, the emblems are placed at the "top" of the field (Bohannan, Paul and Laura, 1968, p. 44); a compound head usually places his residence and reception hut at the "base" of the compound; *ityough ki taregh* means "east," while *ityo tar* indicates "west." I am not sure what these associations add up to, but there may be a sociogeographic dialectic at work here that complements the sociotemporal conflict alluded to earlier between dry-season dance and wet-season work. Certainly the lyric in this version makes the latter contrast more explicit. During the yearly cycle, dance activity picks up toward the end of the wet season, September into October, as various grain crops have already been harvested, notably millet for beer, and yams can be dug. Dance activity climaxes in December and January, when dance groups take the styles they have been rehearsing for months all over the countryside. The Christian holidays happen to coincide neatly with this dance-touring period. But, ideally at least, this is the same period, November through January, when new fields should be prepared for planting. So there is a clear conflict of interests. Clearing and digging a new field require cooperative labor, and the compound head who calls in help may have to contend with young men, and women too, who would rather be taking their dances around to markets and compounds, where potential spouses are sure to be watching and food is part of the fee. A clearing event is a kind of festival—workers sing, the meals provided are heavy—but it is nothing like a dance, and it is easy to see how a little drumming or fluting from the hare can turn one event into the other.

The drum the hare plays in this version is specified as a *genga,* the largest skin-covered (both ends) drum among the Tiv (see discussion of the giant slit-log drum, *indyer,* below) and an instrument that traditionally symbolizes the solidarity of the smaller kindreds or "*akombo*-groups; these describe themselves by saying *se mba koho genga mom,* 'we beat the same drum,' such a group also being called *ikoho genga* or *ishav genga,* 'drumstick'" (Abraham 1940b, p. 102). Considering the choral nature of the song, I think we can say that the hare drums at the base of the farm not only against the chief but also for the people.

A fourth version comes from a text in Tiv and English written by one of the best young storytellers in the Makurdi area. His version of "The Chief's Farm" was the fifth and last episode in a very long composite story. In the preceding episode *Ihambe,* the wasp, has resurrected the hare and his family with medicine only to have the ever ungrateful hare tie a rope around his waist and squeeze it to its present narrowness. "At that time a friend of *Ihambe* invited some people to come and dig his farm. When the hare heard that it was *Ihambe*'s friend who invited people he said, 'I must stop them.' The friend was chief of the area and said no one had the right to stop his work." The hare makes a hole in a tree by the side of the road that leads to the farm, and on the appointed day he hides in the hole, applies stick to drum—*wa ishav sha genga*—and the onomatopoetic song way-lays workers, wives who bring food, and the chief himself. The lyric in the text is not divided into calls and responses, but one line repeated alternately throughout—*shav gidi gidi gidi dian*—is probably the chorus. Though not explicit, as with feather in flute, the hare in the hole with his stick on the drum could easily be taken as another double metaphor for song as coitus. Uninterruptus.

A fifth version, written in English by a student, phrases the story as a pure status competition between *Nor,* the elephant chief, and the upstart hare.

> One day the hare went and challenged the elephant, saying that though the elephant was the chief and biggest of all the animals, nobody respected him as much as he, the hare was respected. When the elephant heard this, he was very angry and cried out with rage that if the hare repeated what he had said he would kill him. But the hare just laughed and told the elephant that they should both suggest what they should do in order to prove their respectfulness.
>
> The elephant suggested that they should employ labourers for their farms and see which set of labourers would obey the employer best and work hardest. . . .
>
> To do this they both came to one decision, that they should employ equal numbers of labourers so that there would be no cheating. Very early the next day they went in a forest looking for labourers. As luck would have it they both found equal numbers of labourers with equal ability and skillfulness. On the fixed day they looked for equal areas of land where the two sets of labourers were to work.

With the labor force and land area variables held absolutely constant, the hare and elephant return to their compounds and the teams set to work with remarkable speed.

> When the hare knew that the elephant had reached his compound, he went in the bush and caught a bee. He took the bee and hid with it near the elephant's labourers. He got a rope and tied it around the bee's waist so that it made a humming noise without stopping.
>
> As soon as these labourers heard the humming noise, they were filled with a sweet contentment and started dancing. The noise was so nice that they asked whatever made the noise to keep repeating it. So the bee started singing like this:
>
> Viengem viengem viengem viengem viengemaan
> Viengema viengemaan
> Tor viengema
> Viengema
> Viengemaan
> Tor viengema.

As in the first story, Nor sends his wife with food, and she throws it away on arrival in order to dance. When Nor himself comes, he finds his field half done and the hare's finished to perfection.

> When the hare saw the elephant he laughed and shouted with pride that as from that time onwards, the elephant should be respecting him. So when the elephant heard these killing words, he felt very ashamed of himself and took one of his biggest cows and gave it to the hare.

The song could be a solo or call/response; in a written version we can't be sure, of course. The voice is disguised from the workers. The lyric, aside from *Tor,* "chief," seems almost entirely onomatopoetic, although the *engem* in *viengem* could possibly be a reference to glitter and shine. And again a sexual component may be present as well. In another tale, dipping fingers into honey is explicitly a metaphor for sexual relations; the butterfly is often called "the one who joins in wedlock," and bees are known to perform the same function. Indeed the "bees" part of our "birds and the bees" may be nearly universal as a sexual symbol, and it is not a wasp, mosquito, or flying ant that the hare harnesses to his purpose. If feather-in-flute song and stick-on-drum song have the potency of a natural force, this literal utilization of natural energy may be a logical extension of the principle.

In a sixth version the plot is very similar to that in the third, and the songs are almost identical. Hare and chief both have farms underway when the story begins; the hare is weak and thin; both characters brew beer for their laborers; but the added twist of interest is that the hare meets a toad on the road, kills it, and uses its skin to make his drum.

In all six versions, then, the hare does not sing himself but borrows an instrument (flute, drum) or an animal (bee), or an animal with an instrument (the bird, *ikpienger*), or turns an animal into an instrument (the toad). Is this simply an insistence on the hare's ingenuity? Might we hazard a few hypotheses: (1) song is a third term or mediator between nature and culture; (2) song is a natural weapon against cultural authority; (3) song is exemplary cultural control over natural energies? Is the feeling that one has of song being somehow both supernatural (bees don't sing) and supercultural (men don't harness bees) purely an effect of the folktale or fantasy context? Can we begin to account for all this nature-culture confusion by restating that song is a metaphor for sexual intercourse and, like sex, both a biological necessity and a societal prerequisite, a natural act and a cultural symbol?

78

In pursuing further some of the questions raised in this analysis of "The Chief's Farm Bet," we must concede at the outset that only a fool could take a metaphorical substitution of song for sex seriously:

> My hare's tale did not land that way. My story fell here, went up to the sky and back to the earth.
>
> Once the chief planted a lot of millet and announced that he would give his daughter in marriage to anyone who could guard the millet without a bird touching a single grain until harvest time. So, a certain foolish fellow went there to guard the millet. While on the farm, whenever he held the rope [fitted with shiny tin pieces] to pull it and scare away birds he would sing:

> Leader: The chief has asked me to guard his millet.
> Oh! He'll give me a wife!
> Tsa-tsa kei! Kei!
> Chorus: Tsa kei!
> Leader: Tsa tsa kei! Kei!
> Chorus: Tsa kei!

> That was how he was making his penis move with the action. For he knew that they would give him a wife and he would lie with her.

> (repitition of song)

> So he kept on pulling at his penis and did not take care to guard the millet. All of the millet was consumed by birds. And the fool did not get the wife. That is why if you are told to do something so that a wife will be given you, you should not become too excited. You should only be careful about your assignment.

This is the only story I have collected in which a fool (*bume or*) is the protagonist, the only story in which masturbation occurs, the only story in which the reductionist dangers of taking song as sex are pointed out to Tiv and anthropologist alike. It is atypical, yet it shares some basic features with "The Chief's Farm Bet." Once again song and sex disrupt food production completely. The chief is willing to trade a daughter for a good harvest, but work motions (pulling the rope) prompt a song (in fact most boys who guard millet build small log xylophones to while away the long hours), the song becomes sexual, and the singer, a fool, seduces himself, losing both food and sex to fantasy.

The storyteller followed up this tale with a story in which a beautiful princess who has been playing hard-to-get is guarding the millet. The hare vows to seduce her, goes under the platform where she is sitting, slips his penis between a crack in the boards, and diverting her attention with a song, slips it into her crack as well.

> Leader: Is that the crack?
> Chorus: It is the crack!

The story doesn't tell us what happened to the millet. It ends with the hare boasting to the chief that he has had his way with the princess and that she can now be given in marriage to anyone the chief selects.

In a few stories, sexual intercourse, song, and food preparation occur simultaneously, and the following tale, in which the ground-squirrel, *Ihinga,* substitutes for the libidinous hare, defines that nexus as well as any. A short version of this story was the very first one told at the ill-fated tale-telling competition that I sponsored, and this longer version came from a Tiv living in Ibadan.

> Mine never went so. Once the squirrel made a bet with the chief. He said that he was handsome, and since the chief was marrying all the women, he would surely screw all the wives. "There is not one of my wives that you can get to," the chief told the squirrel. The squirrel then told the chief that he would certainly screw his favorite wife. "It's a lie!" answered the chief.
>
> The squirrel went back, and he started to dig a tunnel from the outskirts of the homestead right into the kitchen. He made a little opening exactly at the place where they used to sit and knead food. When the wife got up to cook, she put water on the fire, and after it was hot she put a cracked calabash on the ground to sit on it. The squirrel ran out of the compound to the outskirts and entered the tunnel. He ran through to the kitchen. Listen, get ready to answer my song. When he reached the calabash, he jumped inside it. He pitched his penis through the lady's wrapper and pierced it. Then he simply let the penis enter the lady's vagina. The woman then began to knead her food.

> Leader: Piana, piana, piana!
>   Piana, piana, piana!
>   Ah! Anangajia!!
> Chorus: Tor terem kujira tor.

[*Piana* is probably from the verb *piama,* meaning "to place one thing on another." *Ah anangajia* is probably just an exclamation. *Tor terem kujira tor* is literally "chief my father low-Hausa-stool chief."]

"Why is that stupid woman doing that sort of nonsense down at the cooking house," the chief started griping, "she has stopped cooking and is singing." He was offended and called his most beloved wife to go and knead the food and give it to the guest. The woman then went to the kitchen.

When she got there, she went and sat on the calabash where the first woman had been screwing with the squirrel. She pushed the first lady away and removed the calabash to the place where the food was on the fire. At this time the food was cooking on the fire, so she sat down and started to knead. She was kneading the food—piana, piana—and the squirrel just shot his penis and it fell directly in; shocking her whole system, she exclaimed with awe, "Aye! Anangajia!" Imagine, the chief's most beloved wife!

> Leader: Piana, piana, piana!
> Ah! Anangajia!
> Chorus: Tor terem kujira tor.

The woman forgot entirely about cooking food, and she started moving about the kitchen enjoying herself with the squirrel's motion.

The chief was offended. He began to quarrel and abuse them as stupid wives. He said that he would go and knead the food by himself. He said that cooking wasn't beyond his power. The chief came out of the reception hall, took off his royal clothes, and jumped into the kitchen. He siezed the calabash from his favorite wife and put it by the fire. He sat down and started to knead the food. The squirrel again came forward and pushed his penis right into the chief's anus—kang! The chief shouted, "Ah! Anangajia!"

(Repeat song)

At hearing even the chief sing, the guest said that it was time for everyone to go to the kitchen and see for themselves what was the cause. On getting there, they found the chief moving about with the squirrel's penis. The squirrel was clinging underneath the calabash and after many people had gathered there, he jumped out of the calabash and stood on his feet. He at once asked the chief to give him his bet. "I have told you before that I am handsome and will have all your wives; I've screwed your wives and your anus on top of that, so give me my stake." The chief brought a cow and gave it to the squirrel. This is the reason why even a prime minister's wife is sometimes seduced by a poor man. The chief thought he was wealthier than the squirrel so the squirrel wouldn't be able to screw his wives on sheer handsomeness. I have ended that one.

Clearly, the thrust of the story is against authority. The chief is screwed at least seven times over by my count: (1) first wife's seduction; (2) his favorite wife's; (3) delay of the meal and inconvenience to guests; (4) must prepare his own food (a great indignity for a man according to Tiv); (5) is screwed himself; (6) even seems to enjoy dancing to the squirrel's "tune" as he loses face before a crowd of people; (7) has to give a cow to the squirrel and listen to his boasting.

But what is the role of song in all this? Within the narrative, it facilitates the work of preparing food (*piana, piana*); it intensifies the sexual act (*ah! anangajia!*) and transforms it into dance ("she started moving about the kitchen") at the same time that it disguises all the action from the chief. Through song, the squirrel gives the chief used wives, burnt porridge, and a sore anus in exchange for sexual satisfaction and meat on the hoof. The storyteller anticipates the squirrel's penetration for the audience (*piana, piana*) and responds to it (*ah! anangajia!*), while the audience responds to the narrator's calls by mocking the chief as father (*tor terem kujira tor*). Song mediates the tension between food and sex as it overthrows the chief's efforts to control both.

In every tale in my collection that has an instance of sexual intercourse, a song accompanies the action. Some examples: A princess out hunting with bow and arrows sings "a funny song" as she is raped by Takaruku, an *ijov* or sprite-monster of some kind. At a time when vaginas were considered sores, Penis finds that he has the cure and sings as he administers it. The widow who wants to trade meat for the biggest possible penis (there are three versions of this story, including one in the Frobenius collection) sings of her insatiable desire even as the Giant Penis is killing her—the last chorus is sung in a strangled thin voice to indicate that the penis has reached her throat. When the women of an earlier era put their vaginas on the bank of a stream to warm in the sun while they wash, a monkey steals the biggest one and scampers to a tree top where he sings a song mocking the owner as he "uses" it. A husband who has moved far into the bush in order to keep his wife away from possible adulterers sits at his loom and sings as he weaves, while a passing stranger "offers honey" to his wife. And so it goes; no sex without song in the Tiv collective unconscious.

Food and song can also work magically together in Tiv fantasies. In a story written out by a student, the hare and his large family are in the grip of a terrible famine. People are eating dried mucus from nostrils, taking blood from the few remaining animals for lack of water. The hare announces that he can not care for his family and that it is every man, woman, and child for his or her self from now on. Anjieke, his wife, is very angry and goes to seek food for her children. She finds a pot of beans by the roadside, brings it home, and prepares part of it for her children. The hare returns, famished, spots the beans, and taking first one spoonful, then another, soon finishes them off. When Anjieke discovers the empty pot and asks who ate the beans, everyone protests innocence.

She told the hare and her children that if that person would not tell her that he was the one who had eaten the beans, she would sing, and that person's stomach would become huge. Then she would know him. She started singing:

Hare, if you are the person who has eaten my beans
Your stomach will become large
Child, if you are the person who has eaten my beans
Your stomach will not become large.

A very short time after she sang, the hare's stomach became so big that he was unable to breathe. The hare then told her that he was the person who had eaten the beans. Anjieke then started singing another song so that the hare's stomach would return to normal.

That is why even if there is famine or if you are in trouble, you never leave your family or brothers to fight for food alone, but you help them. In the olden days, if there was famine, everyone would eat alone whatever he got. But nowadays, if there is famine, we still eat together whatever we get, small or big.

In a number of stories, song is used by one character to point to the guilt of or pin the blame on another. Although this is the only instance in which the song itself has divining powers, analogous miracles are worked by food and song in two other stories. The first of these is "The Chief's Grinding Stone."

Once upon a time the chief had a very beautiful daughter whom he did not want to give away for any bride-price. He used to say that he had migrated from a distant place, but the grinding stone which he had left behind at his deserted home was the one that helped him to eat food. So he said that anyone willing to marry his daughter had to bring the grinding stone to him first so that it might be used for grinding grains for his meals. He said that it was the only substantial use he had for his daughter, therefore anyone wishing to marry her had to do that for him. For he was in a desperately hungry situation.

The distance was very great. It was about twelve miles, and the stone was very huge and extremely heavy. No one was able to bear its weight. So one animal after the other would go to bring the stone.

But the chief had left his principal wife in that old home. She was a very old lady. Very very old. They left her alone at the deserted homestead. Whenever the person had gone to carry the stone, she would cook a lot of food and give them to eat. You know it is after one has eaten plenty that he loses strength to bear the great weight of the stone. When the stone was lifted to the person's head, and while he was going, the old woman would start to sing a song:

Leader: The chief has asked me to carry
Chorus: Amenabiu iier! Kie kie amenabiou!
Leader: The chief has asked me to carry
Chorus: Amenabiu iier! Kie kie amenabiu!
       My meat is in the stomach!
       My beer is in the stomach!
       My food is in the stomach!

While this song was being sung, the grinding stone would escape from the carrier and come back to the old lady. She did this for a very long time with many people. At last the hare got up to have a turn. He told the chief that he was certainly going to marry his daughter because she had attracted him too much. The chief mocked the ability of the hare to carry out such an heroic feat, saying, "Even the bigger animals like the elephant tried to carry that stone but were unable. How then could you, hare, as tiny as this, think of doing that which others have tried and failed?" But the hare affirmed that he would go and surely have a try. He got up and went there. On his arrival the chief's old lady said, "What? Hare, you appear to be too small for the sort of food that I used to prepare for others —what am I to do?" The hare told the lady to prepare enough food for his belly so that he might eat and go. The lady then prepared a meal which was enough for the hare's belly. After she had given the food to the hare, he told her to go, for he said, "I don't eat while there is any person in the house together with me. Get out so I may eat alone in the house."

After she had gone out, the hare took a hoe from the corner of the house. He dug very quickly a hole in the ground and buried the food and the soup. He poured the beer that the lady gave him to drink into the hole. He poured even the water into the hole and closed it. He quickly called the old lady to come and carry away her utensils, saying he had finished eating his meal. On her arrival, the old lady was amazed and said, "What? Have you finished eating this food, hare?" He said he had finished and called her to come and help him carry the stone so that he might go. She came out and helped the hare carry the stone on his head.

Immediately the hare set off very quickly with the stone. The lady

84 said that, since it was the hare, she would make him go with the stone for about seven miles before calling the stone back. This would show the hare that she was mightier than he. After seven miles, going into the eighth, the lady took up her song:

(Repeat of song)

But when the hare heard this, he sang:

Leader: The chief has asked me to carry.
Chorus: Amenabiu iier! Kie kie amenabiu!
Leader: Your beer is in the ground!
Chorus: Amenabiu iier! Kie kie amenabiu!
Leader: Your food is in the ground!
Chorus: Amenabiu iier! Kie kie amenabiu!
Leader: Your meat is in the ground!
Chorus: Amenabiu iier! Kie kie amenabiu!

The old woman then cried out, "This hare has not eaten his meat; it is in the ground. Is that why the stone failed to return even after I had sung my song?"

The hare went with the grinding stone till he threw it in the chief's homestead. He told the chief to take his grinding stone and give him his wife so that he might go. The chief was very much amazed, for he had said that the hare was the smallest of animals and couldn't carry the stone. But as he had proven his ability and brought it, all the chief could do was call his daughter to come out and go with the hare. She was very displeased, but as it was a matter of compulsion, she married the hare. For that was the promise the chief had made. This was what the hare did at the chief's homestead, and he got a wife.

There is more to this story than our old adage that "the way to a man's heart is through his stomach." Would the old woman's song have worked on the hare if he had not countered immediately with a song of his own? Or is it simply that he sings on an empty stomach and might just as well have shouted his defiance?

Is there anything to be made of the fact that the very old woman in this story and wise Anjieke in the preceding story are able to sing with controlling power (no other women do in any of the other stories) when the bellies of men are full? What *do* women have to say about the food-for-sex or labor-for-wives trades that older men make with younger men in the tales, and in real life? Why was the chief's senior wife left behind in the old compound? Normally, it is only a witch, a senior man, who is ostracized in this way. How is it that she has a plentiful supply of food and can provide meat for one suitor after another while the chief is "desperately hungry" and sees a stone for grinding grain as his solution? The argument for a prior and idealized "matriarchal state" (men hunting, women farming and tending the hearth) would be long, complicated, and ultimately inconclusive, but this story and a number of others might be more readily interpretable in such terms. Even without historical assumptions, however, a tension between male (control over women and meat) and female (control over men and millet processing) forces is obviously central to the plot. "The hare has not eaten his meat; it is in the ground. Is that why the stone failed to return even after I had sung my song?" The men have their way: the chief gets his grinding stone (the big bottom one which needs a smaller stone on top to grind grain) against his senior wife's wishes, and the hare gets a wife ("meat" in the sense that it is said of a new bridegroom, "he will eat meat tonight") even though she goes with the hare "under compulsion." In fantasy the men win; in reality, the old women maintain greater control over the tools of production than men would care to admit, and young women have a monopoly on powers of reproduction, of course, that men must cope with as they can. Perhaps men do most of the singing in Tivland, and storytelling as well, because of their "empty stomachs."

As further evidence of what singing on an empty stomach can do, we have the story of the orphan who resurrects his mother. (This version was told second in a series of tales by one storyteller; his first tale was "The Chief's Farm Bet," version number 3. The "grinding stone" story was the last one told by another narrator, and it too was immediately preceded by "The Chief's Farm Bet," version number 1! Why is the most popular tale in Tivland followed by a "food and song" yarn each time? Eventually there may be much to learn from an analysis of story sequences by individual narrators.)

My tale did not go so. Once upon a time a man had two wives. There was the rich wife and the poor wife. This poor wife, after delivering a child, died. So the child was given to the rich lady to adopt. This stepmother began to maltreat the motherless child. When she cooked food, she would give the orphan only a very little; for her own child she would fill a very big plate full of food for him to eat. But whenever she gave this motherless boy food, he would carry it to his mother's grave and start crying. He put the food down; he wasn't eating. He would just sit weeping and calling the mother.

Leader: Oh, my mother! Oh, my mother!
        You have certainly given birth.
        Oh, my mother! Oh, my mother!
Chorus: You have certainly given birth.
Leader: She pounded her food, scooped it,
            set it in the plate for her son.
        She only dipped out a tiny piece
            and gave it to me.

The grave gave a crack—*sakwe!* Again the boy went back to the house. At home they cooked beans, and the lady gave a miniscule portion to the orphan. He took those beans to his mother's grave and, putting them beside the grave, started weeping and calling his mother:

(Repeat song as above)

The grave gave another crack—*sakwe*—and his mother's head and chest appeared. The boy returned and went back home. On the following morning, they cooked yams, but the lady gave him the peels of the yams and said that the boy should eat that because "no one has killed your mother." So he packed the yam peels and carried them down to his mother's grave. He sat there calling his mother:

(Repeat song)

At this time the mother came out of the grave, and only her legs were still under the ground. The boy continued in this manner. He had never taken any meal since the death of his mother until the mother came back to life again and met him. After this poor woman's resurrection, the other boy's mother, the rich woman, died. When they gave this rich woman's son food, he would eat all of it up greedily, lick his fingers, and then carry the remnants to his mother's grave before he started crying:
(Same song as above, but the storyteller races the tempo and sings haphazardly.)
But the grave never cracked again. That's why co-wives don't abuse children when their mother has died. In the past, they used to heap sufferings on motherless children. I have certainly ended this.

In a written version of this story, entitled "Why Mothers Are Never Brought Back from Their Graves after Burial," the first orphan gets nothing to eat and resolves to dig up his mother. Working with a small hoe he sings:

My mother, my mother, come, I am hungry!
When they cook, they never give me anything.
And when they are satisfied, they throw the rest away;
If I take it, they beat me.
My mother, I have come.

As he digs and sings, his mother rises from the grave by stages, takes him home, and prepares a big meal for everyone. When the rich wife dies, the resurrected mother treats all the children equally. The dissatisfied orphan half-heartedly imitates his half-brother—weeping, singing, and digging—but when he sees his mother's head, he yanks at it and breaks it off at the neck. That's why mothers are never brought back to life.

While this second version gives more power to song alone as a life force, the sacrifice of food is implicit, if involuntary. Though song is sometimes used as a ruse or diversion to escape death, this is the only instance of resurrection through song in my sample. In Tiv belief, the *mbatsav* bring their dead victims back to life before they are ritually slaughtered, and one wonders, first, to what extent connotations from this alleged practice carry over into the story and, second, whether this case of "positive resurrection" is all the more wonderful by contrast.[1] The title or moral of the second version forecloses any hope of future miracles, while the first story leaves open the possibility of mothers returning to nurture sons who sacrifice and sing.

There are also a few stories which suggest some sort of a link to the other end of the food chain, a possible equation between defecation and singing.

In one popular tale (two versions in my sample and one in the Frobenius collection), the chief agrees to give his daughter to the brave soul who can, without spitting once, scoop out all the feces that has accumulated in a barn. The animals try one after the other, but none can stand the smell. The hare succeeds by singing a song as he performs the task which disguises the fact that he is spitting continually. In one version, three daughters are offered to the winner. The chief is deceived by the hare's song, but the other animals are not, and they threaten to take the hare's new brides away. They waylay him on the path, but he defeats each animal with diverse strategies until the fatty remains of the tortoise he has boiled trap him tarbaby-style and he is taken to the mountain top for judgment. There he persuades the ani-

1. See footnote 1, chapter 1.

mals to "repair the land" by giving him "a chief's death": he will leap from the back of the elephant, club in hand, and they can beat him to a pulp as he lands. He drops the club off one side of the elephant, the animals flail away at the noise, and he escapes from the other side. For the Tiv, the moral is that "the cunning will always escape danger," but we might draw a number of other conclusions: to marry, one must not only "take a lot of shit" from elders but fend off your peers as well; it may take a song to fool a chief, but if your peers see through the ruse, rest assured that by taking on the chief's role yourself you can fool them with ritual hocus-pocus and mere noise; all Tiv, whether of high or low status, are vulnerable to good performance; singing is like spitting in the face of feces, if not spitting out shit itself.

In what might be considered a variant of this story, the chief stages a farting contest for suitors. All the animals have a try, and Nor, the elephant, trains on special foods, strains mightily, blasts effectively, only to have the hare carry the day again by tying a bell to his tail and ringing it repeatedly until he wins. A song replicates this ruse for the audience.

A number of other stories and parts of stories might be summoned in support of an "anal creation" theme in Tiv culture. A very popular tale (three versions in my sample and a version in Frobenius) pivots upon the discovery of a "thing-that-shits-food" (Frobenius calls it a "Füllhorn"). In the midst of famine, the hare finds a "thing" in the bush that excretes a broth on request. He brings it home; his people eat their fill; and their celebration in dance and song (song here appears incidental to the main action, though the lyric mocks the elephant) attracts the attention of Nor. The elephant comes to inquire, asks the object to "do its thing," and in his greed, gobbles up not only the food but the thing itself. In contemporary versions, the hare returns to the bush and finds Flayer-of-flesh, gets beaten badly himself, but brings it home in order to stage a celebration and attract Nor to an appropriate punishment. Nor comes to enquire and is whipped till he falls unconscious; moral—never take someone else's thing by force even if you are the stronger. In the Frobenius version, however, the story ends after the first celebration as Nor swallows the "Füllhorn"; moral —"When a man is hungry, one should give him something to eat, otherwise he destroys more with his greediness than one saves when one doesn't give him anything." (One wonders what a thorough search for contemporary versions of the forty-three tales Frobenius collected more than fifty years ago might provide in the way of evidence for shifts in values.)

Also in the Frobenius collection is a story about a man who dies of boils, comes back to life, and kills an antelope. Every person who eats a piece has an antelope in his stomach and later gives birth to it through the anus. The resultant herd is scorned by the other animals because of its origin. In another story the hare is seeking fire, finds it, and pokes a stick into it only to discover that it is coming from the anus of a monster who is unappeasable and devours one compensatory gift after another. In the "flute forgotten at farm" story paraphrased at the outset, the Intestines seem to have special power and arrive on the scene in the midst of a whirlwind. In one of the chief-hare competitions, the hare defecates in the chief's well; when the chief wants to know who did it, the hare mocks him in a scatological song that "names" the chief himself as the culprit in such a way that the accusation sticks.

At present I have no clear idea what the scata-logic underlying such events might be, but if it is taken in conjunction with the "food and song" stories, perhaps we have the beginnings of two coordinates on the Tiv unconscious as a source of songs, as well as a relationship between song energy and the basic "gut energies" of life. The relationship seems to be one of opposition in Tiv fantasies, since men sing effectively either "on empty stomachs" or "by emptying the intestines."

At the core of the Tiv belief system lies the notion of life as energy exchange. In life, as reflected in the idea of *tsav,* one man's gain and pleasure is another's loss and pain; some die that others may live; fertility of women and crops depend upon sacrifice in a variety of forms; the extreme and most vivid metaphor for this world view is cannibalism. Explicit instances of witchcraft are almost entirely absent in these stories; the *mbatsav* are never mentioned; their emissaries, the nightbirds, appear very rarely and "act on their own," as it were, not as sorceror's apprentices. But there are many stories in which cannibalism is the theme or in which "song and sacrifice" are linked together.

The cannibalism stories are long and complex and invite the sort of treatment exemplified in Beidelman's fine analysis, "Hyena and Rabbit: A Kaguru Representation of Matrilineal Relations" (1961). Abraham includes a Tiv analogue, "The Hare and the Leopard," in his collection (1940b, pp. 70–72), with the note, "The theme of one partner cooking the children of the other and giving them to him to eat without his knowledge is very widespread and is to be found in all areas," citing instances in Junod on the Thonga, Helser on the Burra, Boas on various American Indian peoples. In my collection the story appears twice as "The Dog and the Leopard," and a few other stories, even more complex, illustrate a similar theme.

Two very close friends living in the same compound and sharing everything have equal numbers of children (in "Hare and Leopard" the protagonists are fathers, in "Dog and Leopard" they are mothers) and are faced with famine. They decide to go fishing and start to drain a lake (the unconscious?) in order to catch a great many fish, but they soon grow very weak and can't continue. The leopard suggests that they kill one of the dog's children and eat it to sustain them in their work. The dog kills and cooks one of the Leopard's children instead, and they eat it and resume work.

> The leopard took up the calabash and started singing:
>
> Leader: I have deceived someone.
> Chorus: Pour in the river.
> Leader: I have deceived someone.
>   Etc.
>
> The dog got up and snatched the calabash from the leopard, say-ing, "You don't know how to scoop water; it will never dry that way," and she began to work singing:
>
> Leader: Once you go home, then you'll see.
> Chorus: Once you go home, then you'll see.

In one version, this sequence is repeated for as many times as there are children of the Leopard, but in a second the song is more explicit and comes later in the story. The two versions vary in their final seg-ments. In the first, when the leopard finally gets the meaning of the song, the dog hides her children and later escapes to the compound of men, with the leopard in hot pursuit. In the second, the dog's song boasting of having killed the leopard's sons leads to an involved series of chases and deceptions until, finally, the dog's sons trick the leopard, kill her, cut her in pieces, and keep the meat a secret from their mother. The dog discovers what her sons have done only when she comes upon the head of the mother leopard.

Both stories explain "the emnity between dogs and leopards," and perhaps other emnities as well—between co-wives, between lineages, possibly even between nature and culture in the sense that the wild leopard is guilty only of evil intent and the mistake of having eaten her own, while the dogs do all the killing and deceiving and end up in alliance with that other deceptive killer, man. Here again the role of the songs is clearer to the audience than it is to the characters within the narrative. In the older Abraham version, this is the only tale in the sixteen that contains a song proper, and it serves to arouse the Leopard's suspicions:

> This went on day by day, the hare every time killing one more of the leopard cubs till only one was left, and then on that day, while they were fishing, he began to sing, "I wonder what has happened at home?" The leopard said, "What do you mean, Hare? What can have happened?" The hare said, "I didn't mean anything; I was just improvising a song."

If draining the lake in the contemporary versions is a metaphor for tapping or draining the unconscious, then the role of songs in facilitating that "scooping" work is more interesting, the lyrics do not seem quite so obvious, and the very act of draining the lake can be seen as the cause of the emnity as consciousness dawns and is differentiated.

A very popular story (three versions) that focuses upon sacrifice is "The Hare's *Indyer*."

> The *indyer* is the largest of the three ceremonial drums hollowed out of tree-trunks, the other two being known as *ilyu* and *gede gede*. The *indyer* was in former times of immense importance; it has a deep booming note and this is produced by beating it with a mallet. It was made from mahogony or the tree *iyiase,* but the duty of felling this tree devolved on a man of prestige (*shagba or*). It is maintained that a near relation of this individual was used as a living measure of the *indyer,* so that the length of the drum should correspond with his stature, the extremities of the tree being lopped off and the man being killed and his blood being poured into the hollow of the drum. These three drums were beaten when an [important] man was buried. . . . In addition they were used in the *girnya* dance in time of war, and the victor danced round it bearing the head of his slain enemy. [Abraham 1940b, p. 133]

With Abraham's account of the *indyer* before us, and knowing Alɔm, the hare, as we do, the following story, written out by a student, has a certain inevitable quality about it.

> Alɔm, the king of animals, wanted *indyer*. This was because all the kings at that time were supposed to have it. When it is hit, it could sound for a distance of 150 miles!

92

Once upon a time Alɔm journeyed far into the bush. When he saw a big python, he fancied it to be *indyer*. When he came back home, he gathered all the animals and told them that he had found a perfect *indyer* at a distant place in another world. The animals agreed to go and pull it home for their king.

When they went in order to pull it home, the sheep saw that it was not a real *indyer* and complained that they were not powerful, so they would pick up a song while the other animals pulled. As the animals were pulling, some of them were missing. When others asked where some had gone, Alɔm told them that they felt so hot that they went to take a bath. But the fact was that the python was swallowing some.

At last they reached the animal compound where Alɔm was king. Women and children came out in order to see *indyer*. Alɔm saw that his wife, Anjieke, and his children were coming. He thought that it was risky, so he told the animals that he would pick up the song himself. And he started:

Leader: Anjieke, go away with my children.
Chorus: Let *indyer* of Alɔm swallow a man.
　　　　Etc.

Anjieke understood him and went with the children. Since it was a song, the animals did not understand what Alɔm meant but took it to be the sense of the song and disregarded it.

The *indyer* was put in a certain building in the backyard. Alɔm forbid his children to go and play on it. When other children went to play on it, the python would swallow them. The population of animals was decreasing. At last other animals also prohibited their children from playing on the *indyer*. It came to pass that the python had no food, and it slipped off into the bush. Alɔm lost his *indyer*, and his fame went with it. Now no one takes a python to be his *indyer*, but rather a hollow log of wood.

The meaning of song in this parody of prestige acquisition ought to be clear enough: you sing if you don't want to be sacrificed, and it is important to understand songs for the same reason. Conversely, songs energize the work (or sacrifice) of others.

In another version of this tale, the storyteller begins with the formula, "My story fell and killed six dogs!"—a release of energy by figurative sacrifice. In this version the hare holds the tail of the snake as he sings his workers along the path and warns his wife and children. The storyteller kills dogs. The singer has a python by the tail that kills animals before they know they are in danger. Both performers are enacting energies that "separate the sheep from the goats," "the men from the mice," the "hip" energy-gainers from the "square" energy-losers.

The *indyer,* as a symbol, is roughly parallel to the *imborivungu* discussed above; the large slit-log drum is a public emblem of political influence if not authority, while the night-flute or voice-disguiser is a secret insignia of religious power (to the extent that our conceptual categories and distinctions between religious and political apply to Tiv culture at all). "Drum-chief" was a common designation for lineage leaders during the colonial era, and while the title referred to paraphernalia purchased from the Jukun and did not derive directly from possession of *indyer,* the central place of the large log-drum was apparently part of Tiv tradition long before buying prestige from the Jukun king became fashionable, and it has persisted in diluted form to the present; a big log-drum sits outside Tor Tiv's compound in Gboko today.

Unlike the secret *imborivungu,* rarely if ever mentioned in the tales, the *indyer* appears in more than half a dozen stories in my sample. And with the exception of one instance in which an incredibly complex courtship-and-cannibalism plot is climaxed by the hare beating out his accusations on the *indyer,* all the stories are comical, often sexual, and at least two feature something very rare in Tiv singing—a set of different melodic lines sung simultaneously. Of all the composers I recorded, only one, Kuji Iyum, had fashioned a single song in which melodic lines diverged from each other. At women's dances, I have occasionally heard the men drumming in the center break into a song of their own that had no systematic relationship to the song the women were singing. Aside from Kuji's one song and the randomly counterpointed melodies at women's dances, the *indyer* songs in tales are the only examples known to me of overlapping vocal melodies in Tiv.

In one story the chief offers his mature daughter to the group which will bring the loudest slit-log drum. The kingfishers carve theirs, and the frogs make their own. The storyteller lavishes much attention on their preparations and rehearsals, molding the characteristic calls of the kingfisher and the voices of frogs into songs of challenge to each other that imitate the patterns of slit-log drums. Segments of the audience sing along and are confident of the basic frog and kingfisher responsorial melodies by the time the two parties arrive at the chief's compound for the beer drinking and final competition. The two sides have prepared simple songs as well, and parts of the audience pick these up before the slit-log response patterns are added. When all parts are going (though not in any particular pattern), the storyteller calls the varied challenges of the frogs to the kingfishers and vice versa to maximally heterophonous effect. Eventually the kingfishers win by popular acclaim; the drunken frogs try to set fire to the feathers of the birds and sieze the woman, but they are eaten up by the kingfishers. One frog escapes to become the ancestor of all present frogs and to perpetuate the vocal conflict that we can still hear today.

In another story (unfortunately only partially recorded) the hare and the clitoris compete on slit-log drums, and Clitoris calls her daughters to assist her so that a song of three overlapping parts results.

In one of the stories about the battles between the penises and the vaginas, the stage is set for a wrestling match, after which the winners will roast and eat the losers. The vaginas insist on beating the *indyer* before the wrestling begins, but the penises rise to the challenge, defeat and roast them, and that's why all vaginas are black "from the short hairs to the inner parts."

There is also a tale that blends with the first version of "The Chief's Farm Bet." The hare and chief wager on who will have the loudest *indyer*. As the hare plays his, a version of the same song the hare used when he was fluting in the tree top emerges from the drum:

> Hit it *gbieke,* hit it *gbieke,* hit it *gbieke!*
> Sing softly softly: Lion, you'll spoil the Civet-cat's anus.
> Even the elephant has to play and call the cobra "Anna."
> I, the hare, king of the animals, am playing
> Abinga on the elephant, hey, hey, hey!
> The elephant has made a bet with me.
> Abinga—Nyio! Nyio! Nyio! Nyiogbire!

The elephant's indyer song is made up of nonsense syllables—"uci, uci, uci; barabarabara gbulon"—and the hare, as usual, triumphs and takes away meat on the hoof.

"The Chief's Farm Bet" is the most popular tale in Tivland for a reason; it embodies most of the central themes in Tiv lore and song. Parody of patrilineal authority and men's sexual anxiety surfaces in story after story; sexual competition and status competition are blended together in song after song. These energetic struggles with the problems of power and sex are often suffused with a concern for that ultimate energy source, food: the problem of survival and its corollary question of death or sacrifice—that is, whose energies are to be exchanged for whose? Song energy, in collective fantasy at least, seems capable of "solving" all these problems, singly or in combination; power, sexual satisfaction, and food come to the singer in tales. And the storyteller in the midst of his audience can suspend these same problems, temporarily, for the contemplation of his listeners.

Do these fantastic song energies serve the singer in everyday life? This is a question to be born in mind as we survey the careers of composers in chapter 3.

3

Tiv Composers

I N TIVLAND almost any song can be attributed to a composer, an *or u dughun amo.* So far as I can determine, the only songs for which an individual creator is not necessarily assumed are lullabies and the songs that animal characters are likely to sing in the midst of a tale. Some Tiv would even insist that these simple song forms have their composers but that they are unknown. This is not to say, however, that the composers of all other songs are known. Many "old father's songs" can not be traced to an author. Women of a compound singing songs outside the home of a new bride who has just arrived might be able to identify only a small proportion of the composers whose songs they are singing. Indeed, I would guess that the average person does not know who composed most of the songs that he hears. On the other hand, sitting in a *burukutu,* or beer hall, where more current popular songs are being sung, almost every song can be identified by one or more of the participants. And if a positive identification is impossible, an intelligent surmise can usually be ventured on the basis of content (events described, people named, locality implied) or of style (the rhythmic pattern with its suggested dance orientation, but more important, the *ikenge,* an idiosyncratic melodic shape associated with a particular composer). Of course if it's a good day—a Sunday afternoon in town, or a market day in a rural setting—with plenty of beer to consume and plenty of people to consume it, chances are a composer will be present and tending to dominate the singing with his own repertoire. If it is a large beer hall with a company of drummers in residence, the drummers will lead the singing and know very well whose songs they are using most of the time.

In addition to these open recreational settings, a feature of every town and four-day market in Tivland, composers have a number of other appropriate situations to exploit.

At any given time there are roughly forty to sixty named dance styles being performed in Tivland and a few hundred dance organizations scattered over the countryside performing them. Each of these dance troupes either has a composer of songs as a member of the group, often the leader, or will commission a composer to create songs especially for it. Every dance has an average of eight to twelve segments, and songs usually occur at the beginning of segments or between segments, where they serve as "breathers" or interludes. Most of the composers have created songs for or within a dance organization at one time or another.

When asked what kind of songs a particular composer makes, the answer is often phrased in terms of "praising" or "crying" and "begging." While this general category does not exclude a dance or *burukutu* setting for the praising of famous and not-so-famous men, it may mean that the composer in question is good enough to be invited with his assistants to the compounds of prominent elders. There he can sing original compositions extolling the virtues of the *or ya* (compound head) and his extended family in return for a slaughtered animal, some money for himself and his assistants, and assorted other small gifts from members of the compound, usually the elder's wives, who enjoy the way they are mentioned in the songs. The verb *ter* means specifically "to eulogize a person in song," and it indicates a long tradition of praise-singing. One of the most basic song genres, *ibiamegh* (or *aluibiam* or *wanibiam*, literally "child of ibiamegh") is derived from the ultimate prestige ceremony in traditional Tiv culture, rarely performed today, if ever, at which a selected composer was responsible for composing songs and rehearsing the compound in their performance. In the 1960s approximately a third of the composers in Tivland had *akenge* (melodic lines) that fell within the *ibiamegh* or *wanibiam* pattern. *Wanibiam* is commonly acknowledged as the genre best suited to praises, but most Tiv songs, of whatever genre, give honorable mention to one or more friends and past or potential patrons of the art.

An interesting musicological problem that awaits considerable transcription, analysis, and further interviews for its solution, revolves around the question of discerning individual styles within this genre. To my naive ear the melodic patterns of all *wanibiam* composers sound generally the same, but some Tiv listeners insist that some individual stylists can be distinguished.

Another whole content category of songs could perhaps be lumped under the term "abusive," though the English word glosses over a number of subtle Tiv terms and correlated distinctions. Very rarely a composer will be paid by one elder to mock or take verbal revenge on another. In "Drumming the Scandal among the Tiv" (1967, pp. 263–67) Paul Bohannan describes a dramatic song duel which in precolonial times would probably have led to a fight. Interestingly enough, when the opponents and their hired composers were finally hauled into court, the judges spent two hours evaluating the songs before quickly dispensing with the case that inspired them.

> After the case was settled on its jural points, the "mbatarev" announced the winner of the song contest: Torgindi won the case, but Mtswen had the better songs. Then they advised both songmakers to go home immediately and not return to MbaDuku for a couple of months until the feelings which had been aroused had died down.

Often a composer will begin or advance his career by attacking, in a series of songs, someone who he feels has done him wrong, as we shall see in the biographical sketches of particular composers which follow.

Given these Tiv predispositions to praise or blame[1] in song, a marvelous new range of compositional opportunities emerged with the advent of emotionally charged party politics during the 1950s and 60s. Some of the best composers earned handsome gratuities during the election campaigns and riots that accompanied the first years of Nigerian independence. Some earned extensive jail terms as well, or were convicted of libel in the courts and enjoined to remain silent for specified periods of time.

Since the military seized power, army recruitment has been extensive in Tivland. Although only about 2 percent of the Nigerian population, Tiv have a well-deserved reputation as fighters and made up almost a quarter of the Nigerian army during the long war with Biafra. A number of the best young composers and musicians found the offer of army pay attractive, and some were probably enlisted with the understanding that they would be primarily responsible for boosting morale with their music.

1. A rereading of this chapter makes it clear to me that I have tended to overcategorize composers in terms of song content. In effect praising *and* blaming, "crying" (*vaan*) about sufferings *and* "begging" (*zamber*) for help are four quadrants of the same circle. If a Tiv composer emphasizes one or two of these elements, the other elements are certainly implied. Given the web of kinship and the Tiv version of the zero-sum game of life, praise for one elder implies a low opinion of his nearest rivals, asking for help implies suffering caused by someone, and "crying" poverty (*ican*) implies blame.

Still another developing field for composers has been found within the Christian missions. American Dutch Reform missionaries were quick to see the advantages of utilizing Tiv song in their conversion efforts and have supported a staff of composers, led by the prolific Ityavger Fate, to fill their churches with hymns in the Tiv idiom. Less than 10 percent of the Tiv are Christian, however, and most of these only nominally. There are probably not more than twenty composers whose primary emphasis is on church songs.

In general order of importance, then, the social range of composing opportunities includes (1) recreation, (2) dance groups, (3) invitational praise singing, and (4) the church. Again, the reader should be cautioned that these are loose, overlapping contextual categories, no tighter than the content categories discussed above. These days very little praise-singing seems to be specially commissioned, at least I was never able to observe this process first-hand during a year in the field. Yet praising the Lord in return for mission pay, elucidating the virtues of local personalities in a song for a dance group, and mentioning a patron in a drinking song could all be considered part of the third category. Songs originally composed for a dance can be heard in the beer halls, and vice versa. And both can be heard at farming festivals. Only the fourth category, church composing, tends to be exclusive, but even here melodic patterns are borrowed from preexisting Tiv dance styles, and church songs may be sung outside the church. Most composers have been variably rewarded by drinkers, dancers, and specific elders at one time or another.

Obviously, many people among the Tiv compose songs, but it is very difficult to estimate their number with any accuracy. The Tiv population is something close to a million, and I have the names of well over 450 composers in my field notes. Since my surveys were far from thorough, I suspect that many more song makers live in Tivland, probably well over 1,000 altogether, roughly 1 composer for every 750 to 1,000 Tiv. Ninety-seven of the names I know something about come from 122 essays on "my favorite Tiv composer and why I like him," gathered from Tiv students at various secondary and technical schools. I had assumed that this sort of essay topic, focused upon favorites, as opposed to, for example, "the best composer in my district," would help to cluster information and opinions around the more prominent composers in Tivland. The spread of almost 100 different choices, while unexpected, can be taken as an indication that loyalties to clan and lineage area are still strong among young and educated Tiv. A favorite

composer tends to be someone you know who sings about familiar people, events, and problems. If another 125 students were asked for their
favorites, another 80 to 100 names of composers could doubtless be
added to the list. It would seem that only when students from specific
geographic corners of Tivland begin to overlap are we likely to get significant overlapping of composer choices.

The major composers, those with years of experience and pan-Tiv
reputations, are certainly known to most of these students, but are
simply not often favorites. Only four composers received more than
two essay-appreciations: Ityavger Fate was mentioned in 7 essays out
of the total of 122, a very small number, considering the facts that, as
the leading composer of Christian hymns, he was a logical choice for
devoutly Protestant students anxious to affirm their faith to a visiting
white man, and that he was perhaps one of the easier composers to
write about. Six essays praised Tarker "No. 1" Gorozo as the leading
composer of songs for *swange*, the basic town dance or "Tiv highlife."
Anande Amende, alias Ikpamkor London, was acclaimed by four students as a paragon of modern song-making, versatile and politically
astute. And four essays on Iorlumun Wanikya stressed the importance
of his song series chronicling an escape from death by sorcery. Eight
other composers were written about twice, but a few of these probably
reflect an over-the-shoulder factor, two student friends sitting next to
each other and exchanging tips and topics. These exceptions noted,
the predominance of local favorites seems all the more impressive. We
can infer from this pattern that no matter how widely and well a composer's reputation has spread abroad, his basic constituency remains at
home.

Before examining the careers of various composers, a general discussion of the ways in which a Tiv may come to compose songs should be
helpful. I would like to include here in its entirety a document by a
Tiv I never met, Agwaza Abende, who wrote this interesting analysis
of three types of composer-recruitment in the note book of a schoolboy
who was collecting information for me during his vacation. It is a fine
example of the amateur anthropologist within a culture, the "good informant" at work.

There are many different ways in which different composers have
managed to become successful composers. Some of the main ones
are:

1. If a composer has many children and the time for him to die
has come, he will call the most sluggish or laziest of his sons and

hand over to him all the composing material or, in short, the composing career.

The selection of the laziest son affirms one of the most stable elements in what might be called the composer stereotype, that is, that composers are slow moving or, according to the composers themselves, "more meditative."

> By so saying I mean the child will be given things like a tail of some dead cow or buffalo which he uses to wave in the air from time to time when singing, a gourd with a long handle inside of which some tiny pebbles are put so that when it is shaken it produces a very rhythmic tune which corresponds with the tune of the composer. This serves as a musical instrument.

These two items would appear to be part of a bygone or localized tradition, for while I can remember seeing tails and gourd-rattles occasionally in the hands of Tiv at a song and dance event, they were never pointed out as essential insignia for composers.

> He is also given many charms of different kinds which we call "ukurayol" to protect him against any evil spirit or bad thing.[2] Before all these he is given or shown a certain tree and he has to chew its leaves or bark before introducing a new song. This, according to our belief, is to make him not to forget the past words of his song but instead some new, striking and expressive ideas should come into his mind.

The grammatically ambiguous placement of "not" in this sentence must remain ambiguous. Most "medicines" for composing stress memory facilitating ingredients, while ingredients that promote original invention are rarely cited (see chapter 4).

> The laziest child is always given this career owing to the fact that even after his father's death he should be able to maintain his life and, if possible, his family. Such a composer is always a praise singer.

The foregoing suggests that composing is usually a life-sustaining or full-time job. This is probably only true for the physically handicapped composers in Agwaza's second category. Even the best and most resourceful composers continue to do some farming, if only the subsistence crops, and many have still another "specialty"—trading, tax collecting, sack making, and so on—that provides income as well.

2. For independent verification of Agwaza's definition of the Tiv phrase *u kura iyol* see Abraham 1940b, p. 85.

2. Some composers are believed to have been given their careers by some spirits or fairies. Such composers are usually born blind or lame. Their songs are always very interesting to hear. Most of them are beggars. Their songs also are usually very sympathetic.

The spirits referred to are probably *adzov,* the sprites that Tiv believe are living in specific trees and near water holes, but "spirits and fairies" could also be a euphemism for the *mbatsav,* the elders or men of power who are assumed to cause most personal misfortunes, including death, as explained in Agwaza's third category.

3. At times a person may just make up his mind to become a composer. This is usually when a very bad thing happens to him, e.g., his wife may die and simultaneously his child. In his songs such a composer may be begging his relatives not to do any bad thing to him again. For we believe that all the lives of different people are in the hands of their relatives, usually old ones. Therefore, if a person dies, it is one of his relatives that has killed him or her.

As we shall see, it is often a very small "bad thing" that can lead a person to "just make up his mind to become a composer." Reading Agwaza, one might easily think that this third category of self-selected composers, those who achieve the role, is a residual one, and that most composers have the role ascribed to them, either through planned or customary, rather than "natural," inheritance, or through an unkind twist of fate. Even in category three, the harsh example offered, the loss of wife and child, suggests an ascriptive component, as the choice to compose is made under desperate circumstances.

My own estimate (based on interviews with a few composers, fairly extensive data for a dozen others, the aforementioned student essays on an additional one hundred, and sketchy secondhand information on still another one hundred fifty) would be that the vast majority of composers are self-selected, and that "lazy sons" and "cripples" in the profession are few and far between. Naikor Bodanyi, a blind composer based at Makurdi, and Ityavger Fate, the mission composer and a double amputee, were the only handicapped composers I encountered. From a combined sample of about two hundred fifty, only fourteen are described as seriously disabled—blind, lame, or afflicted with leprosy. But the student essayists were not asked specifically for such information, and the facts on file for the rest of this sample are even less complete and reliable, so that any estimate of composers in this category would have to be revised upward, perhaps even doubled. On the other hand, a few of the disabled listed as composers may well be beggars who sing other people's songs. An intelligent guess might be that roughly 10 percent of the composers in Tivland came to the trade because they were physically unable to farm for a living. The percentage of composers who simply preferred to farm less and travel more is certainly very much higher.

Data that might confirm and quantify Agwaza's detailed example of inheritance by a lazy son are lacking, with one tentative but major exception. Bam Gindi, still the best-known composer in Tivland, though he died more than fifteen years ago, is said to have received the career from his father. And since Bam Gindi's death, his younger brother, Hule Gindi, has been continuing the tradition. I was never able to ascertain whether he composes himself or simply performs the songs from Bam Gindi's extensive repertoire. This passing on of the role from father to son to younger brother is, however, unique in my experience and based on mere hearsay at that.

While Agwaza Abende's analysis may not stand up very well to closer inspection, it remains important, for it may reflect and articulate at least one segment of Tiv opinion on the subject of composers. One can infer, perhaps, from his emphases, that many Tiv would prefer to think of composing as a role given to an individual by his cultural situation rather than as a skill gained by an individual which requires cultural validation. My discussions with composers on the issues of inherited roles and talent versus training are quite similar to discussions we might have here in the West: some sons follow in their father's footsteps; most don't. Some people are born with talent; some aren't; but even the talented must work to acquire craft. Medicines work for some people, but not others. Some gain a wide following, while the reputations of others do not spread beyond the local lineage and the nearest beer hall. But this is a premature and impressionistic summary, and a closer look at specific composers is overdue.

First, I would like to give a fairly detailed account of Anande Amende's career and opinions, an account which includes the story of an admired composer from a somewhat earlier era. Then we can compare points of interest in this biography-autobiography with material on the careers of seven other composers.

I first met Anande Amende, known to many as Ikpamkor London or Ikpamkor Kwande, at a *burukutu* in Gboko. After we had put away a little *tashi* (millet beer) together, I invited him to the place where I was staying on the outskirts of town. He came the next day with two assistants, Loho Akper and Iorcagh Akume, and a small hourglass drum under his arm. I conducted a brief interview, and he sang twenty of his songs, which I recorded. His style seemed unique to me then and still does, although increasing familiarity with Tiv lullabies, sawyer songs, and the styles of prominent composers in his area has clarified my sense of the resources available for his shaping. Some months after this first recording, I returned to Gboko again and recorded more extensive interviews with Ikpamkor, in the course of which one of my tape recorders was stolen by the thieves of Gboko under the direction of their universally acknowledged leader, Ambi, whose name, literally translated, means "feces." During the rather protracted and foul smelling negotiations with Ambi for the return of my run-down machine (I eventually got it back for a few pounds because, I suspect, he couldn't get it to work either), Ikpamkor served ably as a mediator. So expert were his mediations, in fact, that I was often inclined to suspect him of more than a sympathetic observer's interest in the whole affair. This incident, combined with information from the interviews and the lyrics of his songs, gives me one of the clearest pictures I have of a composing personality.

It is a clear picture of confusion, though my clarity may well be a substitute for real understanding, and his apparent confusion could be a mask for wisdom of a kind. It is clear to me, for example, that Ikpamkor is a man of divided loyalties, a marginal man. His composer's nicknames express the split: "Ikpamkor" means "cob's horn" or "buck's horn" and carries connotations of a war horn or signal that covers great distances; "London" seems an explicit identification with the metropolitan powers that be. Taken as a paradigm, the name suggests a traditional Tiv medium with a modern message. Taken as a syntagm, the name might be construed as "a call to arms against imperialism" or "a communication from the British capitol," like "radio Britain calling." I never asked him how or why he took the name or was given it, but it seems appropriate in many ways. Some Tiv refer to him as Ikpamkor Kwande, restricting his role of worthy spokesman to his home district of Kwande.

Of all the composers I met in Tivland, Ikpamkor seemed the most eager to be modern. Before sitting for a photo portrait, he powdered his face for a contemporary Tiv "glow" that seemed to me a ghoulish grey (see plate 9). In a corner of his Gboko room sit the remains of a locally crafted miniature jazz drum-set that once was part of his ensemble. His daughter is one of the very few girls in Tivland to be receiving a secondary education. He remains the president and secretary of a composer's union or guild, though that organization may only have existed for the few hours when meetings were held and officers elected. He is one of the few composers to drop pidgin English phrases into his songs every so often. But no evidence for an urge to be modern could be more convincing than Ikpamkor's quest for a birthday, the one marker that most reliably sets off the modern man from the timeless traditionalist in Tivland.

I went and asked my parents. I asked them whether they could tell me the exact date of my birth. They said they did not know, for at that time there was no education and so they could not write it. Then I asked them for an event. They told me that Kpiato Adikpo was installed as chief then. So I asked them the number of days after his installation that I was born. They informed me that my mother was a potter, that she used to make large pots called *zwar*. She molded pots at the time she was pregnant. And she molded one to take to Adagi. Then, when one's farm was yielding well, he would take the crops from the farm to give to the eldest member of the community. Or when you are a potter, you would make the best and largest pots for the eldest. It was Adagi who was the senior man of the land, Nanev. She told me that when she got there she did not meet Adagi; he had gone to install the chief at Adikpo. So she left the pots for him. After she had returned, Adagi came back and sent for her but she told him that she had delivered a child on the previous night. She told me that it was midnight. Then I went and searched the records for the date of Kpiato's installation and they told me that it was on the seventeenth of August, 1928. That was how I came to know my birthdate!

It is also noteworthy that Ikpamkor gives evidence of being a monogamist. Since his first wife left him, he has not remarried—"I don't want to marry unless that one should come back." He lives in a bachelor's room with the photographs of his wife and children on the wall. Ordinarily, a man of his age who is unmarried, "who cooks for himself," would be an object of derision, but Ikpamkor is a modern major voice in Tivland and an exception to a number of Tiv rules.

During our tape-recorded conversations he rambled freely over much of his life and career as a composer so that most of his story can be given in a translated version of his own words.

My home was a very large homestead, for my father was a man who had lived for a long time. And as he was in a large area, some

would just come and stay with him. At times a person might fall
sick; since there was a "doctor" at his homestead, after the *ityɔ* [patri-
lineage] had passed judgment, the person just stayed there, receiving
his treatment until his sickness was cured. Sometimes, after the
treatment, they resolved to remain with my father, and they would
make their own houses to settle there with him. There also came
another man and his name was Anviongo. He was there even before
I was born. He had up to forty children, and most of them were full
grown.

My father was with one of his brothers; his name was Kuta. That
Kuta had two wives. Another brother was Fier Adee, who also had
two wives. And there were many people. There was my father's
junior brother; they had the same mother and father. His name was
Agba Tongo, and his only business was defiance, to go out spoiling
the land. In any fight he would go out to kill people; while they were
sleeping he went and burned them up in the house, standing by
the door, threatening to shoot anyone with his arrows that attempts
to break out. Whenever there was a war, if he went, not many would
have to go to the war. For, once he saw a person, he would try to
capture him with his bare hands. Even when arrows were being
shot from all directions, he would certainly capture the man. That
was his business.

But my father was not a troublesome person. He was very peaceful. Even if you tell my father that this thing here is not earth and
you happen to raise your voice up high, he would agree with you
that it wasn't earth. If you told him that the sun was the moon, he
would only say that he had thought it was the sun, but since you
denied it, it was alright with him.

My father had four wives then. Also he had children from other
places, other wives. But in those days they were not considered reliable wives, that is, they were not gotten by "exchange."[3] They
were married in terms of money. And the Tiv never cared very much
about money in those days. It wasn't a very serious thing, so they
wanted a wife that they had married by exchange. My mother was
married by an exchange at Shangev. So they made the exchange
and begot eleven men; I am the twelfth person. My mother did not
bear any after me.

3. See Laura and Paul Bohannan, 1969, pp. 69–71, for a clear and concise
exposition of this extremely complicated marriage custom. Prior to its prohibition by the government in 1927 it was the preferred and most honorable form
of marriage; a number of other customs, rituals, economic practices, and interlineage relationships were tied to it. When Tiv say "the white man spoiled the
land," the first evidence they cite is the prohibition of exchange marriage.

108

As in many another culture, the last born is often a favorite, especially if it is a son, and the son of the most prestigious wife at that. One can safely assume a very pleasant childhood for little Anande.

My father had many children from his other four wives, but those wives were not from *ingol* [marriage ward exchange], so the condition was that even if you have many children from such wives, and even if the children have grandchildren, when the woman's people want to, they can come and go with their daughter and her children. My father had only one *ingol* to exchange, but he had many wives. So people often came and took away their daughters.

Dyo Amende, another of my father's brothers, had four wives with children. He is now head of the compound. My father's oldest son was called Iorliam, and he had five wives. Of my older brothers, Hule had two wives, Iorsula had a wife, and also Hindan, but the others were not yet married then. I was just a small boy myself. All of them had children later.

Idyo too, my father's grandson that he went and carried home from his patrilineage, had wives and children. Agba Tongo, the wicked one, had sons. Another of my father's brothers, Nienge, had two wives. Kyagh Bashi, he too had a wife, and the one called Ajo, Ajo Canca, he also had two wives at that time.

By Tiv standards of twenty to thirty people in a compound, the settlement that Ikpamkor has described is very large indeed, an eloquent testimony to his father's abilities as an elder.

As for my father, he used to play the female *genga* whenever there was a dance.[4] Playing *genga* was his work. He was a farmer and he was a weaver too. He knew how to weave *anger,* those expensive cloths. He could carry three pieces of *anger* and marry a woman; his cloths were always very fine. At home, whenever there was any ceremony or gathering, he would go there to play the *genga,* although he never used to sing. I was told that the father of his father, the one who begot Ajio, was once a song maker. That's how it was explained to me. And then Agba Tongo, my father's junior brother, he was a fighter and a fierce crook.

Again, one of my father's nephews was also a composer. He used to make songs for *amar,* especially the songs for *ishongo.* You can hear the same melodies in those church songs, the ones by this man

4. The female *genga* (see plate 5) would be the largest of a set of drums, with heads on both ends, slung under the arm and beaten with a stick. Some have a string stretched across one head for a rattling or snare effect. (See Abraham 1940b, pp. 102, 103.)

Ityavger. When the missionaries came to Tivland, it was the *ikenge* of *amar* that they chose for making church hymns. Before, when you took a wife, they would call the *amar* and kill a cow. Then they could play and dance on a "stage" [*ivom*]. It went on throughout the whole night. As for this matter of *ishongo*: if I happen to marry your daughter and I'm about to make *amar* for her, I would go and hire a composer to insult you. The songs would abuse the bride's father and all the people of her land. This was being done in my land, Kwande, and in Jecira, but I don't know of it in any other place.[5]

You can say that *amar* and *ishongo* have the same *ikenge* [melodic shape, or in this case, "general intonation" might be a better translation] as *gercam* [from *ger icam*, literally "to shout a call and response song"]. Aginde Agena, the most famous composer before Bam Gindi, he was singing *gercam*. I think it began when Tiv went to war. When they won a victory, after their return, it was *gercam* that they used to sing. Then different types of dances started springing out of it. In the beginning the Tiv composed only *gercam* and *ibiam-egh*. *Ibiam* are noble songs; they are songs of greatness. But you had to sing *gercam* in order to express an emotion. At times you would sing it to advise your people, the *ityɔ*; others would sing it to express their calamities; another to express a pleasurable mood or the beauty of his land. So the *gercam* was being sung in many different ways, and my cousin was doing his when I was a boy.

As for myself, when I was of age I left my father's compound and went to my brother who was at Adikpo. His name was Jande, Jande Amende. His mother was not married by exchange but by bride-price. This being the case, he was carried back to his mother's home. So I left to stay with them and was going to school.

Ikpamkor goes on to talk extensively about the incentives offered by the Catholic mission for attending school. The medals worn around the neck by pupils who could recite the catechism became very popular with the ladies and had a high trade-in value. But someone wearing a medallion without the requisite knowledge was likely to be embarrassed in the market place by a question like "Who made you?"

When you did not know how to answer, they would pluck off your medal, they would pluck it and go with it and all the ladies

5. For more extensive information on traditional modes of marriage and conjoined musical events see Akiga (1965, pp. 121–55, esp. pp. 128, 140, 145–52) and also Abraham (1940b, pp. 138 ff.). It would appear that in earlier times most song styles were linked to particular marriage ceremonies. Ikpamkor notes that *iye*, the term for "honorable marriage by capture," also designates a distinctive song style, unlike any other.

laughed. When the ladies laughed at such a man, he was compelled, there and then, to go and join a school, just for the shame of not knowing English. And so the school at Adikpo was becoming very large.

A bigger attraction at the school developed toward the end of World War II, when Ihambe, an exserviceman (many Tiv were recruited by the British and served in the Burma campaign), came back with a trumpet that he could blow very well. When this was added to the school band, the combination of flutes, drums, and chorus, with trumpet solos, proved irresistible. They sang:

This land of Adikpo is more than I can stand,
Oh, let me go.
ABC is really too hard for me,
Oh, I'll go to Kashimbilla.

Kashimbilla is deep in the bush across the Cameroons border and a long journey!

The boys who blew the flutes were about thirty in number, and after they had finished, then the trumpeter would start to blow his trumpet. This would always attract many people. They would sometimes admit over forty students on such a day. So I came and stayed. As I really deserved to go to school, I began attending—that was in 1939 or 1940—until at last I came to be singing there, songs for dancing "maringa."[6] That was in the year 1944, and those songs of mine spread far and wide. They used to dance; the whole school assembled there, and they would start dancing "maringa," and I started making songs. Some of them were very popular, like "I am Unable Anna" and one about a Tiv man who went to Canada. But my first song that was blown on flutes by the band was

Anande Amende, this thing has been more than I could bear
And I am standing numb.
Anande Amende, the young man from MbaGen
I'll never stop singing, this thing is more than I could bear
And I am standing numb.
When I called Mr. Amende—
Amende has divided his fort with me, and he is living
    in his own land.

6. Quite possibly this is a reference to the Latin style, "merengue," since 78 r.p.m. records from the West were being promoted in Africa just after the war.

The last two lines refer to the death of Amende, Anande's father, which occurred a short time after Anande began to attend school. With the death of his father, Anande had trouble paying his school fees of three pence a month. Asena, a Hausa lady, paid his fees for a while in return for domestic service, but he was always refused assistance at home. "They kept asking me to come back and farm."

By the end of 1945, when his debt was approaching five shillings, he left school and began a life of wandering. First he went to Ogoja, in the Eastern Region, where he worked as a farm laborer and saved a pound, only to have it stolen. Then he moved from town to town among the *Udam* (a Tiv term designating twenty or more small ethnic groups to the south), picking up a few shillings here and there as a farm hand. His aim was to save enough capital to begin trading, but somehow every accumulation of earnings was "stolen." Anande recounts three instances of theft in considerable detail, but I wouldn't be surprised to find out that he gambled his savings repeatedly in the hope of getting rich quick. We can assume that, during his extensive travels over a two year period, 1945–47, he heard a wide variety of musical idioms. My limited survey work in the vicinity of Ogoja gave me some inkling of the rich assortment of musical patterns to be found in this small corner of the continent. Although Anande stopped composing during this period, he must have heard and learned a lot.

After the third and most serious "theft" of his savings, he gave up and returned home. "At home I started pulling rafia and making twines. I wove almost two hundred sacks in less than two years. I sold those sacks at one shilling and three pence each at Obudu, and I got about seven pounds. Then I started trading." By the end of the first year his seven pounds had grown to thirty. He married by proxy late in 1947, "the lady that I was in love with at the time I was a boy." While he was off trading, she lived with his sister Kwaghsor, until at last he could send for her. In 1948 a child was born.

> I went and brought my wife to Kyado. I bought a bicycle and I was in the position of having about fifty pounds. I started going to Onitsha market at that time. Then I began singing songs again.

> Anande Amende,
> He used to step on his bicycle and move,
> La, la, la, la . . .
> Amende's son is surely pleased,
> Anande Amende,
> The son of Amende is surely pleased.

I used to ride the bicycle with this song. It was the only one I sang, on and on, whenever I traveled. After some time I made another.

> Mr. Oan has come to be proud.
> If one foresakes me,
>   even if he is in the land of Ibadan,
> Mr. Amende won't bother,
> Mr. Amende won't bother.

This song spread all over and everyone knew it. Even today they still want to know it. Then I continued with my singing. I was trading, but before my life could be happy, I had to sing. When I am worried, if I sing, then the whole thing will cool down. Even when I am very annoyed, it just means that I will compose one of my best songs. I liked the life in trading. I had a lot of money, but I couldn't feel comforted. So at last it was simply that the song became large, then it took over, it became a means of making money. The money came by itself; the money "got up" and came into the song by itself. But it is not only for the sake of money that I sing now; it is still what brings me peace of mind. So I have this much, I don't have many worries, I can always sing and cool off my mind. One of my first songs in the school was done when my father died. It helped me to forget my sufferings.

Later it was sometimes my wife who used to offend me.

> Anagange, carry your child and go!
> A fierce beast doesn't bear many young.
> Don't increase Amende's family.

Later, by the time she was far away from me and had finished with me, I was asking her to come back.

> Anagange, return to our land.
> We Tiv have got a saviour.

After singing songs about women, I always feel as merry as if I had taken sweet beer. I used to forget everything. But the whole matter is this: I was afraid of things that could possibly get me in trouble. I have the fear of God in me. So I've always been afraid of assaulting someone and would usually try to do it indirectly. At times I would be vexed when I had no money. And again it was sometimes the troubles of my people. I would get offended when I have little and they were thinking that it is more, expecting me to give them something. It makes me unhappy.

And the other things: when the land is in trouble or when the elders don't agree with one another, when something is going wrong,

then I can sing. If an important event occurs and someone is sending
for me to come and sing, I will go; if it is a marriage and he says that
I should sing for the wedding ceremony, for his enjoyment, then I
can sing for that. Though I have only been to one marriage recently
at Mkar. The only thing I am not doing is abusing someone, spreading gossip, quarreling. There are many composers in the bush to do
that. If one is abusing people in songs, the song won't last; it will
spoil people's hearts, it won't go forward. When envy is emanating,
one can go to the man and appeal to him by word of mouth. If I
know that he can understand songs, then I will sing about what is
worrying him, and the thing will go out of his mind.

I am almost persuaded to take this picture of the God-fearing Anande,
individual and group therapist, at face value. Yet the reference to his
wife as a "fierce beast" doesn't seem so very indirect, and it hardly
seems conceivable that his reputation as a political-party composer in
the 1960s could have been won without involving himself in the bitter
quarrels of that period. In addition we have his extensive testimony to
the fact that Auta Anwuna was "the only composer" worth listening
to in his home district at the time Anande took up composing seriously
in the early 1950s, and Auta was nothing if not a master of abuse.

And a certain man in my own land, at the time I was a boy, was
called Auta, Auta Anwuna. He used to abuse Bashi, Bashi Agi. And
the songs went everywhere. So eventually he was sued in the year
1954, for there was a law that no one should abuse another in song.
When this man mocked Bashi, he was arrested and taken to court
then; yes, they asked him to sing those songs. And he sang them. But
when he was asked what prompted him to sing so, he answered them
that he was only soothing his baby boy. His son was crying, so he was
trying to comfort him; it was just a lullaby. Or so he said to the judges.

Bashi is a person that one shouldn't follow!
When he gets into your house,
    then he would start making fussy noises.
He will be peeping to look outside.
When he sees no one coming,
    then he would begin to blink the eyes.
"Woman, come and let's lie down.
If you will give me, I
I will just suck it."
Huu! Huu! Huu!
When ascending, it is by the left side;
When returning, it is by the right side.

114

He took a big pot and put it by the roadside,
But the bees never entered in.
Oh! Bashi! You haven't got *igbe*.
Even if you "repair" it,
The *igbe* will seize you again!
When you see someone coming,
You just rush there with your hullabaloo!
It appears as if you are the fat *icaregh*
By the banks of the Ukungu.
Akpenzan—the earth has gone with my son.

So, even though Bashi was in court, the judges discharged Auta. The chiefs heard his songs and they were amused, so amused they couldn't stop laughing. Then they released him. And after this he continued abusing the man on and on. The man was really very offended, and in my opinion, I think it was because of the abuses that the man died.

The reason why Auta was abusing him was that he once seduced his wife. You can even hear it in his song. And he is singing that the man used to talk very much, like *icaregh*, that bush bird with many voices.[7] Then he shows Bashi going up and down the road, looking for a place to put his pot for bees to enter and make honey. With us it is usually a person who has been initiated into the *akombo igbe* who can cover a pot for bees.[8] Auta is criticizing Bashi, saying he hasn't the power of *igbe* and that it will seize him even if he "repairs" or propitiates it.

Auta came back and made another song which offended even the chief of Nanev, Kuhe Adagi. Although it was not Bashi who said such a thing, he put this song in his mouth.

I was thinking that it was a way to help.
I will stand by the roadside and be saving people.
When I was ill, Kuhe Adagi, who used to eat with me amiably,
Oh, Kuhe came and passed at a distance.
Nowadays, even if Kuhe tours all of MbaRumun,

7. *Icaregh* is indeed a versatile song bird and a Tiv favorite. Its heart or tongue or eggs are frequently used in the medicines for composing, and the weekly newspaper of the primary political party in Tivland, the United Middle Belt Congress, was called *Icaregh*.
8. For a description of *igbe* see Akiga (1965) and Abraham (1940b), and for the workings of *akombo* generally, the Bohannans (Laura and Paul 1969, pp. 85ff.). In brief, *igbe* is one of the basic *akombo* a man must control if he is to be considered a man of power and prestige, *shagba or*. It is implicit in Auta's denunciation that Bashi will be suffering from dysentery for having transgressed the *akombo*.

Even if he visits me, I won't bother to receive him.
The stout man; you are shouting!
I realize now that Bashi could make the chief a toy.
Akpenzan—the earth has gone with my son.

When the chief heard of it, he was not pleased. He believed it
was Bashi who had said it and that Auta only made a song out of
what he had heard. The chief became angry, but it was only a lullaby. And so Auta went on, imitating the *ikenge* for singing to children, saying that he was comforting his son Akpenzan, but it brought
no comfort to Bashi. Usually we pat the child on the flank and the
ear, back and forth, singing:

U, u, u, let him sleep.
Ah! Kpah! Let the tiger catch the baby.
U, u, u,
The bull is lying in the stable.

But he did not want to scare his son with the tiger or the bull, so he
would just dwell on Bashi, calling him a pig. Auta was a fiend, so
he knew just how to introduce his songs. Bashi never had any peace.
Even though he was struggling with ill health, he got up and went
to Utange [a small ethnic group assimilated to Tiv culture but generally looked down upon] and took a wife there. Auta made a very
painful song about it:

He married a wife from Utange,
Killed a rooster and cut the breast,
Taking it to the Utange. They praised him,
Saying their in-law is a man of great wealth.
Akpenzan—the earth has gone with my son.

Usually when the Tiv marry, after slaughtering some livestock, at
least a goat, they send the "waist" to the bride's people as proof, for
they might think that their child has gone and eaten nothing. So the
Utange were praising Bashi for nothing, a small piece of chicken?
All these songs and more—he once challenged Bashi to fill a basket
full of crickets before he would forgive him, and every Tiv knows
it by now—all these songs were crowding in on him and making
him miserable.

Even as Bashi was about to die, Auta composed another song:

Oh! Will you stop my *ityɔ*?[9]
Leave Bashi to stay here,

9. The "patrilineage" and source of sorcery.

So the land would be good.
If Bashi is dead, the land of Kwande will be cold and dull.
There won't be again such a target for songs.
Ayombee, my son, on a certain day I will send you;
You will go to MbaRumun.
Tell them I have commanded that Bashi should not die.
Oh! If you happen to dig with a pig's nose,
No one will eat such a pig.
When the pig sees what they do not,
Then it would pick it and start beating its jaws:
Eat it! I picked it!
Eat it! I picked it!
Huu! Huu! Huu! Huu!

After Bashi heard this song, he was thinking about the case he had lost, and he was filled with rage. When he heard this song, then he died.

You see, Bashi was a wealthy man, while Auta was a poor man who had nothing. There was no way to mock him that would fit well. The only thing to hold against him was that he sang abusive songs. When he lost his case, there was no way for Bashi to retalliate.

Auta Anwuna's story does not end with the death of Bashi. In 1957 he found a new target and dramatized a series of "bicycle songs" focusing upon the accidents and general ineptitude of one Gbar Anshase. Peddling an imaginary bike over hill and dale, coasting and struggling by turns, he recaptured in songs Gbar's pride and shameful pratfalls, interspersed with shouts of "Give way! Give way! Gbeeng! Gbeeng! My bicycle has no bell! Gbeeng! My bicycle has no bell!" This song cycle earned him almost as much fame as the lullabies for Bashi, but Anande Amende was not living in his home district then, so he didn't learn the whole series. Explaining Auta's success and his own admiration, Ikpamkor stated:

People often like wicked acts, so while he was abusing others, people were usually pleased and they offered him both drinks and money. Also, they invited him to different places to sing for them. Listeners would pass the songs along. Wherever he went, his songs would spread all around. And he made many songs, so many. If I had known that someone would come to search for them, I would have taken the time to know them all. Yes, I would have arranged them in an orderly fashion, and we who are from one place, elders like Ierkwagh and Asongo, could sing them. Whenever they are gathered, they sometimes sing these songs to remember Bashi and Auta and Gbar.

Still, people were rather afraid of Auta. When he visited anyone, that person might take fright. For if you offended him, even slightly, after he went he would start to curse you and the world would know of it.

If I have gone to some lengths to recount Auta's exploits, it is because Ikpamkor did. Clearly his fascination with Auta's songs contradicts his earlier opinion that an *icam i anger* (song of gossip, intrigue, envy) can only "spoil people's hearts" and "never go forward." No one has forgotten Auta, least of all Ikpamkor. Loho Ashibi, a friend and assistant, who helped with the interviews and their translation, was convinced that Ikpamkor's own *ikenge* was heavily influenced by the much modified lullaby form that Auta developed. While I can hear certain similarities in style, I am not sure whether to attribute these to a shared lineage-area of Tivland, to Ikpamkor's voice (for his versions of Auta's songs are the only ones I have on tape), or to some factor other than actual borrowing. Extensive transcription and analysis of a variety of Tiv genres and individual styles within genres would probably be needed to prove any points of influence.

In any case, Ikpamkor insists that his style is uniquely his own and that he was born to compose.

Anyone who has been born with the inspiration could learn and know how to compose. An uninspired person, although he could compose a song, might later forget it. He might be making a song, and as he is going ahead with it, he would forget the beginning. As for those who are not born with it, we can take an example from the Tiv people. Some are Tiv and are farmers; others are Tiv but are lazy and don't farm. They may be able to farm, for if you go to the fields with them, you will all be farming together, starting a heap at the same time, but later on you might dig your own line of heaps and leave the lazy ones behind. At times you might be able to finish three lines while they may be striving to finish the first line. We can't say such people are "not born with farming." We can't make any distinction about this and say these are born to farm, while those were not born for it. A man might be a great worker. He works the hardest on the farm; he loves work very much. But this is always the case when the person has been very meticulous about that type of work. He has given all his might for it. He wouldn't realize this in the beginning, but by giving all his heart to the act, he might, after some time, start making real progress in it.

Some people, however, might sit where one is doing something and after a short time know how to do it even better than the person who taught them. They are so born; they are endowed to be so. For at times a father might be a hard worker, but his children might turn out to be lazy ones. So it's no matter of heritage. It rarely happens that one does what his father has done. So it is with songs. You may be a singer, but your child may turn out to be one who doesn't even like to sing. Some of my children don't like to sing, not even my songs. Some like to sing once they have heard one sing it, but others don't even like to go where others are singing, they just don't like songs.

So they can't gather together and say that a person should do a thing because his father was once doing it. But once one's mind turns to anything, people will come and say that the person was gifted with the power of doing so, that he had been given the thing as an inheritance. But it is not so, it is when your mind sticks to coping with a problem. It is only when your heart likes a thing, and as you progress with it, people will say it is your heritage, that you were given it. But no one can claim to be the giver—that he was the one who had given you such power. At least that is my own opinion.

I once knew a certain man in 1945, he was from Ipav and his name was Aunde Jon. He was a composer and most people liked his songs. But one day his *ityɔ* [patrilineage] gathered and told him that they were the ones who had given him the talent for composition; therefore he should make a dinner for them. They said the man was gaining too much from his songs; they had brought him into the world; he should make a dinner for them. But he refused and said in his song that his *ityɔ* didn't give him his talent for making songs.

The foregoing statements on talent and recruitment seem reasonably explicit, yet Ikpamkor often cites his musical lineage, his father's drumming, a greatgrandfather, uncle and cousin who were composers. It would seem that coming from a musical family may help, but it is neither a sufficient nor a necessary condition for composing. Composers are born *and* made. Though the weight seems to lie with nature, whose gifts are arbitrarily distributed, rather than with nurture, Anande's views could be interpreted in different ways. On the one hand, he concedes at the outset that anyone can compose, tacking on the weak qualifier that those not born to it may have memorization problems. Elsewhere he suggests that slow and steady application and memory training can make a composer successful at last. The farming analogy also suggests that all Tiv are able to farm and compose, but that those who are "very meticulous," give their heart to it, will excel their neighbors. On the other hand, "some people," and Ikpamkor clearly considers himself one of them, are learners who very quickly surpass their teachers or models; "they are so born." Is farming, then, really like composing? Can we call someone who doesn't make songs "lazy" in some sense? I infer from his remarks that in his conception of the nature-nurture scale each individual's talents and training balance out differently, with desire a heavily weighted factor and family inheritance carrying almost no weight at all.

As he talks about "the typical composer," this emphasis on self-selection and desire acquires texture.

Composers are different from other Tiv, quite different. Composers, in the first place, are those who want things free without doing any service in return, things that they wouldn't want to do by themselves either. They only want to get things from their songs. When they visit you and sing, even after you have given them something, they always want more. So they have more stubbornness than other people. And that is why when they are praising one and the person is giving them money, the very instant he stops giving out that money they will start to abuse him. At other times they would simply cease praising the person. And there are many who behave this way. But the old Tiv did their own things differently, not like this present generation. Those of the ancient times never made the mistake of going to the house when they were praising anyone unless they were invited first. Then only the elders were drinking beer, *ahopue* [the best ten-day brew], and being praised. At meetings a composer was obligated to give his *ityɔ* warnings and advice, telling them things they should not do, and anyone that you are praising in songs used to be to you as a brother, your very brother.

But today composers are in "a rough state of living"; for some it is gambling that starts them going from place to place singing songs. They stay at a place when they get things, but once it starts dwindling, off they go to another place with the hope that they might get more there; when they have got there, they may find nothing and this would urge them on to still another place. In fact, they are like chickens, for a chicken is never at rest. It eats here and there, always thinking it will get more somewhere else. But with me, when I am praising a person, it is his own business whether he gives me something or not, for I can't with my own free will go to him and demand anything. I would feel ashamed to do it. I don't move from place to place just to beg.

Still, composers are never at rest. Their minds are always working like a clock in order to bring about a new song, always restless. They can't be moving up and down like other people, for that would "take away their minds." So they are usually slow.

120   As for women, composers at times do have the luck of marrying
quickly and at times have the misfortune of very quick divorces.
Sometimes they marry women that are not theirs. Perhaps the woman
likes songs but can't make them, and when she sees you, she would
quickly fall in love with your songs. You marry. But on arrival home,
she might not find it possible to settle. She may want to travel with
you all the time, and in a situation where there are two or three wives,
you may find it difficult to move about with one of them. But others
have places where they could take the women before going on their
travels. They travel, return to them again for domestic affairs, and
then keep moving.

One would not have to spend long in Tivland to know that the differences in personality and behavior Ikpamkor describes are very much
differences in degree rather than kind. Many Tiv are exceptionally
stubborn, forthright about asking for gifts and favors, prone to take
trips on slight pretexts, quickly married and as quickly divorced. Every
compound has its "hunter" or "gambler" or "composer," prodigal sons
that may fill one or more of these roles and have trouble keeping a wife
or tending to a farm. Indeed, rugged individualists, self-styled part-
time specialists, are as much the rule as the exception, and competition
for leadership and influence in all the various spheres of Tiv interest
is always intense. People with a problem invariably consult more than
one divining specialist and compare their opinions. If one cure does
not work, a patient and his relatives are quick to call another specialist.
One who is an influential elder today can be abandoned by his people
tomorrow. There is a rapid and constant calculus of self-interest beneath the flow of Tiv activities. As the Bohannans have noted, to relax
a moment in Tivland is to stand with your elbows out.

One does not do justice to the competitive intricacies of the Tiv cultural context in a few sentences; I wish only to bring home the point
that Tiv composers like other part-time specialists, watch their careers
rise and fall in something that resembles a free market. If Ikpamkor's
nostalgia for a time when composers were tightly linked to their respective patrilineages reflects a former reality, the market for music is
becoming more frantic all the time. The image of composers as chickens, scurrying about Tivland in search of corn, raises the question:
Where is the corn? How are rewards distributed? What are the limits
of competition? Can we plot intersecting supply and demand curves
for song products? What does the community, the audience, the final
arbiter of a composer's success or failure, want? How do they make

their wants known? Informed answers to questions like these are difficult in any sociocultural setting, and Ikpamkor addresses himself to
these issues without much success.

At times one can produce songs, but they won't be much admired.
But one might come and be admired; most people try to know it.
After such a song, you go on making other songs, and at last another
song comes out which most people would want to know. During
political times people tend to like only political songs, and during the
"time of free movements" [after the military ban on politics] people
like free songs. But conditions change; although they are my own
songs first, there must be something connecting people to them;
these connections change. When you sing a song and the audience
turns to examine it, you know that they like the song. But there are
other songs which the people hear but think less of. While you
are singing such a song, the audience will call to you and tell you
to sing others. Maybe one man starts to say this, and the rest follow
him and urge you to sing something else. But for one to sing and be
scorned, no, they can't treat a composer that way. They can't drive
you away or chase you away or say the song is not good; they can't
say so, although they can tell you to sing one of their favorites. When
you have sung one and sung another, then they ask you to repeat the
one that pleased them. First, they sit quietly, but after you have
done the song over three times, then they can start learning how to
sing it. When you come to a place where it isn't hard, they will join
in. They will try to persuade you to stay still, holding you back in
order to know the song.

A composer peddles his wares and hopes for the best, that is, extensive oral transmission of selected works by those who care enough to
learn them and sing them to others. Song supply exceeds demand, and
it is always a buyer's market, even for Ikpamkor, who is one of the best.
Is the threat of abuse and its actual use needed to keep the market from
collapsing? The excess supply of composers and songs can be seen as
a localizing constraint, that is, a particular composer may see all of Tivland as his audience but be forced to concentrate on a particular corner
as his market, praising a carefully selected few of the local notables
who are most in need of a spiritual boost, in order to maximize the
financial return on invested time and energy. Everyone may hear his
songs eventually, but only people as near as his hand, will pay for the
privilege, hence the local emphasis in song lyrics and in student essay
preferences, and hence the necessity of travel, if only within one's
own district. The song peddler must take his songs to different con-

stituencies to enhance, simultaneously, his own reputation and the fame of those he praises (or the blame of those he abuses).

One exception to this pattern, a composer for whom the song demand remained constant, was the late Bam Gindi.

> Bam Gindi was the father of all composers in Tiv Division because he was the first to compose in a "high-life" way. His songs were very gentle and full of sensation. In dancing too, he used to dance in a gentle and pleasurable way. He started composing in the army, and when he returned in 1947, no one in the whole of Tivland had ever sung so, had used such an *ikenge*. Even now that he is dead, no one can sing with that very same *ikenge*.

Bam Gindi spent much of his time in Ibadan, six hundred miles to the southwest of Tivland, but it is said that whenever he composed a song there, traveling Tiv would bring it back in a few days, and within a week it would be common currency. Any Tiv over twenty knows at least one or two of his songs, and many can sing over a dozen. It would seem that no song of his was wasted.

Bam Gindi, as well as Ikpamkor, was one of the charter members of an interesting attempt to form a composer's union or guild.

> It was Kyaater of Ukan who first started it. He was the one who originated the dance *Nyipa*. He began it during the time that composers began abusing each other in earnest. It seems to me that it was around 1957. Maza Nomhwange and Jiagwe, the two best singers of *aluibiam*, were in it from the start; Ayoo Angwe, Bam Gindi, and Abaye, with a few others, joined. They all wanted to be one, for it was not good for them to be cursing each other. Tine had just settled a dispute in which Maza and Jiagwe were attacking each other in songs. They thought that what Tine had told them was wise and that they should be unified. If they were singing songs in praise of someone and that person did not give them anything, then all of the composers would stop praising the person.
> But they were soon divided by politics. Each went to a different party, and there was no more cooperation existing among them. But after a long time, as politics was still going on, in 1962 I called all of them and appealed to them, saying that we should have one policy even if we are of different parties. Let each sing for his own, but if we are disunited, the politicians won't consider us. It is the composers who raise any party's name, but since we are all separated, when it comes to things like bicycles or money, they give them only to those from other communities and exclude the musicians. They said that the composers were not reputable persons, and they failed

to give us those things. I told them that if this was the case, we should all leave politics. We did so, and when the politicians noticed it, they began to care for certain composers. Today I am still both president and secretary. Aondo Iorbo is vice president, and Maza is treasurer. Even though he has been made a chief, he has not stopped making new songs. But the time of politics is finished.

And with that time the climax of Ikpamkor's career may have passed as well. He was understandably reluctant to say much about his political role in the presence of the tape recorder, since at the time of the interviews Gboko was heavily garrisoned. Soldiers, who were unpredictable, wandered the town, and the ban on politics was taken very seriously.

I did not like politics during those days. I did not like it from the beginning, but most of my age-mates were in it, and that pleased me very much, so I stayed with them. It was not long before they wanted to do something, and I told them such an action was not fair. Then some wanted to arrest me, for I was a very strong voice in U.M.B.C. [United Middle Belt Congress]. When they talked of imprisoning me, I wasn't happy with their reaction; that was the first thing. The second was their distribution of amenities. When they had money, they gave it only to the men who were already rich. They never gave it to the people who were behind them, and this too did not please me. So on a certain day I said, "No, I was mistaken." Later on my friends pulled me into the N.P.C. [Northern People's Congress].

We broke off at this point and never picked up the threads of this conversation, so I don't have an account of his shifting affiliations in his own words. Two of the students who wrote about him summarize what I take to be prevailing public opinion on the matter.

Anande Amende devotes all his time to planning the production of songs that are very effective. His songs were mainly against the politicians in the division. He sings against them so that they may give up their former parties to join others. He himself was an outstanding member of the U.M.B.C., but he changed to *Baja* [a Tiv name for the N.P.C., meaning "slaves"] because of their influence. When he resigned, many other people followed him. I believe he was paid by local chiefs to support this party. Nearly everyone in the division liked him, for he was working for the progress of his townspeople. He wanted the Middle Belt to be separate from the North. Some native chiefs would judge cases very unfavorably against the people who were not *Baja.* So after the general rioting in Tivland, this man left the *"Adzov"* [the term for U.M.B.C. members, meaning "sprites"] to join the *Baja* so that he might claim money by way of damages for his property. In 1964, after the general payment for the riot destructions, he went back to join the U.M.B.C. Since the massacre in the division, "party" has been wiped out, so he has not changed from one to another.

The second essay confirms the first:

His songs were first for the party of *Adzov,* but later he joined *Baja.* During the time of *atemityo* [head bashing] in Tiv, the condition was so critical that he again left *Baja* party and joined *Adzov.* They received him gladly because his songs were convincing and could change one's mind. Since the take-over by armed forces, he does no more singing for *pati* men or criticizing opposers. At present he sings for the interest of people. Many people appreciate his songs, so he makes visits for entertaining. Women in particular enjoy singing his songs and dancing to the rhythm of his drums. His melodies are simple to understand and striking.

Although Ikpamkor's income has probably decreased since the political era, his popularity seems not to have diminished significantly. As a third essayist put it,

Where there is clapping of hands, laughter and shaking of heads, we know that happiness and loving have embraced all. When people hear Amende's high-life and sentimental songs, they offer many gifts—he is so cheerful and plain in his songs. So we call him "Ikpamkor Kwande," meaning "worthy to be heard by all."

Since 1964 he has been working primarily with dance groups.

I wanted first to confuse people and make my own thing to be quite different. That was why I decided that my songs should be *soya* [sawyer], that I should name my dance "woodcutter." Some just call it "Ikpamkor," for no other person has this type; it is a dance, mine only and a special dance, but many know it by now. When people are in need of it, they can call me. When there is any gathering at Makurdi [Benue Province capitol], or any sort of festival they are about to hold, or when they want to celebrate Christmas in any other place, then they call me to go and make songs for them. They have to give me a list of all the names that they want, those whom I have to call on in my songs. Then I would go and compose my own song and give it to them. The people would rejoice and sing the song, mentioning their names by themselves, and they would be very pleased.

Zenke Buba, Zenke Buba of Wan Akpishiakpa,
Anjor Aba—din! din! din!
Anjor Aba—din!
When you don't see me, I've gone to Makurdi.
Madam Hiem, Atume Ngugh,
Atume Ngugh Awanga, Awanga of Wan Atsagher,
Wan Atsagher of Yaaju.
I have mentioned Tyoyua Hundu Akanga.
I am beating a big drum over the door of Abaga Zungwa.
Kaangwa Nyam Agba, look for a vehicle to give me;
If it is not a bicycle, they should give a motorcycle;
If not a motorcycle, it should be a Landrover.
I'll be riding and going about on it.
The dance has mentioned Doctor Kuenum Akaa,
Wan Zen from Usaa, from the land of Nanev.
Beautiful Kwande women should look for something to give;
I'll go with it,
I'll go and show Gyerkwagh, father of Kwande,
How the journey has treated me.
Madam Mbapuun, Eorvihi Kpokpia, Matela Dajo,
Even you have cut a heap of copper.
The way you are dressing, the sun falls dark.
A beast has come out of the center of the earth,
And it is ripping up trees.
Richard Abuul, Benza Kaungwa, Nyam Agwa,
Give me a *gbagir* cloth.
I'll drape it and "dig into" the dance.
Bebe Abia has brewed beer for my dance.
Kunav sons are determined to see Ikpamkor of London.
Dura Gbinde, chief butcher. What!
Pay attention and I'll give you some news:
Joseph Minde, Kachi Gyum,
He has a strong heart like the Fourth Batallion.
He held an elephant, tied it up, kept it for Ikpamkor.
When Mr. Amende gets down to Makurdi,
My paternal relatives of Kwande would mix meals for me.

That is one I did for the people at Makurdi. I have sung for the death of Tor Tiv's mother and when Ahom Ingbiase was married, when Gaav women were celebrating Christmas, and any time the women of Kwande Improvement Union are traveling somewhere.

126

In the near future a certain man, Avande Agege, will marry; his daughter is going to marry; so after they have prepared for it, they'll tell me and I'll call my group. We'll practice from then until the time comes.

When asked what it takes to be a successful composer, Ikpamkor said:

It is done by fervent work without resting. You should try to have people at all times and know how to manage those people properly, the ones who help you in singing. At times the people might want to drink beer and you have to be going about with them to places where they can drink. You have to give them money now and then for the purpose. This pleases them, and if you are together, this always makes people want you to praise them in your songs.

The fourth student essay begins, "Amende the drunkard lives in Gboko, where he does most of his drinking." It appears that good employee-relations and mellow management go hand in hand. Between invitations to compose, Ikpamkor keeps his throat wet and at the ready, wandering with his friends from *burukutu* to *burukutu*. Other composers of note can be found doing the same thing, although most do not have a permanent residence in town but simply visit for a week or so when the work at home is not pressing. Gboko is a central location, and earning a reputation there can lead to invitations elsewhere.

Sometime in the future I will go home. But for now I don't feel like staying in my own land. There are so many troubles there, troubles like the judges, the police, and so on. When they have embarked on a bad thing, I don't like living under the pressure, for I feel that I have to comment on it, and it always offends them.

Someday he will go home; someday his wife Anagange will return, he is sure of it. In the meantime, he brings his songs to festivities whenever asked, hangs around Gboko in the intervals, and recalls the days when a composer was the conscience and historian of his patrilineage, when Auta could get away with "murder," and that more recent time when a song from Ikpamkor could persuade people to abandon a political party.

The following biographical sketches of seven composers are drawn from the notebooks of students who were hired to collect information during a vacation. Each student was given a long letter of interviewing advice, stressing the need for details, and a list of topics to be covered for each composer or dance group, with sets of possible questions under each topic (see Appendix B). We met for a few hours to discuss the work before the students went home to their respective areas, and upon their return I was able to read most of the notebooks and raise questions on matters that were glossed over or were confusing to me in their reportage. The information gathered is not strictly comparable, nor was it intended to be; I was as much concerned with the kinds of dialogue that might ensue between young students and local composers as with the reported content of their discussions. Indeed, the reporting style and the participating composers vary from notebook to notebook, while the common list of topics and questions generates a network of overlapping factual material.

The biographies are organized according to the following rough outline:

A. Impetus to compose
  1. Background
  2. Motivation
  3. Early training or encouragement
B. Modus operandi
  1. Style and content
  2. Assistance
  3. Rewards

Wherever possible I have tried to supplement each sketch with the composer's self assessment and the opinions of others in his community. Each biography is a brief account of recruitment and expectations for the role of composer.

CHEN UGYE

At the time he was interviewed by the student Joe Yakobu, Chen was about thirty-five years old. He was born at Tse Amachigh, a compound a few miles from the town of Zaki Biam in eastern Tivland. His grandfather Dafo was a renowned warrior and slave raider, and his father was also a hunter. When Chen was still a boy, he took part in a hunt and was alone when a wounded leopard charged him. He shot an arrow into its mouth as it attacked, then he leaped into a nearby tree with a shout. By the time people came, the leopard had died, and Chen was sitting on top of the beast. His reputation for courage and good aim established at a tender age, he has been hunting ever since, usually in the

128   company of another great hunter, Iyorbo Yakobu. At present he supports a wife and four children by dividing his time between farming, hunting, and composing.

When asked why he took up composing, he gives two reasons: poverty and grief. He states simply, "Poverty [*ican*] made me become a composer." But it should be noted that *ican* has a more explicit range of meaning than our word "poverty," a range that encompasses "difficulties, suffering, physical weakness, a feeling of being disliked by others." *Ican* is often concretized in idiom and song as something that can be tied up, thrown down, defeated; a praise singer is forever noting that so-and-so has dealt with his *ican* in a dramatic and convincing way.

His first song seems to have been a transformed cry of grief.

> When his mother died, he was very miserable because there was absolutely no one to provide for him. His father was dead long before that, so not knowing what to do to comfort himself, Chen started crying [*vaan*]. In his cry Chen recalled all the nice treatment and provisions his mother had given him when she was alive. He sang them out in his cry. He did this repeatedly, and it finally ended up in a beautiful song of condolence. Therefore Chen, on being successful for the first time, went ahead composing.

Chen dismisses inheritance and medicines as factors in producing a composer. He tried various medicines on several occasions, but they didn't work for him, so he gave up the idea. He smokes a pipe, instead, to clear his brain. No teacher of any kind is mentioned in Yakobu's report.

During his career, Chen has composed praising songs, including those for prominent United Middle Belt Congress politicians in his area, and songs for two dances, *Benki* or "Bank" and *Jiagwey*. Chen himself was careful to disclaim any connection to political affairs. Everyone in the area, however, knows his political songs, and three of the six people listed as having rewarded him in some way for songs are advisors on the Sankara U.M.B.C. council.

Benki was started by Chen around 1957, when funds in the hands of Chief Aciv Yaven were stolen. Aciv was held responsible for the loss and was hard put to pay back depositors, and so Chen organized the dance to comfort him. The dance was not extensively rehearsed, and from Yakobu's description it seems a standard variation on one of the basic men's dances. It is still being performed, apparently, though it is not as popular as Chen's *Jiagwey*, which was introduced around 1961 and remains his primary source of income from composing. I cite

Yakobu's report in some detail, since it is one of the few instances of a solo or virtuoso song-dance performance that has come to my attention.

Jiagwey is *imo* [voice or song] not *ishor* [dance or play] as such. It consists of only one dancer, called *Zambia*, namely, the *or imo* [literally "person of song"], Chen the chief composer.[10] When it is to be staged, all the participants go forward in a single file. The *Zambia* leads the line, followed by his wife and *or yese* [literally "person who cares for a child," "nurse or baby sitter"], the helper, and all the musicians or "labele" [pidjin English for "laborers"]. The *Zambia* sits on a chair with two spears, two tails, and one sword. On his right-hand side sits the *or yese,* and on the left is his wife. The rest stand in a single straight line facing them and include one *or gbande* [drummer], one *or kakaki* [person who plays the large Hausa horn], four *mba kwen* [double bell players], and four players of *shiva shiva* [probably a kind of shaker or maraca]. The *Zambia* starts the song, the "labele" follow him, then the *or yese* joins the singing. The *Zambia* stands and begins to dance with the two spears in his hands. He wears a dress which is easily shaken by the wind. As the music takes him up he goes to the drummer, brandishes the spears in his face to *cia* him [frighten, challenge, tease], and then he throws the spears. As soon as the spears hit the ground, the music ceases. They rest.

In the second stage, he takes the sword in hand. As he dances, he shakes his body and draws the sword against his wife, starting a false slaughter with the blunt side against her neck. He dances and dances, then raises the sword high up in the air, and descends on the drummer. That's how the second part ends.

In the third and last part, the *Zambia* holds the two tails and dances. The end comes when he throws them high in the air, and the music stops when they land on the ground. Whenever the *Zambia* is tired, the wife leaves her place to wipe the sweat from her husband's face, then goes proudly and sits down.

Occasionally they will get over six pounds from a host, then move on to the next compound. In fact, *Jiagwey* is an expedition in this part of Tiv Division, for they may spend almost a month going from compound to compound. From the wealth they acquire this way, the

10. *Jiagwey* might be named after the famous Tiv composer of that name, but I doubt it. *Ji Agwai* could mean "understand Fulani" in Hausa, and Tiv do enjoy mocking Fulani customs and rites, but without any clues as to folk etymology from Yakobu's report, we are left to speculate. *Zambia* is similarly obscure; it is not a Tiv word and is not found in Abraham's Hausa dictionary either.

130   *Zambia* and his wife take half, and the rest is divided among the musicians.

Six pounds is probably a very great reward. In general, a reward may represent the total value of the goods that are redistributed at a *Jiagwey* event. The rewards[11] from specific individuals listed in the report are as follows: five shillings; two chickens and six shillings; one pound ten shillings; two pounds; "one she goat and four pounds"; "one very big sheep and cloth worth five pounds." I suspect that the first four rewards are for normal praise-singing and that the latter two are compensation for performing *Jiagwey* with the full troupe, in which case performers and audience alike probably partake of the meat the large animal provides (see below).

Although no note is made of it, I suspect that the assistant or *or yese,* in this case one Abur Indyar, gets a larger share than the other musicians. Under normal singing circumstances Abur is the first to learn Chen's songs and, as Abur has the "sweeter voice," he usually sings the lead or "call" parts in performances.

Jiagwey may be a personalized adaptation of the traditional Tiv war dance, *Girnya.*

> The *girnya* dance is an *akombo* introduced from the Dam people; it is a war dance calculated to give prowess in war, and warriors used to dance up to the drums called *indyer* and *poro,* brandishing the heads of many slain enemies. Today it is only a symbolic dance round the drum in a wide circle, the men brandishing matchets and even young boys carrying mock matchets made of wood. The accompaniment consists of the flute *idyua* (also called *kor,* "horn"), the drum *igem gbande,* open at one end, and sometimes the remarkable *poro* drum which is mounted on a wooden base carved to represent a male figure with large membrum virile, no doubt by imitative magic to give virility to participants in the dance. [Abraham 1940b, p. 92]

Modern revivals of *Girnya* for entertainment, minus the heads of slain enemies, still occur today and are highlighted by solo dancers moving toward the musicians (see plate 3 for a similar salute), who stop abruptly on a prearranged signal from each dancer, a feature that epitomizes the Tiv emphasis on clarity and precision (see chapter 1). The

---

11. While "reward" is usually a translation of *injar,* a Hausa term used variably by Tiv to mean "commission," "rent," or "salary," the verb for giving a composer something is *nambe,* indicating a payment for services with connotations of exchange within the prestige sphere, rather than *kimbi,* to pay for goods, usually in the market place (see Paul and Laura Bohannan 1968, p. 238).

clipped ending, perfectly synchronizing the frozen movement of the dancer with the unison silence of the musicians, invariably delights a Tiv audience (the possible reasons for this delight are explored in the final chapter). Chen Ugye's added fillip of thrown spears and tails, and of course the "false slaughter" of his wife, certainly add zest to a performance already freighted with emotions from a bygone era. The feigned attack on his wife suggests, perhaps, the displaced aggressions of a hunter without game, a warrior without enemies. Put another way, this danced performance of his songs summarizes his diverse roles as hunter, would-be-warrior, and composer.

According to Chen a composer is only as good as his thoughts. In addition to intelligence, "he must have patience to endure any circumstances he may have to encounter. He must have pity for human beings; thus he comforts a person in his neighbor's death or in a neighbor's sorrow."

People in his area admire Chen's abilities and consider him a just and upright man. He is particularly noted for his cunning.

ADI BENTE

The interviewing student, Frank Ime, reports that Adi's father had six wives, who bore him eighteen daughters and sixteen sons. Adi's mother was third in seniority, and Adi was the third born of her four children, all boys. Bente's large compound is a part of the small lineage MbaIyuhe within the lineage Kpav in the Shitile clan of eastern Tivland. When Bente died, Zaria Bente became the compound head. Today Adi, roughly fifty years old, heads his own compound and has three wives, all of whom are childless. "When he was still a young man, Adi's mother and father died, and so he had no one to care for him. This is the cause of his composing spirit. His father's other wives did not love him, so as an orphan he would sit singing quietly to himself."

Apparently Adi did not sing of his orphan's woes quietly enough to suit his siblings, and his older brother "drove him away, saying that he did not want a singer." Adi continued singing for his food. His early praising songs were very short and not very well received; in fact, "people at this time only laughed at him." But Adi persisted, and as time went on his songs became longer and better. Eventually some of his brothers joined him and persuaded the elder brother not to drive him away whenever he entered the compound.

The failure of his first marriage seems to have further deepened his composing motivation. "Though as poor as he was, he married, and the woman, on seeing how much suffering she had to go through by staying with him, divorced herself. This brought much sorrow to his heart and caused him to go back to the composing life." He has been composing steadily since around 1940.

Early in his career he bought medicine from Mhembe Toro Baka, a fairly typical concoction of roots, salt, and bird's tongues, and he firmly believes that he could not have become a successful composer without it. Similarly, he is convinced that, in competitive situations at least, charms are indispensable to success, for example, *imborivungu* (see chapter 2), "the instrument breaker," "the throat-drier," and *iondo*, "the attention-getter." (See chapter 4 for a more complete account of composing techniques and "technical assistance.") While a firm believer in medicines, charms, the blessings of the elders, and the cooperation of kinsmen (see below), Adi Bente is in every other respect a self-made composer, never having been apprenticed or taught and making no mention of inherited talents.

While Frank Ime's report is remarkably thorough in most respects, he never identifies the *ikenge* (melodic style) or dance genre in which Adi composes, referring only to the praise content of almost all his songs and providing forty lyric snippets by way of illustration. These single-statement examples seem to be like the first or identifying lines of poems in an anthology, and thirty of them contain one or more names of people. A second list, this one of gifts, provides the names of twenty-five people who did or *did not* reward the composer in some way, and most of these people are mentioned in the lyric examples. Eleven people in the list of twenty-five gave nothing, including Hingir Songo, who is mentioned six times in the lyrics. Tera Ikume, as frequently mentioned, only gave a pound. It may be that these are close friends of Adi's who are mentioned in a conversational way. Composers often address someone in song as a device for distributing praise and blame to others or for relating their own joys and sorrows. In Bam Gindi's songs, for example, he often calls to Churbenga, once a prominent policeman in Gboko, giving him the latest news. The unresponsiveness of the others on the gift list is not explained. Aside from a few people who gave clothing or cloth (including an Igbo trader) and one delightful instance in which Adi and his singers paid two pounds for a lorry ride to Gboko but received the money back with a ten shilling bonus from the lorry master, whom they praised in song during the trip, all

major rewards consist of an animal (goat, pig, or sheep) and a few
pounds.

While these rewards seem substantial, it is clear that they add more
to the composer's prestige than to his pocketbook. Because he is usually
accompanied by a group of a dozen or so singers and instrumentalists,
nearly all of them sons of Bente, there is a broad division of the spoils.
Frank Ime's description of a typical praising situation in which Adi and
his chorus of assistants are involved gives a fine picture of a reciprocity
pattern that supported composers and singers in earlier times more than
it does today.

> When they get any money award, they sometimes buy something
> that can be divided among all of them. This is done so that when it
> is time for going out again, everyone becomes interested and wishes
> to go along.
>
> Everyone wears his own clothes when singing. When they are
> preparing to go out to sing, they meet every evening for about a
> week; then they go out. When they reach the man's house, he first
> gives them a cordial welcome and then he gives them pipes to smoke.
> After which they rest for some time and then they begin to sing. Adi
> usually dances to some of the songs; he demonstrates as he dances,
> thus making the songs more juicy.
>
> After they have sung for some time and the person likes the song,
> he may go back and bring out a goat and slaughter it before them.
> Then perhaps his wife or brothers or sisters or neighbors will bring
> out money to them. After they have sung for a while more, they
> stop. The animal is now dealt with; it is given to one of Adi's broth-
> ers [usually someone from his mother's lineage or *igba*], who cuts the
> animal in parts. They cut the *iwenge* or waist of the goat and keep
> it for their sponsor at home, but the chest (*vanger*) parts they cut
> into pieces and boil it for themselves and the villagers. The meat is
> always cooked outdoors by the men while the women are busy in-
> doors making food to go with the meat. Then the people from Adi's
> "inner clan," after the meat has been cooked, get special shares, and
> other people have different shares. But, in fact, other people eat more
> than the singers. Sometimes Adi himself does not get much meat at
> all, so that he bears only the praise of having got an animal from the
> man.
>
> When they bring the "waist" to the elder, Zaria Bente, he cuts
> one leg (*namegh*) and gives it to the leader of singers, Adi. Then he
> may give some part to the other people. But he seldom gives it to all
> the laborers. Even if they get ten waists, they return them all to

Zaria. The money is then divided equally among the laborers. If a singer gets ten shillings, then all the singers get ten shillings. But the *or u yesen imo,* or the one who helps in composing, gets more money than the other singers, but not as much as the leader. Whenever they come back from a singing expedition, they give Zaria one pound, no matter how small the money they might have gotten. They do this because whenever they are going out, he is the one who purifies their instruments first. He takes their goods into a room and won't tell what he does there, but then he brings the instruments out, blesses the men, and sends them off.

When they go out to sing, because their songs are so pleasing, they get many wives. Women who love their songs just leave their homes and follow them. But the woman's bride price is later paid. Some women become unsatisfied and run away. But others stay with their husbands. When they sing and their singing is pleasing to some women, the women are drawn to them. And when they come to them, they ask them which man they love best. After the woman decides, they send the woman back home to the man's place and move on. Then when they come back, the parents of the daughter come for the bride price. It is at this point that some women go back to their homes. It depends entirely upon the sound of the chorus. If they sing well, then wherever they go people will respond with much food. If, on the other hand, they don't sing well, they don't get much money.

The statement "It depends entirely on the sound of the chorus" and the emphases on women, food, and money which precede and follow it, summarize very neatly what might be called classic composing economics. Zaria Bente, his older brother, seems to preside over all Adi's song activities with a firm grip, probably because every song expedition takes many strong hands out of the agricultural production sphere, for which Zaria is responsible.

In terms of assistance, Adi is as closely tied to his lineage as any composer I know. Ten of the sixteen people listed as assisting him at various times are sons of Bente, and two others are sons of Zaria. Deayongo Zaria is currently his first assistant, *or u yesen icam,* and "he helps him by bringing new verses and sometimes the melody for them; then they connect up the verses to make a song." Almost all the composers vigorously deny any direct collaboration of this kind, yet Adi notes that others in the group besides Deayongo contribute phrases and ideas from time to time.

Recalling his starting point as an outcast orphan and his childless state today, one wonders whether this heavy reliance on kinsmen is from choice or necessity. Perhaps, given his age, it simply represents a more traditional Tiv pattern. He is described by his kinsmen as a "humble, calm, and patient man," almost always at peace with his wives and his "laborers." Like most singers, he drinks more than the average, just "to keep his chest open." Since he was an orphan and is childless in old age, it would appear that composing has been a way of keeping his name and reputation alive in his community.

HURA IYONGO

Another composer reported on by Frank Ime, Hura Iyongo, is also an older man in his fifties. He began making songs as the servicemen were returning from World War II, and he gave up composing during "the time of politics," presumably the early 1960s. He has one wife, three children, and lives in the compound of Aam Gbeave in the Gambe Ya clan area.

Hura was seriously ill as a child, causing his mother much suffering. When he recovered, he led a normal life, was circumsized in due course, and worked on his father's farm with his brothers. He began composing and singing at an early age. His initial motivation stemmed from a desire to get rich quick. "He was so poor that he could not feed or clothe himself. He felt that if he worked on the farm, it would be a long time before he would get money. He started composing to get the money he wanted in a quicker way so as to clothe and feed himself and his mother."

Yila Nume gave him the medicine, the same recipe reported for Adi Bente minus the bird tongues, and it worked well—he began singing in his sleep! Although Yila Nume was "an old uncle" of his and "a great composer," Hura dismisses both training and inheritance as possible contributors to his career. Unlike Adi Bente, he thinks that "any good songs do not depend on whether or not a person has charms, but depend on how gifted he is. There is no truth in those things."

His first songs were for *Iyon man Ikya* (the bird and the monkey). *Iyon* was a basic dance in Tivland thirty years ago, and the monkey addition probably represents a local variation. In any event, this dance was fading in popularity, and Hura participated in the local troupe more for fun and reputation than for profit. As the dance died out, he began composing praise songs. He was working out a marriage possibility when it was discovered that he had contracted leprosy.

He first went to the leprosy settlement near Mkar, the Sudan United Mission headquarters, where he was converted to Christianity after some years of treatment and the arrest of his disease. He was then moved to Haaga where he became a nurse, washing people's wounds and assisting the doctors. His composing career lapsed during this period, largely because he couldn't leave the settlement duties long enough to promote his songs by "going around the clan." When the missionaries asked him to go to Takum Hospital to preach the word of God to the patients there, he asked to visit his home first; finding conditions bad there, he decided to stay and lend a hand. He never returned to the leper colonies.

Only two of the fourteen lyric examples given refer to his disease:

My mother, daughter of Abur;
If she asks for me,
I have gone to the leprosy settlement.

God does not give everything to everyman.
Tell Teraga Tur, God has changed me into a leper
And Wankur Jirla has refused to marry me.

A leper's plight can evoke sympathy in praise songs after the fact, but actual leprosy and a composing career don't mix.

The other lyric examples are full of graceful hyperbole concerning the generosity of various hosts, and I suspect that this flair for embroidering an incident colors Hura's recounting to Frank Ime of the rewards he received when he was in his prime. Certainly the claim that he once got "eighteen pounds and a goat from Zende Ikyegh" for his best and most famous songs should be taken with at least eighteen grains of salt. It seems even less likely that Gevebe Gbeave gave him a hand-woven cloth of great length, "trousers, pointed shoes, and about ten pounds," since they were both living in the same compound, thereby diminishing the prestige and reciprocity possibilities. It may be that Hura Iyongo is trying to indicate the relative popularity of the songs that he composed for these men or that he is attempting to total up the gifts from each accumulated over a long period of time. The other eight rewards listed are all in terms of shillings and hens, making figures like eighteen pounds and ten pounds all the more improbable.

Hura names thirteen people as his assistants: two *kalangu* (the Hausa hourglass drum) players, a dancer, a *gida* player, and nine singers who were prominent, though there were a great many others who participated in his group from time to time. "If anyone wanted to marry, he could come to Hura, learn his songs; and then they would go to the woman's home and, through their good singing, might be able to marry the girl and take her home."

Since Ime's report in Tiv uses the verb *kem* for "marry," meaning the initiation of the standard long-term series of bride-price payments, one can assume that the singers were simply facilitating a courtship rather than performing a customary role in a "marriage by capture" or "elopement."

His primary assistant, Magashi, served largely as a memory aid, learning the songs as Hura composed them and teaching them to others in the group whenever Hura could not be present himself.

As in his Adi Bente report, Frank Ime is again particularly good at eliciting versions of song situations. Much of the description focuses upon song visits as a device for rapid courtship, and it is clear that it is not only the singers themselves who benefit. "When the group wants to go out, any person interested is allowed to follow them. Some follow to learn their songs, but when they are performing, the nonmembers sit separately. Some follow just to eat food and meat and maybe find a lady." Elders advise everyone not to compete for women, but rather to assist a brother who is favored by a lady. Even an unsuccessful trip has this virtue of interlineage contact. "If your songs are not touching enough, the man may give very small food and money; he gives just because you have come from a great distance and are in need, also to remove the shame you must have if he gives you nothing."

An unsuccessful trip reduces the number of people who will tag along the next time out. Hura also states that on occasion, if a singing group is making a longer visit to a man's compound and the man "wants to go to farm, they go along and work with him on the farm," a further deterrent, perhaps, for hangers-on.

Conversely, however, there are dangers in being too successful: "I did not allow a man to go on awarding me for a long time until he has given me everything. This can spoil his heart later. When you see that the man has given enough, depending on his strength, then you stop singing."

Hura's brother, Igabi Iyongo, tells an interesting if contradictory tale:

> One time Hura went to a person's compound to sing. His songs were so pleasing that the man kept on bringing money and everything he had. At last the man had nothing left, but Hura went on singing. The song was so touching that the man went into his house

and brought out a machete. Before anyone could know what he was about to do, he raised the machete to cut the *tor imo* [chief of song] into pieces. As he struck, Hura dodged, and the machete lodged in the ground where he had been sitting. Hura ran away and never returned, though the helpers stayed for some time before leaving.

This story may be apocryphal, part of the lore of composing, or perhaps Hura was not the *tor imo* in question, for he specifically denies ever having been attacked in such a manner. Bogus or not, however, it is a cautionary tale of some significance.

Ime includes in his report a description of two customs sometimes associated with "formal" song situations:

> *Ka mil a mil imo yo,*[12] that is, when he is especially called for a set time, he brings along with him the man who gave him the medicine. At such gatherings the elders also go. The medicine-giver sits and listens to him while he sings, and when an animal is killed, he [the medicine-giver] is given *namegh* (the leg). If it is not *a mil imo,* the man won't come, because there is not usually much food. The first time this person goes, he gets a leg and one pound under all circumstances. Other times he is given meat and no more. The composer calls the medicine-giver to come and eat food and meat only, not to criticize or say anything about his singing. He may only praise the man's singing or say simply "he is a bad singer," but he is not supposed to criticize.
>
> If the man to whom they will be going has someone of his age, he may send a message telling the age-mate that on that day, when he brings out a cow, his friend should "tie a rope" on the cow so that the singers can hold it. If the man wants, he may tie the rope with about one or two pounds; "tying the rope" means bringing money.
>
> On that day, when he brings out the cow and gives it to the *tor imo* (chief of song), he calls his *or kwav* (age-mate) and tells him to tie the rope. If what he brings is too little, the host may drive him away, saying that he called him to "tie it" and be known as an important person, but now his age-mate has shamed him. This stirs up the man to go and get more money. When the money is what the host expects, he tells the "song chief" to receive it. After this they choose an announcer, and his work is to shout out what each person is giving. After the singing has gone on for a long time, he kills a

12. This might be translated as "It is a brewing to brew beer for song indeed"; the verb *mil,* "to brew," unless it is specifically linked to beer, *a mil msorom,* can usually be translated as "to invite people to an important event."

goat or any type of animal for his elders, one animal for the singers and one for the common people.

One would think that after all the contributions, the cow itself would be killed, but this is apparently not the case. But then age-grade customs have always been rather confusing in Tivland, and the age-grades themselves are ambiguous entities; even in Akiga's time they seem to have been variably present or absent from clan to clan.

R. C. Abraham, writing in 1940, states:

> Although there are no progressive age-grades, yet the members of every annual *kwagh* are considered bound together and form a kind of corporation for mutual help; thus, when a man marries and gives a dance in celebration of the wedding (*mil amar*), it is the members of his batch who contribute the necessary funds. Also, when he is courting a woman, it is they who sing his praises to her and interest her in him. Further, if a man buys a horse, horses being considered to confer great prestige on the owner . . . , he mounts and proceeds on a round of the villages of his age-mates; as the acquisition of a horse by one of their number is an honour to them all, each of them gives him a present of money, in order to show their respect. [1940b, p. 124]

The Bohannans note:

> Age-mates often help each other in their love affairs. . . . Age-sets may appear at the wedding festivities of a member, especially when he takes a first wife. There are no ceremonies at which their presence is essential, but if a young man wants dancing at his wedding, he turns to his age-set. The age-set is concerned (but not present) when a man kills a cow for a wife to gain prestige. [Laura and Paul Bohannan 1969, p. 48]

The primary function of age-sets, where they exist, is to defend a sick member from the ill-will of his elders by consulting diviners and "questioning" the appropriate elders. Apparently Hura Iyongo's singing group acted like an age-grade, even though it may not have been labeled one.

> When one of the singers becomes sick, they do their best to make the person well. They bring different types of medicine to the man. They also tell the elders that they are allowing one of them to die. When the elders hear this, they say that they are the people who are bringing happiness to the land, so they will help to make the follower well. Thus they take special care of the singer.

140   When one of them gets married, they all go to the man's house
and give to the lady any money they can "to buy soap and wash."
Elders usually do not go at such times, unless it is to see how the
boys are playing.

There was never any set fee for becoming a member of the group,
because some could not afford it, so anyone could join at any time.

These examples, taken with the aforementioned courtship activities,
all indicate that Hura's singing group served as an age-grade in fact if
not in theory. Hura's singing "age-grade" seems to have encompassed
his composing career in much the same way that Adi Benti worked
within his immediate extended family.

Frank Ime concludes his report with the following assessment of
Hura Iyongo:

People in the area say that he is a good man who has very good
advice. He is quite helpful to them and he is called a Christian.
They say he is a peaceful man, a peacemaker. He does not fight, but
always threatens to bring people to court. People love his singing.
Now that he has stopped singing, people usually keep on asking him
to go back to singing once more. He was a great drinker but has
stopped now. He smokes pipe.

ANEKE TIRE

Adura Imbor's reports on Aneke Tire and Ada Adi, next to be presented, are idiosyncratically explicit, often raising as many questions as
they answer. Aneke is an inveterate gambler, and Ada slips in and out
of insanity, so it may be that Adura's reporting style reflects the lives of
his subjects. It is interesting that the methodical Frank Ime should
select older composers well-integrated into social systems for his interviews, while Adura—"caught by kwashiorkor" and bodily deformed as
a child, early orphaned and long-suffering—should select composers
whose lives are more abnormal, violent, and chaotic.

Aneke Tire was born on the night of a supernova that Adura dates
in 1925. Aneke's father took it as a good sign and predicted great wealth
for his son, but fate was not so kind. When he was about five years old,
his mother left the compound, never to return, and Tire decided to
give the boy to one of his daughters, who was living far from their clan
area of MbaTierev-MbaJem, which is just south of Makurdi. Aneke
grew up there and had a difficult time, never having enough to eat,

stealing often to make his way, until "he stepped into gambling." He quickly lost what little property he had, and meditating on his failure in life, he began to compose songs.

The idea of composing came to him with special force when he lost his left eye. The story goes that while he was gambling one day, the Native Authority Police came, and as he ran away, he fell against thorns and lost his eye. Most of his songs say something about this accident. He composes songs of sorrow, songs of begging, songs of happiness, and songs of terror.

As for medicines, training, inheritance, and so forth, Aneke dismisses all these external factors with a few terse answers: "No one taught me. I learned how while others were sleeping." "The medicine is too expensive, but it's good to eat the hearts of chickens."

According to Adura, Aneke uses his own partial blindness and disfigurement in countless clever ways, mentioning the things that people with supposedly sound vision have overlooked, describing his own appearance so accurately and with such good humor that people who meet him after they have heard his songs always experience a shock of recognition. "His appearance is exactly as he says in his songs, so they like his songs and they do make fun of him while singing them."

Aneke does not shrink from making fun of others either. He was very active during the political period, abusing and praising the Northern People's Congress by turns. At one point he was "cast out by his relatives and was made to run to Gboko. He was ruined and had nothing until he began to compose songs that favored the party of his *ityɔ* [patrilineage] and was welcomed home again."

Once he was hired by a poor and ugly man to abuse Adikyo, a handsome rival for the affections of a young lady. By the time Aneke had finished working over Adikyo, the girl "was afraid the songs would effect her in future," and she married Aneke's ugly patron. Though I find it hard to credit, Adura insists that "the battle went on so nicely that the aggressor [Aneke] was asked for pardon." Apparently Adikyo's senior wife, Ajia, on hearing the songs, thought it expedient for her husband to invite Aneke and his group to their compound for a performance, hopefully a final one. Adikyo killed a hen for him and gave him five shillings, and "both enemies vowed that they would not become enemies again."

Adura describes Aneke's winning style and imagery in considerable detail:

142

He begins by shouting at the top of his voice, pronouncing the name of Adikyo with a scornful face. Then he gives a pause. This allows the audience to think about Adikyo and ask themselves what sort of man he is. He shouts the name again, and pauses again. Each loud shout makes Adikyo smaller and less important. Even after he begins the song, he stops for a while and starts again. And at the end he pauses too, to make pressure, so that the audience can laugh at his account, and laugh again as he ends his song "O-O-O-O-O-O" and stops breathing.

He says Adikyo is a tall, lean man with very long legs and a long, thin neck, so that he looks just like a giraffe. He is nearly bald, his face is very narrow, but his nose is very large and is hooked like a vulture's beak. His ugliness is sometimes like the monkey's face peeking through the leaves of trees, and his laugh is like the monkey shouting when it is hungry. When Adikyo talks, his mouth smells like rotten eggs. In the song itself he shouts Adikyo's name each time to make him smaller and uglier. He goes on saying that Adikyo's skin is very rough, like the crocodile's, and his wealth is to be found only in dark corners. His shoulders are always drooping, as if burdened. Adikyo's eyes are very sharp and red, as if a fierce dog is running after his enemy. When Adikyo stands up to go, he stoops forward and pokes his long thin neck out as if the tortoise is finding its way through tall grass. Adikyo, walking, takes short stiff steps and jerks his head from side to side like a great clumsy duck. Adikyo is a very untidy man, and his clothes are old and shabby; his body seems covered with white wax, as if the snake is chasing its prey. And these are just the things I recall; there were more, and Adikyo appears more vividly in the songs.

An exception to the usual pattern, Aneke has never composed for a specific dance, though his *ikyenge* is well suited to "modernized *Swange*" and his songs can be heard in the town bars, where this dance is the basic entertainment.

His principal assistant is Zanzan, a man in his early thirties, who "helps him to join long sentences so that his intonation should fall 'accordingly' [*sha inja, sha inja*]." Over twenty people have helped with the singing at various times, though he travels with only five or six in his group at present, including Atondu, a drummer, and Ityokyaa, "to blow horns." Presumably Ityokyaa's primary horn is the *gida* and Atondu plays *ngou gbande* (the basic or mother drum), while the remaining parts of a *Swange* band are recruited as needed (see plates 3 and 4).

Speaking of rewards, Adura cites Aneke directly:

"In fact, it is a very good thing to be a composer. For my own part, I have married two wives from my songs. Twenty-one persons have killed goats for me, and from each I received trousers and a shirt. The greatest thing that I receive is praises, though I'm more happy to marry from it, since I was left alone at first, but now it seems to me that the world wants me again."

People in his area say that he claims to be a farmer but roves about instead. He goes on singing and his songs suit his occupation and habits. He is a gambler, but also gentle and wise, so they want him to appear in their presence.

ADA ADI

Ada is also of the clan area MbaTierev-MbaJem and was born during the time of *Haakaa,* an antiwitchcraft movement that was sponsored, after the fact and in effect, by the colonial administrators in 1929. For centuries, the resentments and fears of the younger generations in Tivland appear to have been focused in periodic action against the assumed sorcery powers of the elders or *mbatsav.*

From Akiga's Story:

> When the land has become spoilt owing to so much senseless murder, the Tiv have taken strong measures to overcome the *mbatsav.* These big movements have taken place over a period extending from the days of the ancestors into modern times. One was called the *Budeli.* Many years later came the *Ijov.* The *Ijov* appeared during the time of the white man, in the year 1912. Since this there have been the *Ivase* and the *Haakaa.* The *Haakaa* was started under the control of the white man. Some of these movements have spread over the whole of Tivland, but others are only known locally. People have heard of them, but have not taken part in them, because some of the chiefs refused to allow them in their districts. . . . The most important of these movements, and those which especially pleased the Tiv, were the *Ijov* and the *Haakaa.* These were so popular that the Tiv did not wish them to come to an end, but after a short time they both died out. [1965, pp. 264–65]

With the advent of the British administration and the erosion of traditional localized authority (for example, by the abolition of exchange marriage in 1927), these anti-*tsav* movements appear to have increased in both scope and intensity. Certainly *Haakaa* as Akiga describes it (1965, pp. 275–89) saw a number of elders beaten to within an inch of their lives, as policemen were encouraged by the administration to follow up the accusations of the witch-hunters by bringing in alleged witches for questioning, along with "all the apparatus of the witchcraft 'cult' that could be found"; hence the name *Haakaa,* "to throw things away." Apparently *Nyambua,* in 1939 (see Laura and Paul Bohannan 1969, p. 39), was an even more violent uprising.

Ada, then, was born in the midst of intense generational conflict and experienced another wave of sorcery accusations and violence when he was ten years old. Ada's recounting of his life to Adura shows a preoccupation with the *mbatsav,* understandable in the light of these events.

> Soon after he was born, the government officers came to investigate witchcraft. His parents hid him under a basket and covered him with leaves so the officers would not see him. The boy was discovered, but they did not harm the child. The mother was crying and screaming, thinking that he would be killed; but when they left, he was handed back to her. And so they named him Ada, meaning "bow," for if one has bow and arrows, he is said to be a fighter, and he had fought for life and won.

Although he grew up, prospered, married, he was always bothered by "the question of superstition," as Adura puts it. "From his very first songs to the present day his thoughts have been about disturbances, his feelings about death, envy, and him being nothing in the world." It was about ten years after he had begun composing that "he became a madman."

> What made Ada Adi insane is not fully understood. He becomes mad about four months in the year and then comes back to his normal senses. I was told that he was made insane because he was abusing the *mbatsav* in his songs, saying that they have cursed him to be nothing on earth. Ada sang that they too were nothing, that those who claim to be clever and evil hearted will one day die just as he will leave the earth. He challenged all of them to live peacefully. Because of the suffering they have caused him, because the earth offers nothing to him but death, he will one day order the evil spirits themselves to destroy all those who possess magical powers. For those who share his condition but forget this evil and mock him, he has only pity. Singing such things, they cursed him.

While it seems clear enough that the question of superstition provides the basic motivation for Ada's songs, he describes the inception of his career in terms of a concrete situation. Before he began to make songs for himself, he was assisting a composer named Aza and learning from him as well. When Aza demanded money for the medicine that would make Ada a composer, Ada stopped going with him. When Aza married a beautiful young lady, Ada's envy was more efficacious than any medicine, and it was this marriage that he marks as the beginning of his composing career.

From the beginning, his songs were directed "to the honor of the bridegroom." As Adura implies, or tries to make explicit below, the "sorcery" theme and songs about marriage go hand in hand because competition between elders and young men for wives is the primary source of social conflict in Tivland (Paul Bohannan 1957), a conflict projected into the cultural, indeed metaphysical, sphere in terms of witchcraft accusations. Adura's explanation of Ada's popularity, although somewhat muddled, invites productive reading between the lines.

> His songs make him popular among his people because (a) his songs express a feeling of fear and distress; (b) his songs express a feeling of sympathy for those who need help from their fathers, that is, those sons who want their fathers to marry wives for them by paying about sixty pounds or two cows for one lady, and a young man who needs help from his father has none of these; so Ada Adi is very popular among both fathers and young people because fathers that are rich are proud of what they have done for their sons and those fathers who are too poor to marry wives for their sons, their sons worry them, and then Ada's songs stimulate their minds to marry wives for their sons; (c) in an historical form Ada gives the keynote to what their forefathers did in the past, for example, a boy who is clever does not need help from his father as such, but he goes out and steals a girl. Why is it that I say it is stealing? Because the girl marries the boy without the knowledge of the parents; this act of marriage was known as a kind of stealing. So Ada Adi reminds young boys to keep on stealing girls that way. His songs are both historical and contemporary.

We can see how fathers of "stolen" daughters and poor fathers who don't care to have their minds stimulated might curse Ada in one way or another. His songs are more popular with sons than with fathers, and most of his invitations to sing come from young men who are about to marry. Most often the young men kill a hen for him and give him a few shillings, but if the groom is rich, he may kill a goat and give Ada clothes. Ada never goes anywhere to sing unless he has been invited, and he says he has never refused an invitation. Aside from his general complaints against the *mbatsav,* he has never abused anyone or became involved in political controversies. Nor has he composed for any particular dance. Marriages and related events would seem to be his exclusive specialty.

Ada "moves with Abahange," his only assistant or companion (*ihambe imo*), who helps with the singing. He memorizes a new song perfectly before teaching it to Abahange. They always appear together.

The report gives us little in the way of self-assessment by Ada—in an important sense it is all in his songs—and the only comment solicited from someone in the area is a general statement which lays stress on the importance of composing songs "both of the things in the past and the present life so that both old and young people will be listening to you," probably a reference to Ada's focus on generational problems. In describing the qualities he listens for in "a good composer," however, Ada tells us something about himself.

> "I like a composer when he says outright what has made him become a composer, as when a girl refuses to marry him and he says it out, or when he was chief or a tax collector but lost the post given to him, he composes songs to cry for it.
>
> "I look to see if the poor people, the rich people, and the ladies have sympathy with him and if the man is good at expressing the points he is making.
>
> "If he can convert the hearts of the people to experience the same situation that he has experienced, then he is a good composer."

AKUMBA ANCHAN

At the time he was interviewed, Akumba was about fifty years old, though Anyor Ikyo, the reporter, says that he looked much older. He had one wife, three children, and lived at the compound of Akeran Orshi in the Iharev-Isherev clan area of northern Tivland not far from Udei train station.

Akumba's father was very poor and married late. Akumba was his first child, and the mother died soon after he was born, so the infant was taken by another woman, Usaaya, and did not return to his father's compound until he was four. When he was seven, his father died, and he went back to live with Usaaya. "There were many children there, and only the hardest working were given old clothes to wear. Akumba was one of the 'laziest' ones because he got little to eat and was very lean and weak." The memories of a suffering orphan seem often to be involved in the motivation to compose.

When Akumba was fifteen or so, his stepmother died, and he took responsibility for three children by working as a laborer for the Nigerian Railway. After a year he moved to the railway base camp at Udei and was paid two shillings, six pence each week as a water boy.

"A sixpence worth of food at that time could feed a man for a month, and only very rich people would buy things for half a penny. I began my own farm at the same time, borrowing seed yams from others and making forty heaps. The next year I did over a hundred, and in five years it was too much to do by myself. I was saving all my railway salary during those years until it came to twenty five pounds. I bought cows and took them to my stepmother's compound, and soon after that I married the daughter of Yogbo."

His wife helped with the farm, and Akumba was prosperous enough to send his first son to the Catholic school at Udei. When he was about thirty-five, however, he was laid off by the railway inspector and given a very small pension. So he concentrated all his efforts on farming and joined a farmer's club. There he became fast friends with Uduwua Gbev, a composer who was very busy making songs for the dancers at "horse ceremonies" (*Nyinya*).

"At that time [circa 1953] the Tiv people were very proud to own a horse. Anyone who bought one was regarded as rich and important. The horse owner had to organize a group of dancers, and Uduwua was the only man around who could compose songs for them, so he was getting a lot of money, hens, and goats. So I joined him, and after being in his company for a little over a month, he decided to teach me to compose by giving me medicine. I never requested it. I took some for five days, and two different ones for eight days. Uduwua told me not to leave my house on the eighth day, and soon after I woke up that day I fell suddenly ill. No one thought I would recover, and I too thought it was my end, but the next morning I was well again. From that day I was able to compose my own songs, and Uduwua told me that we should be going to different people."

Anyor wrote down the words of one of Akumba's "horse" lyrics, which may be translated as follows:

Ukange Aja has put forth plenty of money,
    as if he is a white man,
And has bought himself a male horse.

148

Iyortyer Botwev has a mare.
He should beat a good path,
   for I am coming on a stallion.

As in the past people were having children,
The sons of Ako have brought forth
   the wealthiest among us.

Tell Iyorpenda Ugima that Iyorpu Jii
   has left Swende to ride a cob in the bush,
While Ukange Aja is riding a horse.

Shagba Akegh has married WanMbaKwen
   and has even done *amar,*
And while proclaiming his *akombo,*
   people ran in terror.

They have received gongs;
WanMbaAgi came to the horse dance,
   while Swende rode a ram.

Judging by Akumba's imagery, getting on a horse obligates others to recruit some unlikely beasts of burden. Although horses die of sleeping sickness within a month or two in Tivland, if not sooner, the prestige of having owned one is retained, so horses go quickly from one owner to another until the last owner garners the honor of a conspicuous horse grave (Paul and Laura Bohannan 1968, p. 124).

Although the idea of doing a horse ceremony has faded in popularity, it has not died out altogether. I once came upon such an event quite by accident on the road going north from Makurdi. The horse was tied to a tree, and the *shagba or* (man of prestige) sitting next to it was somber and dignified while a great celebration took place before him. Two *genga* drummers, a man playing two *gida* simultaneously,[13] and a line of dancing, singing women seemed to be the primary celebrants. The beer was flowing freely.

When buying horses went out of fashion, Akumba turned to singing praises and to "pleasure songs." The ten people listed as recipients of praises gave the usual rewards—a goat or hens and some clothing—

13. The technique involved is similar to that employed by Roland Kirk, Harry Carney, and an increasing number of jazz horn players—breathing through the nose while storing air in puffed cheeks so that the sound flows uninterrupted (see photograph at opening of chap. 2). This same technique may even have been shared by the double aulos players pictured on ancient Greek vases.

with the exception of Makiir Zape, once Tor Tiv and now deceased, who gave all of that and more, that is, a goat, clothing for the helpers, and a bicycle for Akumba. He has been very scrupulous about staying clear of the political arena (though praise of Tor Tiv implies an N.P.C. allegiance). He has never abused anyone for the more traditional reasons and scorns those composers who do.

Beginning in 1963 he started composing songs for a dance group in the Iharev-MbaGwen lineage area. On the first day that he presented his songs for their dance, called *Agigben,* he and his group were given six cocks and two goats and were made members of the dance group so as to share any proceeds from their performances. He was still contributing songs to this group at the time of the interviews (March 1967).

Unlike most composers, Akumba does not single out one individual as a "first assistant." Six people are listed as available to help with the singing, but Akumba notes that previous helpers have died or quit or moved to another area, while others have decided to join him for their own reasons.

Anyor prefaces a few remarks on Akumba's status in the community with an interesting public opinion of composers, as if to say that Akumba Anchan is a possible but not a probable exception to the general rule.

> Most Tiv people do not like composers. Even if his songs are very good, they will criticize them and always term the fellow untouchable. In his area the only thing people say about him is that he is gentle and does not poke his nose into other people's affairs. Some people say that it is because he is powerful that he does not like joining them in their drinking places.

KAA MONDO

Kaa lives in the Ikov area of Tivland, small lineage MbaYilaban, south of Katsina Ala town. He is in his middle thirties, single, partially blind, and a "dirty beggar."

His father died when he was three, and his grandfather sent him to live with his mother's people (*igba*) until he was eight or nine. Five years after he returned, his grandfather died, and a cousin took charge of him, sending him to school, where he was singularly unsuccessful owing to his advanced age. After leaving school he worked for a time on the farms of others until "disease caught him and he could not see any distance; perhaps it is myopia, but this disease has not finished, and now Kaa is a composer of songs, praising people so that they will help him."

He began to make songs in 1961, "when my reasonable cousin died and I was thrown into a helpless state. So I decided to sit in one place and praise big people." He took a complicated medicine from Imbese and refers ambiguously to "certain charms" that will affect the people you mention in your songs. However, it is equally important, he feels, to "consult the old composers," studying the way their songs are put together "step by step" to include "the real events that affect everyone in one way or the other."

Kaa has never composed for a dance, has not involved himself in politics, and seems to mention names only in connection with one theme, his "helpless state," if the four long lyrics cited are a true indication of his repertoire:

O my Akawe!
The people who give gifts,
Should I be left alone sitting on my heels?
I strive but do not gain anything.
John Aver, God is mighty.
Wan Amase, God is not giving me anything.
People who hate and dislike me should be patient,
For I am a weakling; they shouldn't go after me.

Or from another song:

Mr. John Bur and wife Mbarumun,
Tell the daughter of Hayo
    that I have stayed with you long enough;
        I will go.
Aemberga Usamu has sent for me,
    and I'm thinking what he may give.
I know one thing he will give me is a horse,
But the other thing I do not know the name of at all.

Ahia Ajima, I am in rags completely.
It would be better if all of you would clothe me
So that the monkey will stop cursing me.

In the third lyric he sings of his plight in a jail cell, where he expects to die, and in the fourth he urges various people to feed him, for he will die soon and "you will get your reward in heaven."

Theodosius Akpoo, who is reporting, gives a carefully itemized account of support for Kaa in the here-and-now.

John Injorov has given Kaa many small gifts that accumulate to something great. Sometimes he gives Kaa a pot of beer and sometimes a few shillings for his own use.

Wan Amase at Ikurav Ya doesn't give Kaa money but prepares the best meals she can; sumptuous and delicious.

The gifts from Gbev Igo are pots of beer, shared food, and kind treatment, for they sleep in the same compound.

John Bur of Adikpo has given trousers and shirt and a big duck worth five shillings if sold.

Ahia Ajima once gave him a new mat for sleeping comfortably.

Aemberga gave some toilet articles like paper, soap, towel, and comb.

Zuana gave a live sheep to Kaa and a hoe for working on his farm.

It may well be that the last few donors in particular were trying to send messages with their gifts, for Theodosius is every bit as thorough in documenting the low regard for Kaa in his area, citing the opinions of five different people:

1. "Kaa is a good person in my sight. He cannot work well because he is partly blind. His songs are good and always in praise; he never criticizes people. . . . polite but dirty, since he does not take a bath very often."

2. "Kaa is stupid, a gambler and a drunkard. He is very lazy and thinks he knows everything. His songs have no value . . . dirty . . . no clean clothes . . . once in debt he never pays. No one trained him in his youth. . . . a person whose approach I dread."

3. ". . . not a neat person . . . a great consumer of food and especially beer. Though half blind, he can dance *Girinya* very well, but his songs are only average."

4. ". . . not a good composer, just wasting his time. . . . a perpetual debtor and drunkard. . . . feeble at work. He is a strong-headed man and eats much without contributing anything. I dislike such people."

5. "No one should condemn Kaa Mondo. Poverty has given him bad habits. He is very strange, and truly a glutton for meat; he may steal food but never any other property. It is his disease that worries him."

Perhaps the most striking feature of the composing role in Tiv culture is its flexibility. Almost anyone who makes songs can carve a special ecological niche for them. The knife that carves is praise or abuse. Every Tiv likes to be mentioned in song; no one wants to be mocked; and the raising and lowering of status, including one's own, is every composer's stock in trade.

Yet there must be some excuse, a theme, a raison d'être, a cause for taking up the knife and incising songs upon the public mind, and it is here that Tiv composers exercise their individuality. Kaa Mondo takes every possible advantage of his "suffering," while Akumba Anchan seems to have been a self-made success who became a composer almost by accident. The demand for *Nyinya* song makers exceeded the supply, and Akumba saw a chance to supplement his income. Akumba is a composer of convenience; Kaa pleads for his necessities. Ada Adi was driven to compose by sorcery anxieties and, when sane, transforms his fears into songs that celebrate marriage. Aneke Tire, the gambler, capitalizes upon his bad eye and disfigurement, mocking himself for money, and heaping abuse on others when it is to his advantage. Hura Iyongo had his career interrupted by leprosy but went on to become the leader of a "singing age-grade." Adi Bente, once an orphan and childless in maturity, leads his immediate kinsmen on "expeditions" in search of food, money, and women. Chen Ugye has combined composing with his reputation as a hunter to stage dramatizations of his songs in *Jiagwey*. The very different stories of these seven composers could be supplemented with seventy others equally various.

Often a composer's impetus and subsequent operations appear to stem from a single incident, a twist of fate. Gari Kwaghbo, a young man in his late twenties, sewed up a pair of shorts for a fellow named Tyongi some years ago and was short-changed by one shilling and six pence. Angered, he began to make songs about the incident, describing at great length in *aluibiam* style the troubles he was having collecting this debt and praising those less stingy than Tyongi who have helped him along the way. (See plate 10.) Generalizing from the Tyongi incident, Gari says:

> I don't usually make songs except at a time when I am offended. When I am very indignant, I lie in my house. I have two wives, but I don't allow them to come into the place where I am. Then the song would be aroused in me, rising in my mind; I would be pulling out the song while it is emanating from my mind. I can compose even as many as three songs at that time.
>
> When my heart is vexed, when I have got into something that is

vexing my mind, when my heart is beating faster, I would just go quietly and lie down. I would not fight. It is not my way. I would just go quietly and lie down, and then I would start to make songs.

Kuji Iyum was happily married, trading a little and farming, when he met Dondoaor, an "independent woman" with a beer hall of her own; the rest is history. This femme fatale took all his money, the clothes off his back, even his bicycle, during a few months of hopeless infatuation, then turned him out. Or so Kuji tells it in his songs. He has been composing short, pungent songs in the *Swange* idiom about her mistreatment of him and of her subsequent lovers for almost thirteen years, less one year in which she sued successfully and a court quieted him temporarily. Similarly, Jato Nyamikongo has been rebuking the same runaway wife for over twenty years! And Kundam, a composer living just south of Lafia, has won a wide reputation for songs that chronicle his wife's double treachery in giving rare wild-boar meat that he had provided, to her lover (see plate 11 and photograph at opening of chap. 4).

Ityavger Fate, the mission-supported composer, took up his work in earnest when felled by disease. Now a double amputee, he probably spends more time making songs than any man in Tivland. While other crippled composers-of-necessity could be cited, not all composers take up the task from physical necessity or psychic desperation. Outstanding song makers like Jiagwe, a prominent elder in MbaGen, Maza Nomwhange, now the chief of a large clan area, Anche, a tax chief near Daudu Branch, are rooted in their communities, and their songs do most of their traveling for them. Like Akumba Anchan, perhaps, they took up composing to supplement incomes from more stable careers already in progress.

Even among those composers who are very successful in other fields, it is quite safe to assume a worry of some kind or a series of grievances —no matter how petty—that a composer both alleviates and nurses in song. Maza and Jiagwe, at a time when both were prominent elders, nevertheless indulged themselves in a notorious battle of songs over a woman. No Tiv is too big a man to be bothered by something; everyone has troubles that can be soothed by songs. Kuji Iyum, at the end of a tedious interview on categories of song, turned anthropologist and asked a question designed to deepen my understanding of this Tiv assumption and bring the interview to a close.

I wonder what is troubling you that you persist in asking me so many questions, trying to know all about my life even to the last detail?

I answered at some length in halting Tiv to the effect that the *inja* of Tiv song was eluding me and that the one big question I wanted answered was "Why do Tiv sing?" And he countered with another question:

Yes, I am satisfied with knowing your concern. But again I am asking, since God created the white man and he created the black man too, putting them all together we can call them "man," I am wondering who is happier in this world? Who is never offended, never worried? Who is living in a completely confident state?

I was somewhat befuddled by this question and asked for further explanation.

It is not hard. I am struggling for the answer to put it into my songs; I will one day bring it into my songs, try to make a song from it, that's why I'm asking. I want to know the man who is more confident in the world, the man that people don't abuse, who is never worrying but is always happy and without any troubles. Who is at peace, the one who is accepted by all people, who never has any evil thing happen to him. I won't tell you all my troubles; you will run away and leave me. I won't make a long speech. It is simply that some people worry me, some offend me, some call me a mere composer and ask why I am always complaining in my songs. Then I think this is the confident person, trouble free, so he can look down on me and wonder why I sing. But even the white man who has more money and is above all of us in the world, he does sing just like other people. When you tune the radio, one of the first things you hear will be his songs. He has everything, all the knowledge, but still he sings songs. So we should ask what has befallen him. That's why I am trying to know, who is living in the world with complete confidence?

Ah, Kuji, I wish I knew.

Most composers are deviant in some way, and their paths diverge from other men and from one another. Almost all of those paths cross "the woman question"; Kaa's begging, Gari Kwaghbo's laments for money owed and Ityavger's hymns excepted, the rest of the composers described are either crying after lost women (include here Chen Ugye's "cry of grief" for his dead mother as well Kuji Iyum's criticism of

Dondoaor) or are busy facilitating courtship and marriage (whether it
is Aneke Tire, hired by one suitor to abuse a rival, or a singing group
traveling to explore elopement possibilities). Many paths converge as
composers use the vehicle of song to bring men together around the
problem of women.

This convergence is visible in the very close relationships that sometimes develop between composers and their assistants (see plate 11 and
photograph at opening of chap. 4), and a clue to any composer's status
is found here as well, though again the pattern is highly variable. Kaa
Mondo, of course, and composers like him, beg alone. Gari Kwaghbo
has friends to call upon for a special event, but usually sings alone at
markets and beer halls, where bystanders can pick up his choruses easily at the end of longer narrative solos. And more business-like composers, Akumba Anchan or Anande Amende (Ikpamkor) for that matter, do not depend so much on particular people, but recruit a small
group as needed. Adi Bente and Hura Iyongo are assisted by larger and
relatively stable groups of kinsmen and "age-mates" respectively, though
one man is usually singled out as a "first assistant" among equals. Most
composers, both localized and traveling, have one or two companions
closely associated with them. Kuji Iyum and his two friends were a
striking trio whenever they visited Gboko or Makurdi, for they wore
the same long, striped shirts and neat little goatees; uniformly short in
stature, their very presence predicted a tight unison singing style, and
listeners were never disappointed. A composer's assistant or assistants
provide an important initial small audience for his work, often serve as
memory aides, may even take the lead in performing the songs, and
make every performance a group event. Though they rarely collaborate
in making a new song, they provide indispensable support for the careers of most composers.

Women composers are conspicuously absent from this account. I
never sought out one for an interview, and neither did my apprentice
fieldworkers, all males. The names of women composers do appear on
some of the survey responses at various schools, and of the four hundred
and fifty or so composers on file, about 5 percent are women, all seemingly leaders of dance groups who have composed their own songs
rather than commissioning a man to do it for them. Moreover, the
songs that women sing as they dance to welcome a new bride seem to
form a special and metrically complex genre, and women may compose
some of these for themselves as well.

156   Certainly the songs that are sung by women at weeding parties, as described by Laura Bohannan, could never be composed by men. These "obscene songs" may be traditional or formulaic, new phrases plugged into older patterns at the spur of the moment, but this would be counter to prevailing Tiv practice.

Generally women weed their own farms, but sometimes, because it is much pleasanter to get a month's work done in one day and in company, several women who have adjacent farms brew beer and summon the women of the neighborhood to weed and drink. No man between five and eighty dare venture near such a party. Each woman takes one line of yam mounds. Abreast, dancing as they move, singing obscene songs, they weed their way down to the end of the farm. Meanwhile, in any homestead within earshot, the men prick their ears at the songs and shake their heads disapprovingly if they do catch any of the words, for the songs the women sing in the evening while they drink their hostesses' beer are full of virtuous sentiments and fit for the ears of husbands.

One day I went to one of these weeding parties close to Kako's. Since I had come with Udama, who called me "daughter," I was expected to join in the weeding. My hostess showed me a short row, slightly less than the amount of work expected from an eight-year-old girl. "We know Europeans, like albinos, can't stand much sun," the woman said kindly when I flagged. "Go sit under the tree and start some yams roasting for us."

"Madam!" I looked up from the coals and saw Monday. "Madam!" He was advancing upon us, waving one of my handkerchiefs like a flag of truce and shouting loudly that I had forgotten it. "Go away," I yelled. But Monday was young, curious, and over confident in my will to protect him; he had determined to find out what actually went on at these feminine get-togethers. Udama turned on me: had I broken my promise not to bring or tell any man? I denied my responsibility for Monday's gate-crashing; again I shouted at him to go back. Monday, still etiquette-distance away and not wanting to hear, was deaf. He came on.

With a whoop of pure anticipation, the women surged toward him; they screamed obscenities as they ran. Monday gave one frightened look; he swiveled on his heel and bolted for safety. Only the Furies could have caught him. The women, panting and laughing, returned to the tree. There they proceeded to mime in dance just what they would have done to Monday had they captured him. I appreciated his speed. When I got home to scold him, Monday still looked unsettled, but he seemed only faintly sheepish and not at all repentant. At least, he asked me to teach him some of the songs. Sedately, I refused. [Bowen 1964, pp. 75–76]

Women abuse men by singing collectively and in private in very strong language, whereas a man will rebuke an individual woman in public. At least one composer knows that it is safer to abuse a woman than a man, for the woman "would be counted out of normal society" if she retaliated in kind. Since at least the abolition of exchange marriage in 1927, when "the Europeans spoiled the land," women have had considerable freedom in terms of mobility; virtually all Tiv elders have had at least a few wives run away from them, and many can count over a dozen lost spouses. It may be that the predominance of men in composing roles and their preoccupation with "the woman question" is some measure of the need to soothe bruised male egos.

The failure to collect information from women composers is a serious one. In what ways do the lyrics and melodies of women's songs differ from those of men? Are their motivations significantly different? And what perspectives would answers to these and many other questions provide for reinterpreting male composing roles? All of these unanswered questions become even more pressing when we consider in chapter 5 the ways in which masculine and feminine modes suffuse the Tiv expressive universe.

Technique and Style

T HIS BRIEFEST of chapters should be the longest, but almost all of the work that a detailed ethnographic account of Tiv song construction requires has yet to be done.

Before going to Tivland I transcribed and analyzed eleven Tiv songs from a tape without much difficulty (see Appendix A). After transcription, intervals were counted, melodic formulas derived, modal abstracts constructed, and so forth. The resulting tables, percentages of intervals, and formulation of melodic regularities were compared with similar analyses available for other peoples. With the help of a Tiv student in London, Joseph Werna, and my able instructor in Tiv grammar, Professor Arnott, I was able to make reasonably exact tonemic transcriptions of the lyrics in these songs and then match these patterns with the melodies. Later I discovered an article by Friedrich Hornburg (1948), based upon his prewar thesis, which analyzed a collection of Tiv songs made by Rupert East in the 1930s, and Hornburg's statistics match my own in most respects. Since returning from Tivland, I have done some further transcription work, but as I contemplate the whole enterprise—reducing Tiv songs to black dots on the page in order to quantify, formulate, further abstract them—it seems a heavy investment of time with few returns.

Before considering the merits and demerits of traditional transcription and analysis of Tiv songs in more detail, let me set out what little information I have gathered on Tiv song-making procedures and suggest the kinds of field studies that need to be done if we are to better understand what it means to be an *or u dughun amo,* or "person who pulls out songs."

One of the few things that all composers are agreed upon is the need for isolation when composing, getting away from it all, especially women. It is tempting to exaggerate the importance of this quest for isolation, especially when it seems to be the sine qua non of composing, and because it seems such a natural motive to Westerners. Some concluding remarks from Werner Munsterberger's obsessively psychoanalytic analysis of primitive artists are suggestive, too suggestive.

> At this point we ought to inquire further into the function of the isolation of the artist. . . . The artist relinquishes communication with an inhibiting or disturbing environment. Women are phobically avoided. . . . The oedipal aggression is not as strongly repressed in these societies as it is in Western civilization. The regressive tendency for isolation is a security measure. Affect is being avoided. Objective reality is denied while strength is gained from a narcissistic retreat to a level of omnipotent fantasy. The Australian artists who work in a specially built hut which they call the womb; the African artists who go to an isolated spot from which women are kept away; . . .
> If these are the conditions under which artistic activity among primitive peoples is possible, then two seemingly contradictory tendencies are at work: the necessary isolation indicates that distance from the oedipal mother is sought. . . . On the other hand, reunion with the *giving* mother of the preoedipal phase is wanted. . . . The determining factor is that the men who retreat into the "womb" make use of their pregenital defenses and "steal" the phallic mother's paraphernalia. Under the threat of being overpowered by their oedipal desires, the artists temporarily abandon reality . . . a regressive step toward an early phase in which the attachment to the nursing mother was the source for hallucinatory fantasies and creative imagination. Stealing her paraphernalia would then mean stealing the penis which was originally in her. The creative act would be a form of aggression against the phallic mother. [Otten 1971, pp. 127–28]

There was a time when I hoped that stealing the paraphernalia of the psychoanalysts would help solve many of my problems in understanding Tiv song. I particularly anticipated reading an article entitled "The Voice as a Female Phallus" (Bunker 1934), but alas, when I finally obtained the article, it turned out to be the case history of a boot fetishist who also worshipped strong female opera singers and Sarah Bernhardt, not, on the surface at least, the sort of theoretical statement that would assist in deciphering Tiv tales and the position of songs within them. Still, hope springs eternal, and I'm convinced that a Tiv version or analogue of the oedipal complex exists and that working out the pattern of that complex will account for some of the power inherent in Tiv song. Portions of Munsterberger's remarks ring

very true in my ear; the passage immediately brings to mind (1) all
the composers with "woman problems" mentioned in the preceding
chapter; (2) many puzzling bits of information from the tales—the
hare's phallic flute as inverted by "feathering," the dynamic drumming-
singing female phallic clitoris, the women who sing as a giant penis
reaches for their throats, the male characters who sing powerfully on
"empty stomachs"; and (3) there is, I will argue in chapter 5, a fundamental "source for hallucinatory fantasies and creative imagination"
that nursing babies and isolated composers share as they stare up into
the Tiv roof. But the gap between psychoanalytic theory and Tiv creation of songs is not one that I can fill well without further interviews
with composers in context that expand upon the fragmentary accounts
which follow.

Agojo Utege's account of his procedure is as representative as any:

> If I have been worried for long by a particular problem, or there
> is something to celebrate, or I have a man in mind to praise, I go
> away from the people in my compound. I can go to a hut where
> there is nobody, or at night when all the other people in the com-
> pound are asleep. This is the time when the brain works best. If I
> cannot finish in one night, I leave it without telling anyone, even
> my partner Agu; then I go again and hide in a quiet place to finish it.

Or T. Akpoo reporting on Kaa Mondo's habits:

> He sits alone very quietly in his house, and in his heart (which
> should be brain) the words of the song come. He then sleeps on his
> bed, face upwards, and thinks of the names of the people he is go-
> ing to include in his song. He practices the words, and the melody
> then comes. When the plan he had when sleeping face upwards is
> satisfied, he knows that he has ended one song.

There are a number of interesting ambiguities in this statement:
How are we to take the reporter's equation or substitution of "brain"
for "heart"? Is the "theme" of the song established as he sits awake,
while the "names" of those to be praised are added when lying down?
Is he really "sleeping"? How does practicing the words bring on the
melody? What is "the plan he had when sleeping"? Reading between
the lines we can posit a three-phase process: (1) conscious selection of
theme or person; (2) unconscious or semiconscious planning or blending of words; (3) conscious manipulation of words and melody to
achieve a song. Certainly the consubstantiation of "brain" and "heart"
is suggestive, and "sleeping face upward" is a good phrase for the dia-

162 lectic between conscious and unconscious. All composers favor this position, lying quietly on the back, if they don't insist upon it. Almost as many indicate that the night time is the right time for making songs. That is also, of course, the time for sex, the time when the *mbatsav* are active; and implicitly, at least, song making could be a substitute for or in conflict with both sex and *tsav*.

Four other composers claim that songs are sometimes, at least partially, a result of dreaming. Kundam Agure stated that "it sometimes comes while one is asleep, and on waking I continue the song with the phrases I have snatched from my dream." When asked to sing a few songs that came that way, he said he couldn't remember which ones were which or even how many were dream mediated.

Iorlaha Buga, when asked about such matters, quickly cited two of his songs, and two only, that came to him in dreams.

Chen Ugye's involvement with dreams is more pervasive:

> Whenever I want to compose a song, I smoke a lot of tobacco and swallow the smoke, breathing deeply and letting the smoke come out through my nose. After spitting heavily, my brain is quite clear and is already filling up with the thing I want to sing. Then I lie down quietly and sleep a deep sleep. I sing the song I want to compose in my dream. Then I wake up and lie quietly in bed, never saying a word, thinking of parts and connecting them bit by bit, one after the other, until I get the length I want. Then I sing it over and over that night so that I won't forget it the following day. I teach it to my assistant soon after.

Chen adds that starting the song is the hardest part, and that the *ikyenge* comes before the words because it emphasizes what he has to say. Apparently it is in the midst of the dream sequence that the basic connection between words and melody is made, though the parts can be edited, spliced, as part of a waking or conscious process.

Hura Iyongo is also assisted by dreams, though less frequently:

> Sometimes a song comes to you from a dream. Maybe when you were sleeping you dreamed that you were singing a song. Then when you wake up, you remember your dream and start singing the song you dreamt about. You sing it to the end without hesitation. Everything is easy after you have taken the medicine.

The complex role of dreams (*mnyam* means "dream" or "sleep," but *mnyam ma cien*, "*mnyam* that is frightening," designates "dream" specifically) in Tiv culture makes these instances especially problematic.

Tiv entertain a variety of theories about dreams, for example, that they take shape in response to one's sleeping position, that it might have been "something you ate," that they are brought to one by the power of someone else's *tsav,* that they are sometimes prophetic but usually in a perverse or reverse way (something like the opposite of what you dream may come true), that your *jijingi* (your shadow, reflection of self, that leaves when you die) has something like a mind of its own or is receiving messages from who knows where and then transmitting them to your heart (*shima*). Much further fieldwork in Tiv ethno-psychology is needed to sort out their dream theories as they relate to songs, but generally speaking, dreams have a negative aura about them in Tiv belief, and it was initially somewhat surprising to find them included as a source of songs.

Now let us turn to the medicine that makes everything easy for Hura Iyongo. Opinion is divided on the efficacy of medicines. Even Hura concedes that "if you are not a thoughtful, reasonable person, you may take medicine but you won't compose songs. Every song that you compose will sound childish and false." Every composer knows of other composers who took medicines but found them useless, still others who bypassed the treatment altogether and became successful; but most nevertheless insist that *"saa u ma imo, u fatyo dughun amo ga,"* literally, "unless you drink song [voice], you are able to pull out songs [voices] not." Though clearly neither a sufficient nor a necessary condition for composing, the various ingredients give important clues to the composing process.

Hura Iyongo took a mixture of ground up roots or bark from *zelagba* and *horkula, bar dam* (salt from the peoples to the south whom Tiv call Udam), and *msuram* ("peppermint" or "alligator pepper" seeds used by all diviners in their work and allegedly by the *mbatsav* to revive a dead man prior to his ritual slaughter and consumption).

If you take the medicine and sleep, the saliva that collects in the chest and hinders you from composing will collect in your throat and mouth, so that when day comes you gargle and throw it out of your mouth. Thus your chest becomes clear [*hinger wang*] and you start a song. You never again forget what you have composed.

The *zelagba* and *horkula* roots help in cleaning up the brain and making it sharp for remembering what you have composed. The *msuram* is to bring out the flem that is in the head, making it clear for composing and recording songs. I don't believe there are separate medicines for singing and composing; one serves for both. With the medicine you can sing clearly, mention people's names distinctly; without the medicine you may fall into error, the song will sound very watery [*mgerem mgerem*].

It is almost as if the medicine gives tape-recorder qualities to the composer, enabling him to clear or erase the tape of his mind and put a new song on to stay. Virtually all medicines stress memory facilitating ingredients, and in almost every medicine I've heard about, ingredients for clearing the head or chest, or softening the throat and chest, are prominent. The pipe that Chen Ugye smokes in place of medicine serves the same function—"I . . . swallow the smoke," "out through my nose," "after spitting heavily, my brain is quite clear and is already filling up with the thing I want to sing." The verb *ma*, literally "to drink," is used for both our "to smoke (pipe)" and "to take (medicine)," and in both cases "swallowing" or "intake" precedes "output," first of saliva or flem and then of songs. "Clearing" and "memorizing" seem to have something to do with getting rid of fluids, and singing, according to Hura Iyongo, should not be "watery" either. Fluid imagery or a wet/dry contrast appears in one way or another in most accounts.

Kaa Mondo, listing the medicines he would like to take if only he could afford them, speaks of taking *kuca* ("drinking the water from the mouth of a dead man brings good luck") and *ifough* ("parts of a creeping plant mixed with water to soften the mouth and chest for good singing"). One of the ingredients in the medicine Agojo took was the tail of a particular lizard (*tsa ishondo*) which "keeps my mouth wet with saliva." Iorlaha frequently uses a mixture of *jiagba* and *ikehegh* or *yiye* "for strength and a wet throat." Kundam claims that the ground-up taproot of *nom hur* keeps the throat wet and increases endurance; he sometimes gives it to his assistants before they go out to a major singing event. Occasionally rules are made by the medicine giver, and in Kundam's case he was told never to cross a stream while singing. Another composer in Turan District told me that he was enjoined from urinating in streams and that he had never done so since taking the medicine, for fear of pissing his talent away.

More inquiries might reveal that the wet/dry contrast is one between singing and composing. The meager evidence presented indicates that fluids need to be cleared away in order for a song to flow, while a wet throat, whether from beer or medicines, facilitates singing. The phrase *A mil imo*, "he invited people for a singing event," if taken literally, that is, "he brewed song," turns song into fluid beer, *msorom*, or the "fluid that repairs," from the root *sor*, "to repair."

Some composers say that one medicine serves for both composing and singing; others distinguish concoctions appropriate to each activity. Adi Bente argues for the latter position:

> There are different types of medicine for singing. After you have prepared the usual medicine [in Adi's case, "peppermint" seeds, raw beniseed, something called *yiye,* Udam salt, roots of *seragba*—all of which "help me to compose and remember the composition"], you add to it, well pounded, the tongue of *icaregh* or weaverbird. This helps you to sing fast and compose fast and not forget. The tongue of the bird *akiki* [probably *clamantor levaillanti,* a large species of cuckoo, identified with the *mbatsav* by Tiv] is feared by all Tiv people, and it has a very big voice for a bird. It helps for loud singing so that you can be heard from afar. The tongue of lion too can be added; this lowers your voice, makes it loud and heard great distances. The weaverbird tongue can also help you to sing for a long time without having a dry throat.

The principle of contagious bird magic is favored by many composers. Kaa Mondo would like to eat the breast of *icaregh,* for then "you can sing sweetly and nicely without getting tired." Agojo Uzege has taken the head of *akiki,* "a fierce and mysterious bird associated with evil," but since the other birds associated with the *mbatsav*—various owls and the nightjar—are not, to my knowledge, used in the song medicines, it would seem to be *akiki*'s voice qualities more than his sinister characteristics that composer-singers are trying to emulate. Kuji Iyum cites the *hom* tree as an ingredient that may be doubly contagious or sympathetically contagious: "when it has made fruits, many birds used to come and eat it; so if you take it, many people will gather for your songs." But Kuji does not make explicit the notion that what is good for birds is good for composers as well.

Anande Amende's observation that composers are like chickens, scurrying around from place to place in search of rewards, has its echoes in medicinal practice. Iorlaha Buga, who received his medicine from Maza Nomwange, was asked by Maza to bring along a young rooster so that Iorlaha and the bird could take the medicine together. "The rooster was left to mature, and my *imo* ripened with his. If it is killed, I have to give medicine to another to take its place." Despite the facts that composers sometimes give medicine to an assistant to enable him to compose on his own, or that an aspirant like Iorlaha seeks out the composer whose songs he likes best, Maza, in order to receive the medicine, all informants insist that there is no necessary stylistic connection between giver and receiver of medicine. Maza's device of the parallel rooster might well be a way of giving Iorlaha time to develop a style of his own.

A number of composers, even a few who are skeptical about medicines, say that eating the hearts of chickens can help. And when rules go with the medicine, one of them usually has to do with eating the heart of any chicken you should happen to see being slaughtered or not eating any chicken whose heart you haven't eaten first. Given the heart as the seat of Tiv knowledge, understanding, emotion, and chicken as the commonest animal sacrifice, it is fitting that composers should frequently be laying claim to this delicacy.

Once the elements of "clearing," "memorization," and "bird mimesis" in any given medicine are accounted for, there may be residual ingredients—a stimulant to keep one awake during those good composing hours, something for endurance, an ingredient that makes all the others palatable or acts as a catalytic agent on the others, something that influences qualities and therefore, perhaps, style as well.

Most medicines are said neither to effect the songs themselves nor to enhance the personality of the composer. "Charms" (*imborivungu*) and special devices for attracting attention and defeating others, like those cited by Adi Bente (chap. 3), are a different order of business, if a composer will admit to using them at all. They can assist a performance, intimidate rivals in the market or beer hall, influence the response to singing, perhaps influence the singing itself; but they have no role in composing that I have been able to discover. Occasionally, however, a composer claims that an ingredient does not merely facilitate composing but actually shapes songs. Kundam insists that sheanut oil was the strongest part of the medicine he took and that "it gives an *ikenge* that could attract people." Ada Adi says that the medicine as a whole—in his case, parts of various trees—"helps you to put the words in proper locations, which will suit an audience."

Aside from these two minor instances of "active ingredients," Kuji Iyum provides the major exception, describing the medicine he took and has given to four or five others. As it turned out, he wanted to sell it to me. The salt from Udam that does nothing special for most composers can reshape your mind and make a song start to flow again when you are having trouble. Ikehegh, the "alligator pepper," can "repair a song when it spoils"; "you have already taken the medicine, so when you need help you just touch it on the hands and over the body, then it will come out alright." Parts of the *alom* plant "bring all the ingredients together to stay in your mind at all times" and can "teach you wisdom and tell you how to compose songs." Something called *giegwe* will "force down songs"; oil makes the medicine easy to take. And that special ingredient, *hom,* brings people flocking to you as birds to the tree. Kuji assured me that I could compose in Tiv or English, as I wished, if I took the medicine. At another point in the interview, however, he conceded that "some take a medicine and don't sing; others don't take it and do; so it must be God's gift."

Aside from Kuji's somewhat exaggerated version of medicinal efficacy, we can generalize to the effect that, to the Tiv mind, a medicine may enhance a composer's talents and put him in sympathy with other song makers, both human and natural. It certainly opens the gates for a song to emerge and, most important, makes it easier to memorize what comes out; but it cannot substitute for the "act of creation."

Unfortunately, words are never a very good substitute, in any culture, for that mysterious "act." Not surprisingly, however, composers who are scornful of medicines tend to be somewhat more articulate about how a song is actually made. Aneke Tire, the gambler and master of abusive zoological similes, "has nothing to pay to medicine men" (though he eats the heart of a hen now and again) and is quite explicit about what it takes to make a song:

(a) you have to be good at memorizing; (b) you have to be quiet, alone, no one should be near or disturb you; (c) be alert to good and wise sayings from other people; (d) observe how people move about and what they are doing at the particular period; (e) use your own experience and thoughts; (f) know the life of the person you are praising, begging, abusing, or lamenting for and keep before you a vivid picture of the person or thing you are going to describe in your song; (g) keep all the important points in mind and then add even smaller ones; (h) lying down backwards, you go over the points you have gathered and begin to put them in fitting phrases; (i) use open sounds first, o-o-o or u-u-u, then sounds such as m-m-m-m, and finally some exclamations—*kpash!* or *wii wii!* or *kei!!*—at starting points and in the middle of the song, to give shocking news to the listeners; (j) putting all the ideas together, you have to converse in your heart, making mere words come out in a singing form; (k) when you have covered all the points, you know the song is finished.

The hardest part of making songs is the collection of actual facts and making them good in a singing form. Also, memorization of the song after you have finished is difficult. If you are clever enough, you invite somebody to sing with you, so that if you forget some

168

points or phrases, he will teach you as you have taught him before. Making songs is not easy work because it is brain work and needs concentration. The melody comes first, followed by words. The melody sounds as the words are pronounced, so the fit is easy for singing. Though I don't take medicines, constant singing helps me in doing the melody. When you sing long and often, the throat becomes dry, very dry, and your voice appears small; after a few days it becomes very loud and helps you to get your melody. Once you have your melody fixed in your head, you can compose any song, and the melody and words will fit together very nicely.[1]

Aneke's itemized account corresponds quite accurately, I think, with the views of other Tiv composers, but let us review very briefly the simpler versions of procedure they offer.

For Agojo Uzege, the names of those praised are the hardest part, getting a pronunciation that will please the owner. It is easier when the words are familiar, when you and your own family are involved. Melody comes before words: "I can't explain how the words fix into the melodies, . . . they just fit in by nature."

Adi Bente thinks about the person first, looks for the appropriate praises, isolates himself to put words together, then starts to sing quietly, rearranging the phrases. Usually the words come first, but it can be the other way around. Varying the names of people, putting the same name on high and low pitches in different places, is a necessary skill; you should never use names in a perfunctory way. Remembering is the main problem, and the medicine solves it.

Hura Iyongo feels that finding a way to mention names clearly is a top priority and that usually the words come first. Then the problem, after dreaming of course, is to put the pieces together with enough "hills and valleys" in the *ikenge*.

Kaa Mondo can't explain how the words and melody are mixed together; it seems to happen simultaneously.

Aku Gyenku bears in mind the standing of the man being praised and, once settled in bed, concentrates on attention-getting devices that will intrigue the person. Then he proceeds bit by bit, omitting and adding things. The start is difficult, the end easy. Melody and words go hand in hand.

1. An extended and nearly perfect set of parallels could be drawn between the composing process as Aneke describes it and the apparent procedures of James Brown, one of Afro-America's leading song-makers. And an equally fine analogy exists between Brown and Tivland's leading solo dancer, nicknamed *Norkeghkegh*, literally "waiting erection."

For Kundam, the words are all-important; they can carry a poor melodic line, but not vice versa. So the words come first, then you apply the *ikenge,* and then you edit or change certain phrases that do not match or meet with the *ikenge.* He can compose while going along the road or lying on the ground, if necessary, as long as he is far away from noise.

Jato Ukura cites the importance of interesting proverbs as the highlight of any song and adds that he, like most composers, puts his words into a definite melodic pattern from which he does not wander very much. He gives Ityavger's hymns as a classic example, and even to an outsider, they are instantly recognizable and remarkably uniform in style.

Other composer's procedures are not so uniform, however, and certainly opinion varies on the "words and melody" issue. Some say words first, others melody first, and some say they come together simultaneously or "by nature." Even Aneke the itemizer seems to skirt the issue when he comes to "(j) putting all the ideas together, you have to converse in your heart, making mere words come out in a singing form." This process of "conversing in the heart" seems to correspond to the dream phase or dip into the unconscious attested to by the four composers above. Since Aneke (like most of the composers here) was never asked explicitly about the possible role of dreams in creating songs, we don't know just how close the correspondence might be. Probably he is much more rational or conscious in his efforts than most composers.

Unfortunately, the field data that might deepen and clarify our understanding of the way words and *ikenge* fit together have yet to be collected. It appears that any established composer has an *ikenge* of his own, a standard melodic model into which he plugs the messages of the moment. Composers who say the words come first may simply be taking this model for granted, for in any particular song-making effort the words do come first. Given the desire for a new song, the tonemic contours of any spoken Tiv utterance, and perhaps the patterns of syllables, consonants, and vowels as well, the most rigorously standardized *ikenge* would have to be bent somewhat by the "plugging in" operation. Even assuming a series of drastic lyric readjustments in favor of melodic model integrity, a composer would seemingly have to go through lexemic contortions to retain the identical melodic line of song A for song B without confusing the meaning of words, creating unintentional tone puns, adding nonsense syllables, and so on. But how much integrity or standardization does any composer's *ikenge* have in the first place?

I never had the presence of mind to ask a single composer the simple question that might have made these speculations unnecessary, that is, "Can you whistle your *ikenge?*" Be assured, it is the first question I will ask the next Tiv composer I meet, and the next, and the next. Perhaps the "melody first" composers have melodic models in their "hearts" to be pulled out on request, while the "words first" men can only whistle their latest song. Those who say the words and melody come simultaneously may have more flexible models. If there *are* Tiv composers who have a melodic abstract of their works ever at the ready, what a find for ethnomusicology! Could one, by a careful transcription and analysis of a composer's diverse works, arrive at the same common denominator, and if so, by what rules? With the composer's own abstract in hand, one might decipher how the tonemic pattern of a particular lyric had forced specific changes in the melody. Is it possible that those composers who have melodic models also have the more idiosyncratic, instantly recognizable styles? Given a set of abstracts from a variety of composers in one genre, for example, *swange* or *ibiamegh,* could one arrive at an abstract for the genre as a whole— say, *the swange melody?*

The one experiment along these lines that I did conduct, a few weeks before leaving Tivland, only makes the question "Can you whistle your *ikenge?*" all the more crucial. I asked a Tiv friend, Loho Ashibi, to put together a few topical sentences that he would like to hear sung. In the course of a trip through Tivland, we gave the lyric to four different composers, asking each to turn it into a song. Four quite different songs resulted, even though three of the four composers were working in the *ibiamegh* genre.

As in the eleven Tiv melodies that I have checked against the tonemic patterns of their lyrics, conspicuous violations occur very rarely, that is, less than 5 percent of the melodic intervals move in directions that oppose the tone shifts of normal speech. On the other hand, melodic conformity to tonemic pattern is anything but strict; a downstep drop of a semitone in speech can easily become a drop of a fifth or sixth (seven, eight, or nine semitones) in song. Similar liberties taken with speech patterns can be found in any phrase from any Tiv song. Excellent analytic work has been done on the relationships between lyrics in tone languages and their melodic shapes (Blacking 1967, and references cited therein). I have no doubt that rules for "the setting of words to music" analogous to the eight principles developed by Blacking for Venda children's songs (pp. 167 ff.) could be derived for Tiv; in fact, I suspect that a few of the Venda principles may fit the Tiv phenomena perfectly and can eventually be refined slightly in the Tiv context.

But proving principles of this kind, for example, "speech-tone patterns influence only certain parts of the melodies, chiefly the beginnings of phrases," or "descents in speech tone and melody need not coincide, but a rise in speech tone is generally accompanied by a rise in melody" (Blacking 1967, p. 169), is extremely arduous and frustrating work, given the nature of Tiv song lyrics. The exact meaning or single best translation of Tiv song texts is invariably difficult to ascertain, since they are usually based on specific incidents, mixed with proverbs, colloquial expressions, and snatches of conversation; and the possibility of hidden metaphors, double entendres, tone puns, and so forth, can never be ruled out. Lacking semantic reference points that are precise, it is very often difficult to know which grammatical usage is the correct one and, consequently, which tonal realization of a particular syllable or set of syllables was intended. Indeed, only the composer may know (and have forgotten) the precise tense of the verbs (many of the twelve tenses are distinguished by tone alone; see Arnott 1964, p. 48), the actual sequence of events aluded to in the song, or who the protagonists in a snatch of dialogue may have been, and any one of these factors can reshape the tonal contours of a phrase as spoken. Ambiguity is probably an important factor in some of the most popular songs, for if only the general intent of the lyric is known, for example, to ridicule someone, then the song may be adapted to a variety of circumstances. The outsider, removed from the scene of the song, or a Tiv not present at its premier, can easily become lost in the maze of possible meanings that lurks behind each "simple" phrase.

Furthermore, in the context of a song, vowels may be reshaped, extended, or elided; subject pronouns, particles, and verbal copulae may disappear or be absent in one phrase but present in another, extended in repetitions of phrases. Even when a text is supplied, as in the experiment with four composers above, control over phonemic tone variables is lost, for each composer drops particles, shifts verb forms, and adds vowels in order to fashion a song to his liking. Still, by at least beginning with a tonemicly accurate text, some of the imponderables that a preexistent song presents are removed, and the delicate interplay between purely melodic considerations and the predispositions inherent in tonemic speech is more susceptible to rigorous observation. Even

172   moderate success in the search for basic *akenge,* or abstract melodic models, coupled with further exploration of composer response to pre-set lyrics, ought to reduce the labor otherwise involved in developing "words and music" rules for Tiv and, one hopes, make those rules more precise and informative than those posited for other cultures by Black-ing, A. M. Jones (1959), and others.

Suffice it to say here that phonemic tone establishes an important and complex parameter for the construction of Tiv songs.

The other major parameter for Tiv song construction is motion as reflected in song meters. And at this point in my work, it is the single biggest obstacle to worthwhile transcription. Almost every Tiv song has its foundation in a particular sense of motion. For example, roughly 90 percent of the songs in folktales correspond with a motion of some kind—dancing, beating a drum, lovemaking, hoeing, weaving, pound-ing, grinding, scooping water, traveling along the path. Only the occa-sional announcement or warning in song or a cry of grief lacks a mo-tional support.

Even lullabies are sung to the beat provided by patting the child alternately on the flank and ear. When asked to sing lullabies for the tape recorder, men or women, if they lacked a babe in arms, would apply a patting motion to their knees as they sang.

The Tiv sawyers I interviewed in Ibadan, who work in the mahog-any forests not far away, all agreed that it was impractical, if not im-possible, to saw a stroke without singing. As with so many things Tiv, the reasons for continual singing while sawing are both physical and metaphysical: (1) the work goes much more easily with the saw if the men at either end of it are singing to each other and therefore breathing with each other, pulling in perfect synchronization; and (2) the sprites who use the great trees as homes or resting places can perpetrate acci-dents or other tricks upon those who don't sing.

Similar dual explanations are often offered for the origins of specific dances: on the one hand the motions that go with tin mining, laying railroad track, and so forth, or the movements of an animal, such as the ground-squirrel as it steals peanuts, will be cited as a source, the basis of mimesis. But the same informant, speaking of the same dance, will also speak of the person in a distant lineage who originated the dance after being captured by the *mbatsav,* or after having visited the *mbakuv* (the village of the dead) where the preoccupation of these mysterious beings with certain ritual and dance activities both enabled the person to escape and inspired the observor to create new choreography.

All the composers work with a dance meter or meters in mind. Some claim that their songs can be made to fit a number of dance styles or that various songs of theirs fit one dance idiom while others were designed expressly for another dance. Kuji Iyum, for example, known primarily as a composer of fine *swange* songs, claims that though his songs are often adapted to that dance, they can be used for others as well and that basically his style, like all others in Tivland, in his opinion, springs from the older *ibiamegh* genre. Anche, oldest of the four composers who participated in the preset lyric experiment referred to above and the only one to compose most of his version on the spot, unisolated, as we sat together at the side of the road, said that his *ikyenge* was essentially in the *ibiamegh* mold, but that, as the originator of *Gbangi* style (the forerunner of contemporary *swange*), many of his songs could be used in either dance context. Anande Amende takes a view diametrically opposed to Kuji Iyum's, positing a general *ger icam* idiom (not linked to any specific dance) as the foundation for most contemporary styles, including *swange*. He refuses to label his own *ikenge* with one dance name or another. Though the dance he composes for most often is one that he invented, called "Sawya," he disclaims any direct mimicry of sawyer songs and their meter. He did, however, bring a small hourglass drum to accompany his first taping of songs, and it is just this sort of link to an explicit meter that is missing in most of my tapes of composers who sang their songs unaccompanied by instruments.

Given the welter of conflicting opinions among Tiv composers on the many possible relationships between song and dance, given the equally confusing array of opinion and approaches among ethnomusicologists who have tried to systematize various African metric and rhythmic patterns, I have much experimental and comparative work to do before even attempting to devise a transcription system that at least partially reflects Tiv realities.

The great unasked question that parallels "Can you whistle your *ikenge*?" is, of course, "Could you *tsorogh* (blend) your song with dance?" or "Could you ask one of your assistants to supply a hand-clap or bell pattern or drum beat, or have various assistants supply all three, while you sing it a second time?" But even a response to this second question may not quite hit the mark, for the best metric foundation may well reside in footwork or "buttocks-bounce" that is not echoed explicitly in one or another percussion part.[2] I can remember watching women dancing before the house of a new bride and singing a song I had transcribed before going to Tivland. The simple back and forth shuffle of their feet was in a perfectly regular meter underpinning the song, but in something other than the simple 4/4 time of my transcription, something "very other." I ran for my tape recorder but was too late. Even if I had arrived in time, what would I have recorded? Where did one of those small shuffle steps begin or end? Would even a perfectly sound-synchronized film have unlocked the secret of the song's metrical organization? I wonder now, and I think the answer is "Yes." At the time I didn't wonder enough. I was troubled by that particular incident and a few others, but I was still, in a word, overconfident. Didn't I have over fifteen basic drum patterns for as many dances under my hands and on tape, reconstructible, transcribable at any time? Hadn't I reduced the eleven songs to transcription already? Didn't the complete confidence and tight unison of composers singing their own songs indicate that equally precise transcriptions would be possible upon return?

The negative answers testify not only to my general lack of consistent day-to-day fieldwork with particular composers, to the specific lack of experimental initiatives, and to a missing rudimentary awareness of the ways in which singing, drumming, and dancing must be linked together for analytic purposes, but also to the divisability of song labors in Tivland today. *Ibiamegh* is rarely, if ever, performed as a fully danced ceremony anymore, though the song style continues. One composer in the idiom, Gari Kwaghbo, volunteered the information that he checks all of his compositions by dancing them as he goes along (a point I failed to follow up with other composers for lack of time). Most *swange* composers work independently from the bands that play their songs for dances, and receive their rewards from persons praised at beer halls, markets, and compounds. Similarly, a composer whose idiom is any other dance can and does sing his songs without accompaniment, as the spirit or the occasion moves him. Still, the Tiv ability to separate

2. And the most effective singing may very well thread its way between the footsteps at that. Even after a transcriber has decided to group pulses and place bar lines by some criterion or other, the problem of how to notate rhythms most accurately remains. A culturally appropriate criterion for meter should give some guidance, but we can probably never lock up all the secrets of a living, evolving performance tradition behind the bars of transcription. (For a fuller discussion of these issues, see Keil 1966a.)

song from drumming and dance does not give the beginning student a similar freedom. Especially when we consider the absence of any consistent correlations between emotional states and melodic patterns (see chapter 1), the importance of correlating melodies with motions seems all the greater. It may well be that any semiotic or semantic study of the Tiv melodic universe will find its designata in the dance.

Documenting this sort of hypothesis will be subtle and difficult work. Do other composers "check" their songs by dancing them? How are mistakes discovered this way, and how are they corrected? Does every song suggest appropriate movements to Tiv? And how does one inquire about or measure kinetic suggestibility? Are some songs and song styles inherently polymetric, others monometric, or does a given song take on more exact metric qualities according to the different drumming-dancing contexts in which it finds itself? Clearly the most preliminary questions concerning motion-and-music issues as centered in the Tiv concept of *tsorogh* have to be answered before any kind of transcription can make good ethnographic sense. As with the words-and-music issues surrounding the concept of *ikenge,* plausible *tsorogh* principles could probably be worked out by painstaking work with my existing tapes, but it seems more sensible to postpone intensive structural study of Tiv songs until after further fieldwork has clarified the ways in which these two fields of force work in particular styles.

The following list of Tiv song characteristics is based primarily upon prefieldwork transcriptions (see Appendix A) and is as reasonably accurate as it is superficial and "xenographic." That is, if one takes a set of fairly typical Tiv songs by a variety of composers and makes a rough translation of their melodies into Western notation, the following regularities and prominent features are observable.

1. Tiv songs have a wide tonal range, about sixteen semitones on the average; composed songs invariably have a range of an octave or greater, though rarely more than seventeen or eighteen semitones, while songs within folktales, old war songs, lullabies, may have a range of less than an octave.

2. Songs can begin anywhere in the upper two-thirds of their tonal range, and they usually end in the lower half of it. Occasionally, songs begin on the highest note of the range, though they rarely, if ever, end on the lowest note; though a slightly downward overall melodic slope characterizes most songs, some begin and end on the same note in the middle of the range, and in a few songs the ending note is a few steps higher than the beginning one. The "downstep" or "terrace-tone" na-

ture of the language does not dictate very strictly the overall song contours or melodic levels, but most songs and most melodic phrases within songs end somewhat lower than they begin.

3. In terms of interval frequencies, Tiv songs have a higher proportion of wide intervals, 40 percent (perfect fourths, 28 percent; fifths, 8 percent; sixths and wider, 4.5 percent), especially in descent (60 percent of all descending intervals a fourth or wider—29 percent fourths, 18 percent fifths, 12.5 percent sixths or wider) than any culture whose songs have been analyzed to date. Tiv songs always have a few more ascending intervals than descending ones (also apparently unique vis-à-vis other cultures) and melodic phrases have a jagged or angular aspect that can often be described in terms of "pendular fourths" and "interlocked fifths" (see Appendix A and fig. 2).

4. Repetitive monotones are an equally striking feature of Tiv song; most songs have them, triple or quadruple, but sometimes the same note may be repeated five or six times. Usually these monotones occur at the beginning or end of phrases. As they are interspersed with the angular wide-interval patterns, the net effect is one of mountain ranges and plateaus, or what Tiv composers sometimes call the "hills and valleys" of an *ikenge*.

Figure 2 presents in its entirety a short song (the same call-response pattern repeated many times in performance) that illustrates the interplay of monotones, fourths, and fifths very nicely, and Appendix A offers other examples.

5. Formally, the songs transcribed prior to fieldwork were of simple AB structure, with a few more complicated exceptions. Most Tiv songs follow an AB, call/response pattern, but the songs of some composers are quite intricate. In performance, parts of old songs may be melded into a potpourri that is very complex indeed. In general, however, Tiv prefer short, pungent songs that can be learned after a few hearings.

6. In the transcribed songs and in the longer more complex compositions recorded in the field, the general duration of responses outweighs the length of calls by a ratio of at least two to one in most styles, *ibiamegh* being the notable exception.[3] Compared to other African idioms, there is relatively little overlapping of calls and responses. There seems to be an important alternating phrase-ending pattern to decipher

3. The fact that the closest equivalent of a solo or bardic style in Tivland is historically linked to the ceremonies which once differentiated "big men" from their inferiors, might be taken as confirmation of Alan Lomax's cantometric correlation between bardic style and hierarchical social structure.

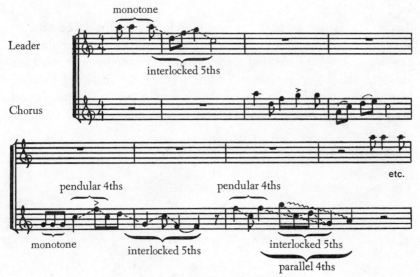

Fig. 2. Typical song pattern

eventually: many calls end on a falling interval, while the last phrase of a response (hence of a song) often ends on a rising interval, giving a sense of openendedness, to Western ears at least. Conversely, the few calls that end on rising intervals seem to invite responses that end on a fall. This phenomena may be linked to a feeling of two tonics or double duration tones that many songs seem to generate.

7. There is little evidence to suggest that improvisation is of much importance in Tiv songs, even in the calls of Tiv soloists or song leaders. Renditions of most songs contain enough pattern repetitions to make most variations of motif or any improvisation stand out clearly. Many versions of a composer's original song may exist, perhaps as many as there are Tiv who sing or blow it, but differences in melodic line are due primarily, I think, to imperfect mimesis, faulty oral transmission, rather than to deliberate individual attempts to reshape a work.

One hopes that deeper understanding of the principles underlying these characteristics will come from field work that explores the *ikenge* and *tsorogh* issues discussed above. Whatever our future understanding of song-generating rules may be, however, these basic features of Tiv song—wide range, wide intervals, angular phrases, repetitive monotones, open-ended responses, "twin tonics," minimum improvisation, and so on—give us variables that may be of value when we attempt to generalize about the Tiv expressive universe in chapter 5.

Viewed from the outside, the song parameters of "words" and "mo-

178   tion" seem, at this point, to be complex limits, confusing constraints on Tiv composers and my understanding of their creative techniques. Perhaps after I have closeted myself with various composers and have joined in the dance, a time will come when I can share the satisfactions of men who have mastered the craft of intensifying speech and disguising dance in their songs.

1. A clay penis ready for tale-telling night

2. Everyday stances with elbows out

1

2

3. *Swange:* A dancer's salute to the mother drum

4. *Swange:* Orshio's *gida* leads the way

5. *Swange:* "Getting down" with *genga* and *kwen*

4

5

6. Tuning up the mother drum

7. Mother and male drums played as a pair

8. Use of stone for changing pitch on mother drum

6

7

8

9. Amande Amende, also known as Ikpamkor London

10. Gari Kwaghbo sings
of his sufferings (*ican*)

11. Kundam Agure with his assistant

13. Atsuku figure (7 inches high)

15. Twel figures

12. Figure carved by Chiki (2 feet high)

14. Common stool (8 inches high)

11

12

13   14

15

16. *Gbercul:* "Strike the forehead" dance

17. *Agatu:* Leader and circle counterpoint

16

17

18. *Agatu:* Witches must
never touch

19. *Ingiogh:* Dancing
their diseases

20. *Ingiogh:* Terror and
paralysis

A

B

A

B

C

D

E

5

Circles and Angles

... melea, *the limbs in their muscular strength* ...
Bruno Snell, *The Discovery of Mind*

She had a picture of a cowboy tatoo'd on her spine
Saying Phoenix, Arizona 1949
Singin'

> *Yiii–i–in yang!*
> *Yiii–i–in yang!*
The Coasters in *Little Egypt*

The papers in this symposium emphasize the tribal artist as
a wood carver, but certainly in West Africa the principal or
central art is dancing, in contrast to architecture in Europe.
K. C. Murray, in *The Artist in Tribal Society*

THERE IS no conclusion to Tiv song. Any particular song is but a part of a deeper underlying process, a discrete piece from a larger continuum, pulled out by an *or u dughun amo*. Kuji Iyum may use the formula *a bin dedadi*—his rendering of a Hausa phrase for "how sweet it is!"—to signal an end to a selection, but the sweetness draws him into another song immediately. Composers putting their songs on tape don't like to stop once they have started. Songs begin with a purposeful burst but end only by accident or necessity, or so it seems.

Though I have no conclusions and few answers to the questions raised about what Tiv song is and does, the explorations of the preceding chapters do point in a number of promising directions for future research. Consolidating these directions, however, giving them a stronger theoretical foundation, is hard work, for the literature on primitive esthetics generally and, specifically, the state of the art in ethnomusicology does not offer much inspiration. As I review previous studies and

182 essays with the Tiv in mind and the intensity of their expressive universe at heart, my dissatisfactions range from vague to angry. It is as if scholarship to date has had trouble in even finding and agreeing upon a "name," a sense of *logos*, for the Tiv phenomena that I would like to understand and communicate to others.

What is it that I am trying to understand: "qualities of experience" (Dewey 1934; Mills 1957), "symbolic action" (Burke 1969), "webs of significance" (Geertz 1973), "the act of creation" (Koestler 1964), "a medium of communication . . . a kind of metalanguage" (Devereux 1961), "vital forces" (Tempels 1959; Jahn 1961), "ontology of energy" (Armstrong 1971), "the science of the concrete" (Lévi-Strauss 1966), "cognitive maps" (Fischer 1961), "patterns of culture" (Benedict 1934)? Of course Tiv "expression" is more complicated than all our conceptual frameworks combined; anything framed is reduced; the more frames introduced, the more drearily microscopic the subject becomes. A culture's expression is probably as complicated as life and perhaps even more complex in the sense that Tiv who *dugh* and *gba* and *gber* (are they "creators"?) may be trying to master all of that life-complexity and condense their sense of it in each particular work.

I find myself using "expression" or "expressive universe" whenever I wish to evade or leave open the issue (what is expressed?), and more pretentious phrases come to mind, like "ontology of energy," "phenomenology of creation," whenever I want to engage the issue. I feel guilty of mystification in either case. Perhaps, as a lazy American pragmaticist, I am unduly inhibited about coming to grips with Merleau-Ponty, Husserl, Heidegger and the other artful European thinkers on matters ontological and phenomenological, but on the one hand I know that the Tiv are singing and dancing without their help ("existence prior to being" or "contextuality before consciousness," as the philosophers might phrase it), and on the other hand I sense that Western thought has been, is, will always be, the primary obstacle between me and Tiv *imo*. The notion of an "expressive universe" as broad as the culture itself—"the Tiv way," anything and everything that seems distinctively, arbitrarily, gratuitously Tiv—at least does not close off, by definition, the possibilities of understanding Tiv song. But it invites a Westerner to "estheticize" the whole culture. And if carving out "an esthetic domain" within Tiv culture seems absurd, describing the ways in which the whole culture has an "esthetic aspect" or "embodies an esthetic" seems just as unsatisfactory. Yet it is something like the latter course that I will be following.

The aim of this chapter, then, might be stated as follows: to begin constructing a theory about the Tiv expression of vital forces that is at least partially free of Western esthetic bias, a theory that can be tested in future field work so as to pinpoint the survival value of Tiv song as one special strategy within a unified range of expressive strategies for Tiv situations.

Ideally, two or three field studies and some years from now, I would like to be able to take the ethnocentric theory, method, and models of Lévi-Strauss as exemplified so beautifully in *The Raw and the Cooked* and turn them upside-down and inside-out, substituting a "way" of understanding dynamic particulars in context for his tables, charts, and static paradigms *ex cathedra*. What could be worse than to take harmonically oriented, architectonic Western music as the model for understanding the world views of "melody-and-rhythm" peoples in South America? Why play our spatial-visual-vertical-heirarchical-intellectual games with their temporal-aural-horizontal-egalitarian life energies? Instead of applying our ordering principles to their energies, we should be tapping their energies to undermine our order, to criticize and revitalize, if possible, our existence. This is, of course, easier said than done, easier spoken than written, obviously better sung and danced than argued.

Getting rid of "art," "esthetics," "estheticism" in the West is not going to be easy; it is the opiate of a very powerful intellectual elite with the strongest possible vested interest in believing that "art" transcends and therefore somehow justifies or makes tolerable all the atrocities and horrors that spring from Western civilization. It seems to me that only a radical understanding of what "art" means in our culture can cope with the confusion, indeed a kind of desperation, that characterizes so much of the literature on "the arts" in other cultures. By radical I mean that the fascinating question often raised, "How could the culture that nurtured Bach, Mozart, Beethoven, Brahms, et al., have nurtured a Hitler?" should be reversed: "Why didn't a culture with such a pathological respect for Composers and Conductors find its Supreme-Composer-Conductor sooner?" Elias Canetti's analysis of "The Orchestral Conductor" (1963, pp. 394 ff.) gives us the metaphor of symphony concert as totalitarian state with frightening clarity:

Someone who knew nothing about power could discover all its attributes, one after another, by careful observation of a conductor. . . .
The conductor *stands*: ancient memories of what it meant when

man first stood upright still play an important part in any representations of power. Then, he is the only person who stands. In front of him sits the orchestra and behind him the audience. He stands on a dias and can be seen both from in front and from behind. In front his movements act on the orchestra and behind on the audience. In giving his actual directions he uses only his hands, or his hands and a baton. Quite small movements are all he needs to wake this or that instrument to life or to silence it at will. He has the power of life and death over the voices of the instruments; one long silent will speak again at his command. . . . The willingness of its members to obey him makes it possible for the conductor to transform them into a unit which he then embodies.

The complexity of the work he performs means that he must be alert. Presence of mind is among his essential attributes; law-breakers must be curbed instantly. The code of laws, in the form of the score, is in his hands . . . the conductor alone decides what the law is and summarily punishes any breach of it. That all this happens in public and is visible in every detail gives the conductor a special kind of self-assurance. . . .

The immobility of the audience is as much a part of the conductor's design as the obedience of the orchestra. They are under a compulsion to keep still. Until he appears they move about and talk freely among themselves. The presence of the players disturbs no-one; indeed they are scarcely noticed. Then the conductor appears and everyone becomes still. He mounts the rostrum, clears his throat and raises his baton; silence falls. While he is conducting no-one may move and as soon as he finishes they must applaud. All their desire for movement, stimulated and heightened by the music, must be banked up until the end of the work and must then break loose. The conductor bows to the clapping hands, for them he returns to the rostrum again and again, as often as they want him to. To them and to them alone, he surrenders; it is for them that he really lives. The applause he receives is the ancient salute to the victor . . . Victory and defeat become the framework within which his spiritual economy is ordered. . . .

He stands at their head with his back to them. It is him they follow, for it is he who goes first. But, instead of his feet, it is his hands which lead them. The movement of the music, which his hands bring about, represents the path his feet would be the first to tread. The crowd in the hall is carried forward by him. During the whole performance of a work they never see his face. He is merciless: there are no intervals for rest. They see his back always in front of them, as though it were their goal. If he turned round even once the spell would be broken. The road they were travelling would suddenly cease to exist and there would be nothing but a hall full of disillusioned people without movement or impetus. But the conductor can be relied on not to turn round, for, while the audience follows him behind, in front he is faced by a small army of professional players, which he must control. For this purpose, too, he uses his hands, but here they not only point the way, as they do for those behind him, but they also give orders.

His eyes hold the whole orchestra. Every player feels that the conductor sees him personally, and, still more, hears him. The voices of the instruments are opinions and convictions on which he keeps a close watch. He is omniscient, for, while the players have only their own parts in front of them, he has the whole score in his head, or on his desk. At any given moment he knows precisely what each player should be doing. His attention is everywhere at once, and it is to this that he owes a large part of his authority. He is inside the mind of every player. He knows not only what each *should* be doing, but also what he *is* doing. He is the living embodiment of law, both positive and negative. His hands decree and prohibit. His ears search out profanation.

Thus for the orchestra the conductor literally embodies the work they are playing, the simultaneity of the sounds as well as their sequence; and since, during the performance, nothing is supposed to exist except this work, for so long is the conductor the ruler of the world.

Canetti's long book, *Crowds and Power,* documents in loathsome detail the role of "rulers" everywhere, their compulsion to murder, and the urge to honor the "survivor" that makes these crimes possible, permissible, perhaps inevitable. From his concluding pages:

Whether there is any way of dealing with the survivor, who has grown to such monstrous stature, is the most important question today; one is tempted to say that it is the only one. . . . Hitherto the only answer to man's passionate desire for survival has been a creative solitude which earns immortality for itself; and this, by definition, can be the solution only for a few.

We worship art and artists because they are the "soul survivors" of our civilization. The other survivors, our leaders, are all killers at heart. At bottom, then, there are two kinds of intimations of immortality available to us: (1) standing alone in a field of corpses and (2) standing at the frontier of feeling and bringing back a definition of that frontier that withstands the test of time.

186   Ours is a society based on sacrifice, human sacrifice of the grossest
kind, not only of the Biafran, Bengali, and Indochinese millions who
die physically, but of the millions of "living dead" within our boundaries. Thousands of blacks die undignified deaths in the ghetto, but
John Coltrane played saxophone like no one before him, Aretha Frank-
lin sings of places that thousands of her sisters will never see. We kill
some "others" every day to postpone an American identity crisis, but
in the meantime we have our Christs, our redeemers, our Andy War-
hols. There may come a time, however, when the screams of the dying
drown out our best singers, when religion, the opiate of the masses, and
art, the opiate of the elite, can no longer dull the pain. And I hope that
time is coming soon.

With our pressing need to rid ourselves of rulers, religion, myths,
and art, the Tiv have much to teach us. They have no rulers: the influence of elders rises and falls, depending upon how wisely they exercise it, and prominent men today can be ostracized tomorrow. They
have no religion; in its place is an abiding and profound awareness that
the survival of some is predicated upon the death of others. They have
no mythology, but tales are acted out with great energy and with relevance to everyday life. They have no art, though there are more song
makers and expert dancers per capita than in any society known to me.

Though the Tiv may be in the vanguard in these respects, "radical
humanists," "extreme existentialists," or "a Canetti culture," if you
will, I suspect they are not alone in the non-Western world. And so I
have often found myself wondering what the two recent anthologies
I've been reading (Otten 1971; Jopling 1971) are really all about. Edi-
tor Otten seems to grasp that much of what she has anthologized doesn't
make sense, when she states (echoing Geertz on sacred symbols and
"their presumed ability to identify fact with value at the most fundamental level"), "In pre-literate or proto-literate culture, the art symbol
becomes the fact; that is it simultaneously represents, defines and manifests its referent." Agreeing with what I take to be the meaning of that
statement, I would point out that "art," "symbol," and "art symbol"
have certainly lost their conventional meanings in any discussion of
preliterate expression, and it's not at all clear that any new meanings
have been added.

If art is something produced only by civilizations, this has not pre-
vented people from looking for it and finding it in primitive societies
even if, for the people who produce it, it just isn't there. I doubt that
the words "art," "symbol," "artist," "beauty," "esthetics," and so on,

translate easily, if at all, into any African, American Indian, or other uncivilized tongues. And I judge that few, if any, of the six factors which Merriam's excellent analysis (1964, pp. 261–69) finds underlying the Western notion of an esthetic, can, if taken as criteria, be met by many preliterate societies: (1) "psychic distance" or "objectivity" or "sense of nonutility"; (2) "manipulation of form for its own sake"; (3) "attribution of emotion-producing qualities to music conceived strictly as sound"; (4) "attribution of beauty to the art product or process"; (5) "purposeful intent to create something esthetic"; (6) "presence of a philosophy of an esthetic." There was a time when I thought it desirable and possible to make a case for the Tiv along these six lines. The very presence of many composers constantly making new songs in isolation invites such an argument. Statements of intent from composers and comments of praise from listeners could be gathered and mixed with the adverbial doubles of perfect-clarity (see chapter 1) to form a "philosophy," and so forth. But all six criteria obfuscate rather than clarify Tiv expression: something quite the opposite of "psychic distance" is at work; for all the emphasis on technique in the descriptive terminology, I don't think form is being manipulated for its own sake; song has strong emotion-producing qualities, but isomorphic correlations between particular songs and affective states is specifically denied. But, to be brief, the fact that a case could conceivably be made either way argues for the irrelevance of the six Western criteria until a Tiv Ogotommeli (Griaule 1965) turns up to prove me wrong.

Before building a theory of Tiv expression based upon more qualitative considerations of the sort espoused by Fernandez and Armstrong (see below), I would like to examine very briefly two quantitative or "hologeistic" studies by Lomax and Fischer, not because I agree with their theories and methods, but because one looks to crosscultural analysis for at least a rough sense of what-might-correlate-with-what. The very inapplicability to Tiv culture of most of their hypotheses, at least as formulated and rationalized, seems instructive. Against all the debits —the inevitable associations of static, ill-defined, and semi-isolated variables; the loss of each culture's complex internal relationships, which makes the study of the arts interesting in the first place; and so on— these studies have the single virtue of attempting to link styles to aspects of social organization while avoiding esthetic verbiage for the most part.

In the first chapter of *Folk Song Style and Culture* (1968), "The Stylistic Method," Alan Lomax summarizes his hopes for cantometrics and its apparent achievements to date:

188   The charts, the statistical tables, and the arguments in the forth-
coming chapters all rest upon the inference that if song performance
and life-style vary together, one is the reflection and reinforcement
of the other. At a first level, then, our demonstrations signify that
features of song performance symbolize significant traits in culture.
      We find that song styles shift consistently with:
      1. Productive range
      2. Political level
      3. Level of stratification of class
      4. Severity of sexual mores
      5. Balance of dominance between male and female
      6. Level of social cohesiveness
      Nothing in the established correlations, however, shows that song
style refers to any particular institution or the behavioral pattern of
any one culture. Rather, song style seems to summarize, in a com-
pact way, the ranges of behavior that are appropriate to one kind of
cultural context. If style carries this load of social content, however,
song can no longer be treated as a wayward, extra, belated, though
pleasant afterthought upon the serious business of living. Song presents an immediate image of a culture pattern. A man's favorite tune
recalls to him not only some pleasant memory, but the web of relationships that makes his life possible. [P. 6]

Unfortunately, as much as I agree with these last few sentences, the
most general Lomaxian hypotheses, though confirmed by his computer
in various ways, either miss the Tiv mark or are subverted by the range
of Tiv expression.

      Solo song characterized highly centralized societies, and leaderless
      performances were most common in societies with simple political
      structure. [P. ix]

But in Tivland most songs can be sung equally well whether alone
or in a group, and solo songs are heard almost as often as group singing.
Some solos, for example, an *ibiamegh* composer performing, might even
be described by Lomax as bardic in length and complexity.[1] On the
other hand, group performances usually have clear leader or "call" parts,
and when composers perform with assistants or a responding group of
beer drinkers, leadership is a very salient feature. But then, how do the
adjectives "simple" and "complex" apply to Tiv political structure or
what some might assert to be the very lack of it?

1. See footnote 3, chapter 4.

Unified choirs occurred in highly cohesive societies and diffuse choruses in individualized cultures. [P. ix]

The Tiv are notoriously individualistic, yet when Tiv composers perform with their assistants, the unison sound is so perfectly tight that a listener might easily imagine that one man with three sets of vocal chords was doing the singing. More informal singing situations with much larger numbers sometimes have a diffuse aspect, but it is not a characteristic valued by Tiv as such. Should we then say that Tiv individualism is expressed cohesively?

A third major classificatory criterion for Lomax is "degree of vocal tension," and again the Tiv refuse to scale nicely, since almost every composed song contains phrases that are delivered at very nearly "primal scream" intensity and passages so "relaxed" as to lull a listener to sleep.

As these hypotheses-criteria-variables are refined in subsequent chapters, my frustrations merge into confusion, and one wonders what cantometrics has to offer the student of a particular culture. A rough preliminary coding of ten very popular Tiv songs by a schoolboy chorus (see Appendix A) and five songs from folktales (all fifteen songs typically Tiv, but certainly not anything like a representative sample of Tiv styles) suggests to the cantometrics coder[2] that Tiv "intervals are proto-African (Pygmoid); orchestra is West African; unison (no vocal polyphony) is North African; melodic forms are mainstream Bantu," and that in a rank ordering of similarity to other cultures, Tiv are closest to "Bulu (73%), Yoruba (68%), Baule (65%), Hausa (62%)." In other words, Tiv are in the middle of Africa somewhere. Further coding of a more varied sample and computer processing for societal correlations may make these posited connections to all corners and historical layers of the continent yield some insights, but for the moment I can only agree with Lomax's statement that "in general, a culture's song performance style seem[s] to represent generalized aspects of its social and communications systems," and add that this seems two times too general for my taste.

Similarly, while Fischer's approach to correlating social and graphic designs, in his article "Art Styles as Cognitive Maps" (Jopling 1971, pp. 171ff.) is, at the most general level, very suggestive for understanding Tiv patterns, all the actual correlations seem, for very potent reasons, to be inapplicable to Tiv reality. That is, Fischer's assumptions

2. Roswell Rudd, long associated with the Cantometrics Project as music analyst, was kind enough to give my sample a preliminary rating.

that "man projects his society into his visual art" and "that the latent social meaning of visual art refers primarily to people, especially to characteristic physical configurations and to characteristic gestures and motor patterns" (p. 173), seem valid and useful as assumptions about Tiv expression. However, in the secondary spelling out of these assumptions, the polar ideal-types "hierarchical" and "egalitarian," on the social side of the correlational matrix, are hardly ideal from a Tiv perspective. It is not, I think, entirely a matter of the real Tiv falling between ideal poles in the center of the continuum. Rather, Fischer defines a cooperative sort of egalitarianism, one with "reduced personality variation" (p. 177), while Tiv equalization is a product of intense competition. In fact, Fischer's definition of "hierarchical," with its emphasis on "higher" and "lower" categories of people and exchange of services for protection, is almost a better model for a society governed by the *tsav* ideology, but for the facts that Tiv pyramids of power are plural, subject to sudden if periodic fluctuation, and statuses are not inherited.

Given "dynamic hierarchy" or "competitive egalitarianism" among the Tiv, the design elements Fischer wishes to correlate—simple repetitive/complex nonrepetitive, empty/full, symetrical/assymetrical, enclosed/unenclosed figures—become problematic, as do the rationales offered for the four specific hypotheses, that is, that (1) simple repetition, (2) empty space, (3) symmetry, and (4) unenclosed figures will be found in the designs of egalitarian societies. A point Fischer makes with respect to symmetry is worth bearing in mind:

> Note also that bilateral symmetry can be said to involve an "original" image and a mirror image that is the opposite or negative of the first. This could suggest an egalitarian society perhaps but with an emphasis on competition between ostensible equals, i.e., some interest in establishing a heirarchy, but without success in stabilizing it. [P. 179]

Like Lomax, Fischer draws attention to "the relative prestige or security of the sexes" as an important stylistic variable. In the latter portion of his article he ventures and tests some hypotheses concerning the relative predominance of straight or curved lines in the designs of (1) "societies which strongly favor male solidarity in residence" and (2) polygynous (sororal and nonsororal) and monogamous societies. He theorizes that male solidarity in residence and nonsororal polygyny foster male security, hence a preference for circular feminine forms—confident males "looking for" women. Having argued elsewhere (1966b,

Introduction) that psychological theories of "masculine insecurity" within colonized cultures may well be a projection of the social scientist unless carefully checked against the culture's own sex-role definitions, I hesitate to pronounce Tiv men "insecure." Yet the following points suggest that patriliny, patrilocality, and polygyny do not contribute necessarily to feelings of male well-being:

1. The *ityɔ,* or territorially based patrilineage, may be the place for a young man to claim land and earn influence, but it is also considered to be the source of any sorcery directed against him. Conversely, the *igba,* or mother's people, are looked to for nurturance, shelter, and security in times of danger, a place to live without fear for as long as one wants.

2. Abolition of exchange marriage seems to have loosened the whole range of possible marital arrangements. The divorce rate is very high, and Tiv men are forever complaining of their inability to hold wives.

3. Polygyny, far from increasing male solidarity, pits all men against each other, but especially the elders against the younger men, who must wait to marry if older men are to have more than one wife.

4. Adding points 1 and 3 together, the same elders powerful enough to bewitch a young man are most able to afford polygyny, hence a doubling of insecurities on both sides of what might be called the Tiv generation gap.

5. As we have seen in the biographies of Tiv composers and in lyric content, the woman question looms large.

We will return to the issue of masculine insecurity and some of the other hypothetical correlations suggested by Lomax and Fischer in the course of speculating about the circles and angles of Tiv expression, but first I'd like to review the two qualitative studies that I have found most helpful in thinking about Tiv forms—James Fernandez's article "Principles of Opposition and Vitality in Fang Aesthetics" (Jopling 1971, pp. 356 ff.) and Robert P. Armstrong's book *The Affecting Presence* (1971).

Following Durkheim's observation that in primitive thought "we are continually coming upon things which have the most contradictory attributes simultaneously, who are at the same time one and many, material and spiritual," Fernandez describes a Fang "aesthetic—their notions, that is, of preferred form in object and action," based upon principles of "opposition and vitality" that he supposes may characterize other "tribes without rulers" in Africa. "A good many peoples on that continent possess uncentralized political systems in which order and stability . . . are achieved through lineage structure and a principle called segmentary opposition. Of these people one might truly say that they cannot live without contradictions" (p. 358).

Aside from the very simple and general definition of esthetics, "preferred form in object and action," which helped to revive the concept's utility for me, I was struck by a number of similarities and differences between Fang and Tiv, most of them occasioned by the fact that Tiv society seems to contain even more contradictions. While these can be phrased in terms of opposition ("a portion of the idea of contradiction," p. 359) and dualities (the popularity of bipolarism in Western thought and the influence of "le grande Claude" exert a strong predisposition in such a direction), it seems to me that the pairing of principles has explanatory value for Tiv expression *only* if it raises questions about the special qualities of relationship between the items or principles paired and begins to answer those questions.

As reported by Fernandez, Fang oppositions are a matter of balance and symmetry and are meant to be merged. The relationship between male and female principles is reflected in complementary filiation of lineage segments. The "mature man," between the ages of thirty-five and fifty, balances male (sperm = brain, bones, sinews, will, drive, determination) and female (blood = heart, organs, flesh, reflection, deliberation, thought) principles in his person.

> Opposition between maleness and femaleness . . . is carried throughout the Fang worldview and is evident in dualistic sets such as hot (male) and cold (female), night and moon (female), and day and sun (male), earth (female) and sky (male). [P. 369]

Sculptured figures (which, as we shall see, share a number of stylistic features with Tiv) bring together both infantile and ancestral aspects and are criticized formally in terms of smoothness, "finished or unfinished quality," "the balance of the object and whether its various quadrants balanced with the rest."

> The stomach, thorax, and sometimes viscera . . . are the centers of power and thought, while the head is simply the organ of apprehension and direction enabling what fundamentally belongs to the torso willfully to be put to use. . . . the head and the stomach should work together in complementary fashion, though they do not always succeed in doing so. [P. 360]

Villages are laid out in "two long rows of huts facing each other across a narrow court"; disputants in the men's council house sit facing each other on two opposing rows of benches.

These principles at work might best be shown in Fang comment upon traditional dances where their gustatory appreciation in the vitality of the dance rises out of the presence of oppositions: the male drummers, the female dancers; the low sound of the drum, the high pitched falsetto voices of the women; and, of course, the customary scheme by which the dancers face each other in two opposed lines.

While innumerable Fang complexities have inevitably been lost in a short article, it is nevertheless clear, I think, that the Tiv pattern of expression is not nearly as neat and symmetrical either in theory or practice. Tiv live in circular houses, arranged in circular compounds, and dance concentricly as well. While a "head and heart" dialectic, parallel in some respects to Fang belief, may well be at work in Tiv life, a Tiv theory about such a relationship has yet to be recorded, and in idiomatic speech the heart is certainly in control: "Tiv think (*hen*), perceive or understand (*kav*) and know (*fa*) with the heart (*ishima*)" (Laura and Paul Bohannan 1969, p. 82) and, as we have noted in passing, affective states are situated there or somewhere in the body. The *tsav* ideology links maturity to seniority, the older the stronger *tsav* in the heart, so that the notion of balanced maturity in middle age is an alien one for Tiv. While *ityɔ* and *igba* are opposed in many respects and ritually interconnected in others, there is no balancing mechanism like complementary filiation to point out, and the processes of segmentation, migration, conflict mediation by larger units, and so on, are patrilineal affairs. We will be dealing with masculine and feminine principles at greater length later, but cosmologically speaking, they are present but not, shall we say, amplified in Tiv belief. "The sun is a boy; the moon is a girl" is a standard benediction at many an *akombo* repair, but seems to be very much a traditional formula rather than an affect-laden invocation. Hot and cool links to male and female modes of expression have been noted in the terminology (chapter 1), but day and night, sky and earth associations with sexuality are not consciously made by Tiv to my knowledge, though they can be inferred from the formula above. Left-hand and right-hand (hands and their gestures, so we shall see, remain something of a puzzle in Tiv) are not explicitly linked to male and female duality as they are in Fang belief.

In short, the Fernandez study raises a host of interesting questions about Tiv culture and its expressive aspect that can be summed up in the following: If "complementary dualism" is the password for Fang contradictions or oppositions, the key to their styling of life, what is the phrase for Tiv that will unlock our understanding of their vital forces?

194   One does not do justice to Robert P. Armstrong's *The Affecting Presence* in a few pages. Its argument is remarkably concise and intelligent. Indeed, in a first reading of the book, I found myself underlining most sentences, reunderlining others, putting notes in the margin of almost every page. I have only begun to cope with its multiple challenges. Though still very much an heir to the noblest Western esthetic biases, as are we all, Armstrong seeks to develop a vocabulary for discussing "the affecting presence" that is free of concepts like "art" and "beauty"—a giant step forward.

Secondly, he wants to substitute metaphor for symbol, simile for sign (or "similetic equivalents" for semiotics), presentation for representation, immediate experience for mediated experience, the concrete for the conceptual, in any discussion of the fundamental inherent qualities of a culture's expression.

> For Mrs. Langer, though the work of art is "nondiscursive" and although no artistic medium may be thought of as a "language," the work is nonetheless a *symbol,* an instrument important in "conceptualizing the flux of sensations," and an act of "reference." The affecting presence, however, is not a conceptualization, nor does it in any intrinsic respect refer to anything at all—in no respect that is inherent to its nature, at least, although it may do so secondarily, or "extrinsically." On the contrary, it is actualization rather than conceptualization, and this not of the flux of sensations but of form via the flux of sensations, a form whose only significant apperception is in terms of feeling, for in feeling lies the only possible intrinsic meaning of the work. Because "presentational" so fits the act of confrontation that characterizes the relationship of the affecting presence to its perceptor, the revelation which the former makes to the latter, I choose to use it here.

> The affecting presence is a thing-in-itself—a *presence* as I have called it here—and not a symbol because the creator does not build into his work cues to some real or imagined affective state external to the work itself, but rather strives to achieve in that work the embodiment of those physical conditions which generate or are causative or constitutive of that emotion, feeling, or value with which he is concerned.[3] [1971a, pp. 29, 30]

His third major accomplishment is to theorize with elegance about what should have been obvious, namely, that the affecting works in a

    3. Contrast this formulation with what Merriam quite correctly posits as the first axiom of Western esthetics, "psychic distance."

homogeneous culture must share and exhibit that culture's sensibilities with respect to the way forms are presented in space and time. It is in working out the conceptual apparatus for this basic idea of "inter-medial equivalence" that Armstrong is at his best, most difficult, and least paraphrasable. Definitions for central concepts like "cultural meta-phoric base," "trope," "style" are perhaps best made by citation.

Affecting presences can be created about one of three kinds of axes—spatial, temporal, and spatio-temporal. Sculpture and painting rely upon an axis of space; music, poetry, and narrative upon an axis of time; and costume, drama, and dance upon an axis of space-time. . . . I assume thus that space and time respond to one master affective set or principle rather than to two entirely different ones—one set of feelings to be expressed in time and another to be expressed in space—and are therefore equivalent. This metaphoric order I call a *trope,* and the trope represents the bifurcation of far more basic meta-phoric processes. The trope is also the elementary order at which the similetic metaphor obtains. The trope itself is neither spatial nor temporal, but rather both. And so it tends to accept either time or space as its dominant mode of existence but subjects them both to a common metaphoric discipline. [P. 64]

The trope thus brachiates the predispositions resident in the cul-tural metaphoric base into time/space, interpreted in the language of a style. [P. 70]

style may be viewed in terms of a markedly economical system of opposites—two, in fact: whether the treatment of features stresses *extension* in space or in synchronicity, or in contrast, rigorous *inten-sion.* Extension/intension are to be regarded as disciplines of the media. Style may thus be seen to be a composite of media and their structures, *in terms of* the *discipline* to which those media and struc-tures are characteristically subjected in enactment. Style is further to be characterized in terms of whether the axis of the work asserts a *continuity* or, contrariwise, a *discontinuity* of development. [P. 51]

whether the form is spatial, temporal, or spatial-temporal, there exist four structural-stylistic possibilities: intensive continuity, intensive discontinuity, extensive continuity, and extensive discontinuity. [P. 72]

The continuous in both space and time is easily indentifiable as that which projects through time and through space with minimal inter-ruptions, for example those presentations of the body in sculpture in which the body most nearly attains the volume of a block or column.

The closer a work approaches that presentation which gives the work the conformation of the natural body, the more it departs from continuity; and when that naturalistic mark is passed and the junctures of the body are stressed at the expense of the long lines, then discontinuity is approached. . . . As concerns time, the drive to follow through with emphasis upon the organic, diachronic development is continuity in time. On the other hand, the careful, simple, or elaborate definition of synchronic structures, with the frequent use of stop-time, asserts the exploitation of the principle of discontinuity.

Extension/intension also exist on a continuum, from the maximally extended to that which is folded in upon itself. Extension is a property of limbs, features, and decorative elements, and thus as a result extension is largely a property of such attributes projecting into space. Extension can also be read as range, however; and that work which exploits the possibilities of wide range is also characterized by extension. Intension is in all cases the opposite. Both extension and intension entail structural and stylistic consequences. Thus maximal extension tends to inhibit the development of strong continuity. [P. 69]

I am not entirely satisfied that Armstrong has grasped the basic "modes" or "disciplines" of style with these two continuums—intensive/extensive, continuous/discontinuous. Two tables describing "characteristics of the media" (surface, volume, color, tone, movement, word, experience, relationality, situation) in each of the four possible combinations, much theoretical discussion, and a second half of the book devoted to exemplary analysis of Yoruba (intensive continuity) and Jogjakarta Javanese (extensive discontinuity) expression, raise as many doubts as they remove, in my mind at least. Satisfaction with these concepts is crucial, for without it, the idea of a "trope" bifurcating in space and time seems rather mysterious, and the trope's emergence from a "cultural metaphoric base" downright mystical. Mystery, complexity, man in all his metaphorical diversity, are inevitable and ineffable realities; we both recognize that any discourse on affective or expressive works is just as inevitably reductionist and that dissatisfaction with any one man's reductive schema is to be expected. Despite my reservations about the quality of his two-continuum reduction, despite my abiding, and indeed primary, interest in what Armstrong would call the extrinsic or secondarily referential aspects of expression, and with all its flaws, discussed below, Armstrong's invitation to humanistic anthropology is one of the most eloquent I've encountered.

Though Armstrong tries to confine his argument to an affective sphere roughly equivalent to what are conventionally viewed as the arts, his recognition of a wider affective universe is relevant to the theory that I will be developing for Tiv.

> There is every likelihood that as the cultural metaphoric base speaks through the affecting presence and the metaphoric system, so does it speak through the total affective life, giving a consistency of style to the ethos, touching not only sculpture, dance, music, painting, but food, clothing, fighting, house styles, interpersonal relations —all the soft, viable, fleshy, feeling parts of culture. [P. 65]

> Although I have cast this study in terms of the affecting presence, and shall indeed permit it to stand in this way because of the special role enjoyed by the affecting presence, there is a vaster field of affective activity. It is in this total universe that the decorative design is a part of the affecting sensibility, as surely, though less powerfully, as a paramount affecting presence. In this universe, the affecting presence is thus but one kind of phenomenon among many. In this universe, the factors of importance are the cultural metaphoric base and its immediate function, the space-time metaphor, or the trope. [P. 194]

Armstrong's theory is grand, and its few flaws, I believe, are major as well. The first flaw is that, like so much of the Western literature on non-Western arts, a static visual bias prevails throughout. On page after page it is clear that Armstrong has a statue in mind as he theorizes. He states, "Of all the forms, it is in sculpture and painting, and most especially in the representation of the human body, that one may commence his search. Further, one will choose the human body as it actually is as the standard against which to perceive deviations" (p. 94). We are in agreement upon the importance of the body as primary reference point, but it is the body in motion, not in frozen statuary, and least of all in painting (a very civilized medium of expression), that must command our attention. I have cited Snell and Murray at the outset, for it is from "*melea*, the limbs in their muscular strength," that melody derives, and the origin of Tiv melodies in *melea* is clearly at the heart of Tiv expression. It is dance and dance only that can make Armstrong's concept of a space-time trope as mysterious and vivid as life itself, for dance embodies the very "turning" in space *and* time that the word "trope" denotes.

A second major flaw is the exclusion of masculine and feminine modes of expression and dimensions of feeling from the entire theory.

If the Tiv affecting universe is an acceptable test case, "male and female" probably ought to suffuse the whole model (p. 57, table 2) from bottom to top, from "universal metaphor" and "cultural metaphoric base" through "trope" to all the forms as mediated. It is certainly not a variable to be tucked into the theoretical superstructure. Nor do I think it can be regarded as purely extrinsic to affecting works, a matter of sexual symbolism attaching itself, clinging sensually, to the abstract and intrinsic disciplines of the space-time trope. In the light of Tiv men's and women's dance styles, it is certainly tempting to substitute feminine/masculine for continuity/discontinuity in Armstrong's scheme of things. Since a similar substitution of masculine/feminine for intensive/extensive in another cultural context is hardly inconceivable, we might consider adding this continuum to the first two, giving eight structural-stylistic possibilities rather than four. In any case, it is not necessary to rebuild Armstrong's theory in order to borrow from it unsystematically. My own inclination at present is to posit "intensive discontinuity" as the basic Tiv trope, with the intensive carrying strong feminine elements and the discontinuous being a predominantly masculine dimension.

A third flaw might be called a "romantic hangover" or leftover in Armstrong's thinking about affect or the emotions. It is a diffuse sort of error, a lack of any precision about what the actual emotions, feelings, values presented in any particular affecting presence in any particular culture might be. Without an intimate inside or ethnographic sense of how the Yoruba or Javanese respond to or experience their own works (what Armstrong would term the "pathetics, pathemics and parapathemics" of the system), he leaves the impression that their responses are generally like ours to works of art—awe, mystery, transportation to dreamy realms, vicarious joy and anguish, and so on. Recent personal communications and an article in progress, "The Role of the Storyteller in Relation to the Aesthetic: The Yoruba," indicate that this is one weakness Armstrong is busy eliminating. Referring to the Yoruba, he noted in a letter:

> the work of the affecting presence is not apart from the rest of reality, as "something of beauty." On the contrary, it shares the same ontological estate as every other formed thing in the world, which is to say that it participates in universal energy. If we must speak of aesthetics, then, we have to speak of an esthetics of energy. I prefer to speak of an ontology of energy. . . . we haven't taken the care to realize that emotion can be attendant upon seeing energy achieved via affecting works.

And upon hearing energy personalized in perfectly clear melodies by a composer-singer, I must add.

Perhaps in shifting the conceptual frame from "emotion" to "motion," from "beauty" to "energy," from "esthetics" to "ontology" we are creating an illusory sense of discovery; certainly I am little clearer at present about the qualities of affect generated by witnessing energy achieved. Yet I have the sense of very basic ethnocentric cataracts and ear plugs gradually being pulled away.

At bottom the flaws in Armstrong's theory are but manifestations of ethnocentrism: a preference for written rather than oral narratives—for example, his preoccupation with Amos Tutuola (pp. 137–73)—and for statues that sit still; a bewilderment with the dance; the ease with which sexual dialectics can be overlooked; the assumption of happy/sad emotional states; and so forth. Armstrong argues very carefully that his theory is intentionally "xenographic," that his methodological prescriptions are a first effort to parallel linguistic rigor (the natives needn't be any more aware of their aesthemes than they are of their phonemes), that ethnographic data need only be drawn upon in certain narrowly specified ways in order to define the works suitable for xenographic analysis. I am more than sympathetic to humanistic anthropology, xenography, and crosscultural studies of being rather than behavior. But it will be very difficult work, for a genuine xenographic analysis assumes a nonexistent vantage point outside all cultures! Perhaps the best that we can hope for is a marginal perspective on "being" that contrives, after considerable struggle, to borrow some values and methods from other cultures for analytic purposes in still another cultural context.

And so I have very modest claims to make for the following theory of Tiv expression. It is based upon meager ethnographic data, and most of that collected by others. I dare not call it xenographic for the reasons just given. Much of it may very well be an idosyncratic projection of pattern into spheres where no pattern or a different pattern obtains. Furthermore, I have little sense of either the degrees or qualities of affect that may be attendant upon this pattern as mediated in each of its various forms—pot surfaces, roof construction, stools, walking sticks, calabash carvings, sculpture, body scarification and costume, verbal narrative, drumming and blowing, narrative dramatized, song, dance —though I would like to think that this list, certainly incomplete, is in general ascending order of affective importance, moving from the visual-spatial works through the aural-temporal forms to the ultimate time-space spanner and audio-visual climax, the dance.

If I may borrow another statement from Armstrong at one of his more tentative moments, "I shall attempt merely to see, after a hypothesis, what congeries of order there are to be seen and to show these at work in those works we call art" (1971, p. 2). His hypothesis for the Yoruba is sufficiently general to serve for Tiv as well, namely, "the idea that power, or force, or vitality, or energy, or dynamism is in fact the informing principle of the Yoruba schema, and thus of the Yoruba affecting universe" (p. 6). Armstrong has borrowed this hypothesis from William Fagg (though Father Tempels or Janheinz Jahn might have been cited as easily), who observes:

> Of all the thousands of pre-industrial tribal philosophies in the world, it is unlikely that any two will ever be found identical; yet in this one fundamental respect they would seem to be all alike, that their ontology is based on some form of dynamism, the belief in immanent energy, in the primacy of energy over matter in all things. That is to say that whereas civilizations see the material world as consisting of static matter which can move or be moved in response to appropriate stimuli, tribal cultures tend to conceive things as four-dimensional objects in which the fourth or time dimension is dominant and in which matter is only the vehicle, or the outward and visible expression, of energy or life force. [1963, pp. 122–23]

Yet it seems that belief must have its basis, energy its source, and that human vitality or life force must be culture specific. And so I would like to move beyond the idea of energy to explore a number of related and overlapping hypotheses that I hope will take us from relatively simple, easily perceived visual-spatial designs to a clearer sense of the particularly Tiv kind of energy generated in the more complex works of song, enacted narrative, dance.

1. The Tiv schematic, at its simplest, is one of "circles" and "angles"; "circles and angles" within quotation marks because the graphic design implicit in such terms is but the plan for an energy generator or the trace of energies expended. The circles are moving or moved once upon a time; the angles penetrate or escape the circular boundaries, fields of force.

In more expansive moments I think of calling this particular "web of significance" (Geertz 1973, p. 5) a logogram or "logo" heralding the rebirth (earlier anthropologists relied heavily on the concept of "pattern," after all) of a discipline in anthropology that might be called "whole-logo-istic" studies, defined in exact opposition to hollow "hologeistics." Searching for a Tiv logo, one thinks of the contemporary peace symbol, with its angular "rocket" contained by a social-cultural perimeter (figure 3). An angularized version of the Chinese yin-yang

Fig. 3. Peace symbol

symbol (figure 4) might be shaped to reflect the Tiv dynamic. But per-

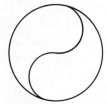

Fig. 4. Yin-yang symbol

haps there is no one best way to reduce or abstract the "expressive grid" (figure 5; see also fig. 1) of Tiv culture to simpler elements. Though

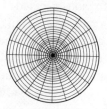

Fig. 5. Tiv expressive grid

there would be irony in it, it might be helpful if some op artist could draw this grid in such a way that the eye is encouraged to see various angles converging on the center.

2. Circles are or represent forces of society and culture, femininity, melodic stability (monotones, duration tones, or subjective tonics) and continuity (responses), "intension" and centripetalism, "the ground of being," and are normally "good."

3. Angles are or represent forces of individuality, masculinity, melodic change (intervals, especially wide ones) and discontinuity (calls), extension and centrifugalism, "modes of being and becoming," and are potentially "evil."

4. It is the friction and tension between circles and angles that generates energy, dynamism, life.

If, in the course of developing and documenting these hypotheses, I seem to be going around in circles and flying off at tangents, take it as but a pale stylistic reflection of kaleidoscopic Tiv reality imperfectly known.

THE ROOF

On the first day that I moved into a Tiv hut in a Tiv compound, children came to visit me and to teach me Tiv words. At some point a child pointed to the top of the roof and said, "*Ikyuliko*," as the other children giggled with delight. I wrote it down (quite accurately I think, aside from a lack of tone markings) with the help of many repetitions from my teachers and much discussion in Tiv that I couldn't follow. But I gathered that if you knew that word, you were an *or u fan kwagh*, "person who knows things." I still don't know that word, so call me *bume or*, "fool," and share my frustration at having missed what might be a key to the "sexual politics of Tiv song" and the center of this theory.

Bearing in mind the previously noted Tiv analogy between praise singing and constructing a roof over a man, let us look at Tiv roof construction in loving detail as reported by the Bohannans and by R. C. Abraham, and then explore the terminology they give us in still more detail before returning to the central issue, that is, the issue of the center.

Some excerpts from the Bohannan account of house construction (Paul and Laura 1958, 2: 312–25):

> In either type of building, the first task is to lay out the circle. The first hut we saw built was laid out by driving a peg into the ground; a loop of rope was then put over the peg, and the leg of the builder inserted in the other end of the loop. He pulled the rope tight, giving it the radius of the hut. Then, with his bare foot on the ground, he shuffled around the circumference three times, leaving a marked impression. We have never seen a second stick used for marking the circumference, but almost always the bare foot. Often, no attempt is

made at all to get the hut round, but an approximate ring is scratched out, again, by shuffling about with the bare foot. Lack of symmetry does not usually disturb Tiv, though they may admire it if it is present.

The roof can be put on to either type of hut in a variety of ways. The two most common are (1) building the framework of the roof on the ground, upside down, and the lifting it into place, and (2) to erect a scaffolding and build the roof in place. The roof framework which is built on the ground is usually built inside a circle of upright posts, joined by saplings. The cone-shaped framework is then made. . . . Since the waterproof qualities of a thatched roof are almost entirely determined by the pitch of the roof, it is sometimes necessary to dig a hole in the middle of the ring of posts (in lieu of higher posts) so as to increase the angle of the pitch. Sometimes the circle of posts is dispensed with and each individual rafter of the roof is held by a different man. We have seen as many as twenty men in a ring, each holding a rafter pole while they were tied together into a cone.

In cases of a large roof, a scaffolding will be built around the temporary center post, and the roof framework built in its permanent location.

A ring some fifteen inches in diameter or so of a dozen strands of *pungwa* is made; taking it, three men climb up into the scaffolding, and one places the ring over the top of the extension of the central pole. Then the rafter poles are slid up, on top of the "surrounding" (*ukase*) and, guided by men standing below and supporting them with forked sticks, they are inserted through the ring by the men on the scaffolding. Five poles were inserted into the ring, which now held its position because the poles were bracing one another. The peak was carefully centered and tied lightly to the central post extension. The rafter poles are called *hwange;* the first five (there may be more or fewer), which go through the ring and support the main weight of the roof, are called "male rafters." These rafters should be straight.

A foot or so below the apex, held in place by its ring (the whole is called *ikuraikor*) there are bundles of twigs of *agela* (each twig is about a quarter of an inch in diameter and two feet long) tied in rings to the male rafters with grass rope. One bundle is placed inside and one outside; the two bundles are then wrapped together with the grass rope which has been wetted so that it will draw tight when it dries. This wrapping is either repeated in rings or spiralled down the cone of the roof, one course a foot or so below the last. This process is called *kuva hwav*, "to frame the roof." Supplementary rafters are added by pushing them into place, their points thrust between the two bundles of twigs of the lowest spiral, fastened into place when the next lower spiral is made. Thus, some of the rafters are only half, or even less, the length of the male rafters, and are held in place by the tied framework.

The spiral of tied twigs continues all the way to the lower edge of the roof. The supplementary rafters are usually all in place by the time the half-way mark has been reached. . . .

Bundles of grass are then braided into rolls of thatch . . . thatching grass is spread out on the ground . . . then plaited into strips . . . squatting on the ground, moving along the row . . . Strips of thatch made in this way can be as much as a hundred feet long.

The thatch is put onto the roof frame by putting one or two "courses" of thatch with the root, ends *down*, at the level of the wall. Then, starting at the lowest level of the roof framework, thatch is unrolled onto the roof, spiralling upwards, with the root-end of the grass up, and the point down.

Finishing off the thatch at the peak of the roof is a complicated process. The easier way is to tie an extra bundle of thatch around a short, sharpened pole inserted into the apex of the framework, and then invert a large water pot over the peak. This method, used widely in the south, is all right for sleeping huts: but the pot is recognized —as it is throughout much of Africa—as a female emblem, which makes it unsatisfactory for reception huts, which are the property of men.

Abraham notes, however, in discussing the most important crop *akombo, ihambe twer,* that "two pots, *akuve,* are buried in the earth inside, one male, which is inverted and the mouth buried in the soil, and the other female, buried with the mouth upwards and above ground but covered with a piece of stone, to prevent women looking inside" (1940b, 88).

The most common topping for reception huts is a device called an *nduruku.* . . . It is a sort of tufted crown made by thickening the thatch around a central stake driven into the top of the thatch and framework. Then a roll of thatch is rolled around, rootends down, and bound into a small cone around the stake to form a point. The roots are cut off, and sticks are inserted to hold the whole more firmly in place. Decorative objects may be thrust into it as well. Sometimes an upright pointed stick is left sticking a foot or two into the air above the thatch. This recognized male symbol is usually used only by compound heads, and must be removed, broken and thrown into a stream on the death of the compound head.

The next step is to pound the floor. . . . The beating is woman's work—usually it is done by teams. Several old women, each grasping her beater by the handle, work in rows or around in a ring, pounding and singing the songs they have made for the occasion. [Paul and Laura Bohannan 1958, 2:325]

And Captain Abraham on the roof:

The roof-frame (*haav*) consists of rafters (*ihange*) of Raphia (*ichor*) which are lashed together on both the outer and inner surfaces by rings (*akov*) made from the trees *agegha* or *ikavel*: these rings are spaced at intervals from the lower part of the roof up to near the apex, but the lowest ring (*gbor*) is on the outer surface only. The extreme top (*deda*) of the inner apex of the roof-frame is tightly laced with several contiguous concentric rings (*ikoro iko*), the outer peak of the apex also being firmly bound together with the *nduruku* rings; as an ornament, sticks are often passed through the outside of the apex or it is adorned with an inverted pot. The actual thatch is very ingenious and consists of bunches of grass placed in an up-and-down direction and passing through the open plaits of a grass rope (*iginde hila*) which encircles the roof-frame; this is repeated in layers (*kpo*) all the way up the roof-frame, each layer being superimposed so as to overlap the one below it. [1940b, 119]

Perhaps we need not belabor the obvious: the roof is made by men, the floor or foundation by women. We must note, however, that two of the terms for rings in the roof are also used in connection with age grades: *kóv*, "roof tie ring," and *ka kóv wam*, "he is a member of my age-grade"; *gbor*, "the lowest circle of *íkóv*," can also be used for "the edge" of a platform, or in the sense of "age-grade" or "age-grade member." Still another term in construction, though not of houses, *teran*, is angular—"the cross-pieces placed between two forked branches to form the lowest layer of a platform"—and can also be used to mean "age-grade," so the analogical principle would seem to be one of "essential structural support" rather than angularity or circularity per se. Still, the image of concentric circles rising to the peak of the cone as a model for age-grades which do diminish in size as the members become older is very striking indeed. It is reinforced by the usages of *kpò*, "layer of thatch" in the roof, but also designating "a type of tie-died cloth" (circular in pattern?), "size," and "generation," for example, *kpò ù tsúaá*, "previous generation," or *kpò ù àyíaá*, "the present generation."

That the roof is in metaphorical relationship to society is clear enough, but what is happening at the top, where age-grades, genera-

206   tions, and the three to five "male rafters" meet inside a ring? (I assume
that it is but a pleasant coincidence that one of the best known composers in all of Tivland is named "male rafter," Maza *Nomwange!*)
The "inverted water pot" for sleeping huts, and "the upright pointed
stick" for reception huts which "must be removed, broken and thrown
into a stream on the death of the compound head," make it clear that
it is a sexual nexus as well as a political apex; but the specifics, the
nuances, of that union at the top remain to be deciphered.

Four careful scholars—the Bohannans, Abraham, and even the
writer in this instance—have recorded three different versions of that
crucial term: *ikyuliko* (Keil), *ikɔrɔ ikɔ* (Abraham) and *ikura ikor* (Bohannans). As it happens, each of these sets of syllables has more than
the usual large number of possible meanings in Tiv. The "open O"
(sounding like "aw" in English) is often confused with "*or*"; "r" and
"l" substitute for each other in various Tiv dialects; "y" can be heard
after the first consonant and before the next vowel in words beginning
with "i"; so the three transcriptions are not as disperate as they seem on
first inspection. Still, working out the possible meanings for the phrase
with the aid of Abraham's dictionary, I have listed over thirty possibilities, some of which could be woven into this theory very nicely, for
example, "solidified echo," "the vagina that siezes," "guarded horn,"
"the *akombo* seizes," and so forth. Could the first word be *ikúr*, as in
"bunch (of beads worn by women as a girdle)," "nest (of wasps),"
"treaty (with another people)," or might it be *ikúùl*, "claw, talons," or
ikùr, "another tribe," or *íkúr*, "vagina"? But speculation is fruitless
without further discussion with "men who know things." Some of the
ambiguities may be intentional (also intensional), tone puns are possible, meanings ascribed may be variable throughout the clan areas of
Tivland and as open to Tiv speculation as to our own.

Similarly, other terms used for the rooftop—*dèdá, ńdùrùkù, igbéri-
gbu̇e*—require further exploration with Tiv elders before we will know
which connotations, derivations, speculations are the relevant ones and
how metaphors for song, society, and sex are built into the roof. But it
is comforting to know that the "cultural metaphoric base" is almost
certainly up there in the roof, protecting my theory and providing the
essential grid for it.[4] If the roof leaks, and every roof does eventually,
we can make minor repairs until forced to build a new one.

4. A Marxist McLuhanism for this phenomenon: "The base is in the superstructure."

It is this roof that every child looks up into from the day he or she is born. A composer stares into it for a while as he lies on his back in isolation, the universally approved position, to pull out a song.

TREES

The expressive grid (see figure 5) can be seen not only by looking up into a roof but by looking into a tree as well, where the medullary rays and growth rings define the same pattern. Trees provide most of the ingredients for Tiv song medicines. No Tiv sawyer would cut down a tree without singing as he saws. Most of my interview with Chiki, the only Tiv sculptor I met (see example of his work in plate 12), was taken up with discussion of the *adzov* ("sprites" or "spirits") and methods for identifying, propitiating, and persuading them. Are they using the tree you wish to carve as their living quarters or only as a resting place? What happens to various foods left at the base of the tree will provide answers; gifts of other foods may persuade them to leave. *Adzov* are sometimes related to the *mbakuv* ("the dead," and only by inference the ancestors) in Tiv belief; they reside in trees, streams, wells. I would like to learn more about Tiv ethnobotany, not so much their classificatory system as their conceptualization of tree growth. Do they understand the cambium layer, the xylem and phloem? What are their terms for rings, rays, pith, and core? Where exactly do the *adzov* reside? Do the Tiv draw any analogies whatever between roof pattern and tree cross section or is this evidence entirely "circum-stantial"?

STOOLS

Common Tiv stools, carved from the cross sections of logs, present this natural version of the expressive grid on the upper seat surface. The friction of Tiv bottoms on this surface over the years brings out the pattern of rings and rays with considerable clarity. Viewed from the side, the base and seat are joined by three angular legs, bent at the knees, as it were (plate 14). The leg surfaces are given angular form by the adze as well. Anyone who sits on such a low stool, only seven or eight inches high, will find his knees jutting out quite naturally. The edges of both seat and base are decorated with a lozenge or joined-triangle pattern that can be "read" in a variety of ways—a thick jagged line moving between circles, triangles pointing up and down, an echo of the stool's overall structure.

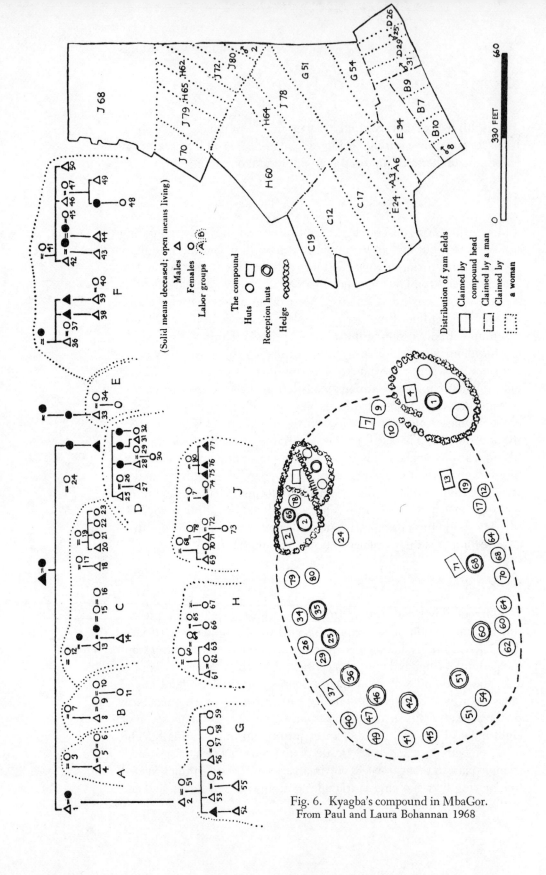

Fig. 6. Kyagba's compound in MbaGor.
From Paul and Laura Bohannan 1968

COMPOUNDS

A tree, often a large one, stands near the center of many Tiv compounds, and the open space around it, the *tembe,* is the arena where events take place. A few reception huts, in a large compound many, might be construed as forming an inner circle, when viewed from above or in diagram, as in figure 6 (Paul and Laura Bohannan 1968, p. 21). The clearest, and middle, circle is made up of sleeping huts and graineries. We might define an outer circle of smaller storage huts, mat-fenced washing areas, interspersed with a circle of small trees—paw-paw, mangoes, some overgrown cassava or bamboo—and finally a circle of kitchen gardens.

Perceptually, the circular roofs become cones and angles when viewed from the ground, and the sightlines from each door to all others in the circle suggest an imposition of cognitive angularity.[5] People view each other's homes, and events in the center, from a particular point on the perimeter, a special angle that has its "blind spots" to the immediate right and left, where one's wives, closest kinsmen, and allies live. The Bohannans have described factionalism and divisions within the compound as reflected generally in oppositional residence patterns, and they have described the ways in which these divisions become actual splits. When a split occurs, it is as if a piece of the pie, a slice larger than half at times, is removed.

At least three or four paths enter the compound from different angles.

LANDS

Most of the myriad paths which criss-cross Tiv country lead from one compound to another, although there are a few main paths which people avoid when choosing sites for their compounds. Seen from the air, the paths form a vast network covering the whole of Tiv country, with compounds forming the nodes. This arrangement, in which each compound appears as a hub in communication patterns, is unique in this part of Nigeria. [Paul and Laura Bohannan 1968, p. 16]

While Tiv fields are laid out in rectangles, rows prized for their straightness from all angles (see figure 7 borrowed from the Bohannans), and borders between lineages fairly evenly delineated, Tiv nev-

5. See Introduction, footnote 1.

210

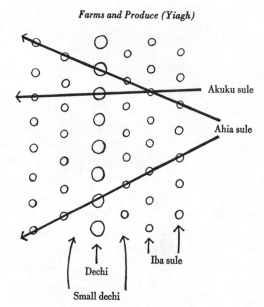

Fig. 7. Mounding of yam field
From Paul and Laura Bohannan 1968

ertheless conceptualize their lands (*utar*) concentricly, as the following case reported by the Bohannans makes clear:

> We asked one of these compound heads if the new settlement did not run him short of farm land. "Oh, no," he replied. "All MbaDuku has given land to the Hausa."
>
> We didn't understand. "You *saw* us," he continued. "All Mba-Duku met and decided that this was the place for the market and village to be built."
>
> "But it's *your* food land!" we insisted.
>
> His reply stated the Tiv view precisely: "All MbaKov [the minimal segment] are the sons of one mother. When you need more land you go to your brother and you say, 'My brother, give me land on which to make a farm for my wife so that she may eat.' The brother says, 'Of course,' and if he in turn is short of land he goes to the brother at his back [i.e., the person who bounds his land but who is more distantly related than the first man. . . .]" [1968, p. 85]

The Bohannan account continues through two more "brother at his back" dialogues, that is, to ever wider lineage segments.

Discussing this later we received a fuller explanation. Our informant drew a diagram on the ground. First, he said that MbaKov

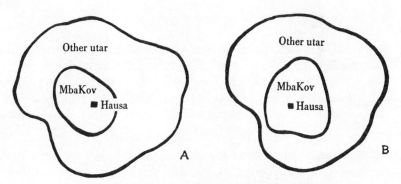

Fig. 8. Land adjustment of a Hausa market.
From Paul and Laura Bohannan 1968

land looks like this (a circle), and it is surrounded by other *utar* (which he named; see the larger concentric circle of Fig. 14 A [figure 8 here]). Then he explained again the process of extending holdings at the expense of the genealogically most distant kinsmen whose land adjoins your own. As he went on he changed the diagram until it had the appearance of that shown in Figure 14 B. "You see," he ended, "all MbaDuku—all Kunav [for the concentric circle surrounding MbaKov could represent either]—are giving land to the Hausa!"

While the Hausa community was being laid out, the men who were being dispossessed from part of their farms shouted and argued foot by foot. They were opposed by the government chief and a few of the more vocal elders; the Hausa very wisely stayed out of the dispute. On the surface one might have assumed that the chief had a right to move his people off a given piece of land or that he had some sort of superior right in it. No Tiv, including the chief, saw it that way. By shouting over this specific piece of land the farmers were impressing on all comers their rights to sufficient land. When the time came for them to take more land, they wanted their case to be remembered. The shouting and argumentation were, in a way, a mnemonic formality. (1968, pp. 85, 86)

Tiv never give an inch at the center, even though they can lay claim to land for miles around.

WORLD

For the purpose of indicating the points of the compass, the world is regarded as a stooping man with his head pointing towards the east, so that the east is "the head of the countries," the west is the "world's fundament," and the north and south are "the soft flesh below the world's left and right ribs" respectively; the metaphor of the stooping man is carried still further and the indication of direction is a serious difficulty to Europeans, the Tiv themselves often being inconsistent, even when two individuals are speaking of the same point of departure and the same destination. [Abraham 1940b, p. 27]

The confusion stems from conflicts between the allegory and actual topography, plus the intervening variable of whether the trip is short or long; "normally 'south' and 'east' are 'up,' while 'north' and 'west' are 'down,' " but a short trip from high ground to low, and most journeys to a river or riverside town, however long, will be "down," even if the destination is to the south or east.

The concept of nearer and farther distance dominates the whole of Tiv thought, "inner" being one's immediate surroundings and "outer" being that with which one is not so familiar; thus "the world" is expressed by "outside" (*sha won*) as contrasted with one's house. [Ibid., p. 27]

According to the metaphor of the stooping man, the earth would seem to be more round than flat, semiglobal, even some what conical. Tiv orientation posits what might be called a "near-high-center," the middle of the back, between the shoulder blades, on a stooping man, a mountain top or high plateau on earth; and the Tiv believe (quite correctly, I think) that they originally lived on a mountain to the southeast before moving into the Benue valley. Psychologically, the near-high-center is probably the place where any particular Tiv happens to be standing at the moment, as measured and modified by where he has been and where he plans to go.

But why is the "earth-man" stooping? What is he doing? Hoeing? Making a pot? Looking for the true center? Having intercourse with the firmament? We must ask.

THE POT PATTERN

The expressive grid appears again in the mat used for impressing the design on the exterior of Tiv pots (see figure 9, borrowed from Murray). Kenneth Murray (1943) describes the final stages of making a pot:

The mat—*Kpwer u Kumen Itiegh*—is about two feet in diameter and made of raffia. There are different degrees of coarseness in the mats suiting the different sizes of pots.

Place the pot on its side on the mat . . . and in the hole and sitting down hammer the inside against the mat with a round stone about three or four inches in diameter, turning the pot little by little (Fig. 19 [figure 9 here]).

With the pod, smooth the inside. The potter usually stands for this and moves partly around the pot, which is upright, but as much as she can she works from one position. Smooth the inside at first

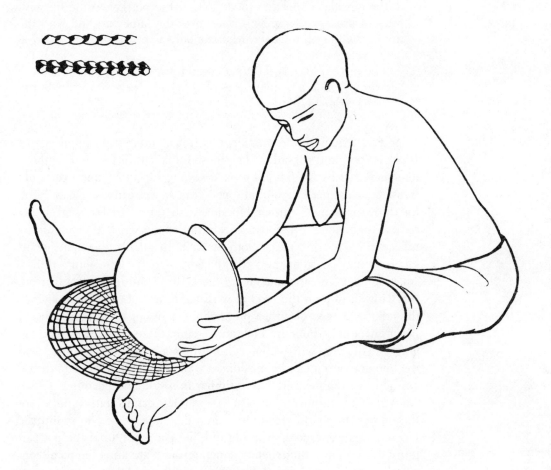

Fig. 9. Pottery mat
From Murray 1943

214

and mainly downwards, but also upwards and horizontally round just below the lip.

The hammering thins the walls of the pots and imprints the outside with circular and semi-circular patterns from the mat. It also helps to shape the pot, but that is chiefly done by the smoothing of the inside with the pod. . . .

Place the pot upright on the mat and pat the bottom of the inside hard with the stone. Turn the pot on its side and turning it bit by bit pat the sides hard with the stone so that the pattern of the mat is well impressed.

Smooth inside with the pod.

Pat outside round the upper part of the pot below the lip with piece of broken pot. Smooth water over the same part and with the tips of the fingers roll over it horizontally a special piece of wood to make a decoration.

The piece of wood—*Uwer u Ngeren Itiegh* or *Shindi*—is a piece of twig in which a regular series of cuts have been made [fig. 9, upper left]. [Pp. 147–56]

As ever in Tiv, the terminology is full of interesting implications. *Itiegh* is "pot" and pot only. The phrase for "mat" (given to us without tone markings by Murray), *kpwer u kumen itiegh,* is almost certainly translatable as "net for pounding pot." But *kpwèr* can also mean "sling for throwing stones"; in combination with the word for "bat" it becomes "umbrella"; it designates a kind of spider (and its "web of significance"?) and a type of cloth as well. In all likelihood the noun *kpwèr* is derived from the verb *kpwèrà,* used for "dragging" things, "making" soot-line adornments on the body, "spinning" coarse thread, "drawing" a line on the ground with hand or foot, and for "playing" the *adigue,* a type of zither presumably now out of fashion, since I never encountered one in Tivland. In sum, there is probably a "dragging" or "drawing out" motion behind the noun for "net" or "mat," and the line drawn out can be melodic as well as graphic. Abraham distinguished two "*kume*" verbs, very similar in sound and meaning: *kùmè,* "to roar," "to thunder," "to beat" the slit-log drums, either *indyer* or *ilu; kúmè,* "to pound" food, "to stamp down" a grave, "to stamp the feet" in a dance. One verb would link the pounding in of the pot pattern to drumming, the other to dancing; there are aural-temporal connotations for the creation of a visual-spatial design in either case, again because of an operational or motional similarity.

In the designation for the notched piece of wood, *uwer u ngeren itiegh,* used for rolling in the under-lip decoration, *úwér,* "a vinelike plant used for sewing broken calabashes," is probably the referent. In future field work I would like to check Murray's transcription, however, for if the noun were *iwér,* it would fit this theory very nicely. *Iwer* is a kind of manual ululation, as in *a gbwidye iwer,* "a person uttered a sharp staccato series of cries by alternately rapidly blocking and uttering the cry with the hand on the mouth (this is used for either trouble or joy)" (Abraham 1940a, p. 316). The notched pattern and intermittent staccato cry would not only fit well with each other in theory but with the alternate term for the notched stick as well, *shindi.* There is only one *shindi* in the Abraham dictionary, the verb "to push some smaller object into a larger (as hand into pocket, straw into roof . . . key into lock), to haft an arrow," from which the name of the little instrument must be derived. One would like to know more about *shindi* as verb (can it be used in sexual connections?) and as derived noun (is it the quality of the notched design or the way it is used that earned it its name)?

It could be argued that "the expressive grid" does not really deserve this name because it is not genuinely expressive or affecting. The roof top is largely, if not entirely, functional, and while form-follows-function is an esthetic credo for some Western architects, we needn't assume it for Tiv. The tree cross section is natural; while we ascribe beauty to "found objects," Tiv do not, although they draw analogies between natural perfection and human, for example, the adjective *swande* is applied to birds in their best plumage, sleek leopards, and fine women. And if any Tiv pattern is merely decorative, the "web" of cross-hatchings that pots pick up from the mat grid must be so considered. Still, functional, natural, decorative, a cognitive map of society, or a model of the world, the grid is, I think, the ground for expression in Tiv. One begins to generate energy and affect, perhaps, by rearranging the grid, breaking it up and playing with the "circles and angles" in various ways.

CALABASH DECORATIONS

Kenneth Murray's very brief report "The Decoration of Calabashes by Tiv" (1951) introduces a very interesting set of sketches copied from rounded calabash surfaces:

During a visit to Gboko, the headquarters of the Tiv Division, it was noticed that many women who came to sell at the market kept their money in calabashes decorated with rich-looking designs. Most of the calabashes were small, varying between three and seven inches in diameter, sometimes with a handle two or three inches long made by the gourd growing a kind of stalk. No decorated calabashes were seen for sale, although many men living in the district could do this work. It seemed therefore that they were probably made to order or as presents. It is said that at a ceremony which takes place after a woman has married and conceived she is given a calabash which her former male companion has carefully carved.

The designs were notable for their freedom and for the beauty, precision and delicacy of their curvilinear shapes. The latter were based on those painted as decorations on the bodies of girls by the young men and are very similar to the body designs of the Ibo and Ibibio. The hook shapes were called *maa,* from a design painted on the face. The triangular shapes were called *kusa* from the name of a tatoo mark made on the necks of men. The traditional designs were evidently abstract, but in recent years representations of birds, animals, fish, palm trees, and motors have appeared. These were introduced among the abstract patterns and often drawn with much verve. This was especially the case in Ihugh in Kunav Clan, south of Gboko. [P. 469]

The designs carved and burned into these calabashes (figs. 10, 11, and 12)[6] probably do not qualify as "affecting presences" in Armstrong's terms; if it is true that former lovers or "old flames" burn in most of these designs, they might be called "after-affects." Still, they are far from perfunctory reflections of the expressive grid.

Paul Bohannan reports:

My most revealing experience in the matter of art criticism among the Tiv passed, like some of the others, in misunderstanding and a minor annoyance. A man named Akise, who was of my true age-set (not one of the men some fifteen years older with whom I was associated, by Tiv themselves, on a prestige basis), told me that his kinsmen from central Tivland was coming to see him and to sell deco-

6. Of the designs reproduced here, all of those in figure 10 and designs A, B, and D of figure 12 are taken from Murray's article. The four calabash designs in figure 11 were given to me by Mr. Murray from his files at the Nigerian Museum of Antiquities in Lagos. Figure 12C is taken from Paul Bohannan's "Artist and Critic in an African Society" (Smith 1961). Figures 11D and 12A do not have arrows indicating top and bottom and may not be "pairs." The single design 12D is from a calabash lid.

Fig. 10. Calabash decoration
From Murray 1943

Fig. 11. Calabash decoration

218

Fig. 12. Calabash decoration
From Murray 1943 and Paul Bohannan in Smith 1961

rated calabashes in the local market. I said I would like to meet the kinsman and watch him work. Akise told me to come up to his compound the evening before market.

The artist kinsman was friendly, but not very communicative about his work. He showed me his tools and his wares. He reconvinced me of something I knew already: Tiv designs have no mystic or religious symbolism, and are at most only a stylization of natural elements like lizards, swallows, and drinking gourds. When asked when he worked, he said "When my heart tells me"—a standard Tiv answer for anything they do which they have not particularly thought about. When I asked him what his favourite design was, he said that he usually liked the one he was working on, so he liked them all. When I asked him why he carved calabashes instead of carving wooden figures, he replied that he did not have any talent or training for carving wood (literally, he did not "know the root" of it), and in any case wooden carvings were sometimes used by the *mbatsav,* or witches, and carved calabashes were only used as gifts to girl friends. This man, I decided, had no aesthetics.

At the time, I was a little put off by Akise, who insisted on breaking into the conversation. During my questioning of his kinsman, he carried on a long harangue about which of the calabashes he liked best, and which one least, and placed the two dozen or so in a row, in order of merit. I asked the artist if he agreed in Akise's judgment. He said he probably did, but he liked them all well enough. I noted (without realizing its full implications) that Akise considered himself a considerable art critic, and I finally turned to copy some of the designs and some of the reasons why he liked them. We were unfortunately interrupted when I had completed only one copy, and we never returned to the subject. [Smith 1961, pp. 92–3]

Perhaps these calabash designs can best be regarded as a potentially instructive midpoint between grid and presence—expressive experiments, diagrams of fields of force that represent rather than present energies, "exercises in incisive eccentricity," we might say, although lines which actually cross each other are conspicuous by their absence.

Yet each carver seems to play with the center of his design in his own eccentric way. Some designs could be said to have perverse elements, giving an illusion of symmetry. A few are thoroughly asymmetrical. In only one or two designs can we point to perfect balance, and here we might recall Fischer's observation (above) concerning the mirror or oppositional aspect of bilateral symmetry. In general, an overall balancing of varied elements—lines, black and white spaces—can be inferred as a common aim, but each calabash asks to be examined individually, and one suspects that dimensions (probably unconscious) of carver personalities are being projected onto these spheres. The carver of calabash A, figure 10, has used only curved lines in his designs; even the tiny angles at the ends of the "umbilical" lines linking the hooks to the circumference and vice versa, are curved. And what a first glance construes as a triangle in the left pattern (reminiscent of a camera shutter mechanism) is obviously curved. Conversely, the carver of calabash B, figure 10, has used straight lines and angles almost exclusively, though the design at the circumference suggests the beginning of curved spokes moving toward center, rotating the pattern.

In any case, there is enough variety within the very small sample to make any hypotheses of the sort suggested by Fischer untestable in this

genre. Though we learn from Murray that the triangular *kusa* marks
are borrowed from the tatoos on men's necks and the curvilinear forms
are like those painted by men on women, this correlation has so many
exceptions that we will want to reverse it when considering scarification more carefully later. Then there is the problem of the "hooks"
appearing in about half the designs, a problem for which I have no
solution.

Murray notes that geometric designs were giving way to represen-
tational patterns when he made his observations (prior to 1951), and
it is my impression that little calabash carving of any kind is being done
these days in Tivland. Perhaps field work in remote areas will uncover
calabash carvers who have presented their work to former girl friends
and who can explain a preference for curved or angular or hooked de-
sings, or combinations of these, but this is a lot to hope for. Could the
carver of calabash C, figure 10, give a reason for putting triangles or
"teeth" on the outer edges of his "hooks"? I doubt it.

Another approach might be to develop a simple projective test made
up of a series of designs, design elements, variably schematic drawings
of common Tiv forms, including some calabash and scarification patterns. Presented in the abstract and "on the flat," missing dimensions
of space and time (that is, a sense of the motions, processes, and occasions that have left the traces of a particular design) might make any
sort of identifications difficult for older respondents, but it might be
interesting to administer such a series to samples of male and female
students.

WALKING STICKS

Reflecting upon an incident in which a youth criticizes the "three
knobs" on his grandfather's sculpted figure, only to have the old man
knock off the breasts and navel with three swift adze strokes, Paul Bohannan goes on to describe walking sticks as further evidence for the
communal aspect of Tiv art.

> When the artist had finished his work, and I had paid him for it,
> his only comment was, "It did not turn out too badly" (*iduwe vihi
> yum ga*). I recorded this comment at the time only because I did not
> really agree with it.
> This incident should have told me that Tiv, in many instances at
> least, care who creates a given object as little as they care about the
> creative process. Art is, among them, an epiphenomenon to play,

religion, prestige and most other aspects of life. Indeed, much of it is a sort of "community" art, a true folk art in which the artist is as unimportant as the composer of folk music.

It was several months later, in another part of Tivland altogether, that I became fully aware of this communal aspect of Tiv art, and that I again noted the phrase "It didn't turn out too badly." This new area was swampy, and I cut myself a stick to help me traverse the slick swamps without falling. After a week or so, a young man from a nearby compound told me that I must not use that stick any longer: it was an old woman's stick and did not become a man of my position. When I asked what sort of stick I should have, he replied that he would make me one which was suitable. A few days later, he returned with a staff which he called a "stick of a young elder." It was about six feet long; on it were several bands blacked with soot which he had set with the sap of the *ikpine* tree. Into the black, he had carved several series of designs.

The stick was very handsome, and before long almost every male in the countryside was making himself a stick of this sort. I copied several of the designs and watched a number of them being made. The most astounding feature, to me, was that comparatively few of the designs were made by a single individual. As I sat watching a young man of about thirty carve a stick one day, he was called away. He laid aside his stick and the double-edged knife with which he was cutting the design. A guest came in a few moments later, picked up the stick and added a few designs. A little later, he handed it on to someone else. Four men put designs on that stick before the owner returned and finished it. When he had done so, he held it out for me to copy and said, "It turned out pretty well, didn't it?" [Smith 1961, p. 89]

The verb for "turned out" or "to come out," *due*, may well be related to *dugh*, "to pull out," the key verb for "composing" discussed in chapter 1. A strict etymological derivation of one verb from the other is not needed to establish a shared concept of "emergence" for song and carving that supports the basic linking verb *gber*, "to cut, to sing, to scarify, to carve incisively" (the latter meaning as distinct from *gba*, "to carve out, as with an adze," in sculpting). To add a note to themes explored in chapter 1, in song one "pulls out," *dugh*, in order "to sing," *gber*, whereas in carving a calabash or a walking stick one "incises," *gber*, in hopes that a good pattern will "turn out" or "emerge," *due*. This possible reversal of processes might be roughly equivalent to the difference between "art" and "decoration" or may simply reflect different Tiv con-

Fig. 13. Carved staffs
From Paul Bohannan in Smith 1961

ceptualizations of aural and visual emergence (see Edmund Carpenter's "The Eskimo Artist" in Otten 1971, p. 163).

What emerges for me from Bohannan's discussion is not so much a "communal aspect of Tiv art" but rather a sense of different individuals leaving their marks, all of them angular with one exception, on another man's staff. Once Bohannan and his friend set a fashion, a typical Tiv status competition ensued, "almost every male in the countryside was making himself a stick of this sort," with friends lending energies, as occasion permitted, to each others sticks. Who carved the angles that transgress the circular bands (figure 13, 3A)[7] and who left the seemingly random angles-within-angles design (figure 13, 2c)? I don't know, but I suspect the owner knew who was on his staff when it was done.

7. From Bohannan in Smith (1961, p. 90).

BODY SCARIFICATION

In considering body scarification we are moving from representations, playful experiments with the expressive grid, to serious presentations of energy—the "affecting presence" alive, in person, and in action. Recalling the four hypotheses that introduced these sections, we may now ask What *is* Tiv scarification; how does it manifest intensive discontinuity?

Paul Bohannan's excellent article, "Beauty and Scarification amongst the Tiv" (1956), concludes:

> The aesthetic of beauty, in so far as it is represented by scarification and chipping of the teeth, is involved with pain. I once asked a group of Tiv with whom I was discussing scarification whether it was not exceedingly painful. They turned on me as if I had missed the entire point—as, indeed, I had. "Of course," one of them said, "of course it is painful. What girl would look at a man if his scars had not cost him pain?" The effort to "glow" must be ovious; the effort to be dressed up must involve expense and trouble; scarification, one of the finest of decorations, is paid for in pain. The pain is the proof positive that decoration is an unselfish act, and that it is done to give pleasure to others as well as oneself. The probable pain is the measure by which Tiv regard scarification; a second measure is the good taste with which the scars fit the face and augment the personality. [P. 121]

"Intensive," we can say, in the sense of intense pain endured and an enduring record of that pain presented at all times thereafter. The person scarified is intensified, augmented; his or her personal characteristics are further specialized, rendered unique. The marks must not only fit personal body shapes, but the shape of a growing personality, a glowing personality that will command the center of attention. I disagree with Bohannan's contention that "The pain is the proof positive that decoration is an unselfish act, and that it is to give pleasure to others as well as oneself." While the element of self-sacrifice is obvious, indeed a blood sacrifice, the god being sacrificed to is the self. The more people will look at you, the more energy gained, the more affective your presence.

> A girl who is lucky enough to be born with "good" legs (full calves and prominent heels) will probably call attention to them by having a design put on them. . . . A really handsome set of leg scars will be famous for many miles around.

The most effective job of tooth-chipping I know had been done on a young woman afflicted with large buck teeth. Particularly, her two front teeth were large. Instead of having them knocked out, she had a nick put in each of them, which gave the effect of her having four narrow teeth where the two broad ones actually were. One always looked at her, then, when she smiled, looked back at her again to be sure that one had seen correctly. I was told by someone else that her tooth operation had been successful because now everybody looked at her twice. She had, indeed, *wanger;* she glowed. The proof was that people stared at her.

The ultimate purpose of all scarification, Tiv insist, is to make themselves more attractive.

Complete scarification may take decades. It begins at the age of 13 or 14 and may go on until one reaches 40 or 45. I knew one woman of 35 who had saved an empty space on her forehead for the time she would leave her second husband. She had now done so, and was casting about for a design to fill the space. She spent days trying designs in ashes and gazing into a mirror. She insisted that I offer a suggestion; I was relieved when she decided against it. [Ibid., pp. 118, 119, 120]

This last passage recalls "Little Egypt" of the song lyric cited at the outset of this chapter and suggests that, like the "after-affect" of a carved calabash, scarification can present clues to a history of personal action, more specifically, of male-female interaction. The body as "ground of being" can be physically altered by a personality's "mode of becoming"; decisions made leave their marks. Incision follows decision; intense pain for intensification of self with intent to draw energy into oneself and gain the center.

Discontinuity is asserted in the very act of attacking the smooth surface of the skin, emphasizing features, breaking up the rounded contours of the body with predominantly angular patterns. Paul Bohannan describes the effect of nail scarification of the face as follows (see fig. 14, A):

"Nail" marks are mainly decorative; both the *abaji* and *mkali* marks, however, actually alter the planes of the face. They are cut very deep, and their effect is on the fall of the shadows on the face. Prominent cheeks, for example, can be made more prominent by doubling the shadows cast upon them. A nose can be made longer—or shorter—by use of a deep mark. [1956, p. 118]

Bohannan states simply that Tiv are worried about "fit," that "a nose can be made longer—or shorter," that patterns will be tested with

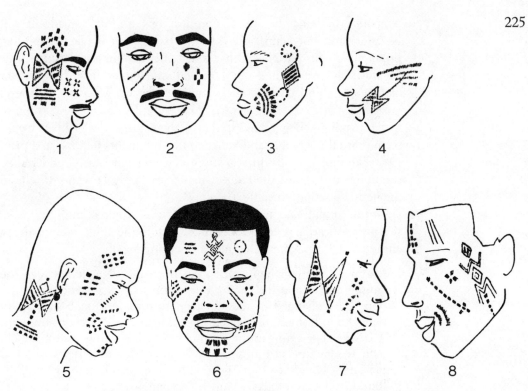

A. Nail scarification patterns (all male except no. 5)

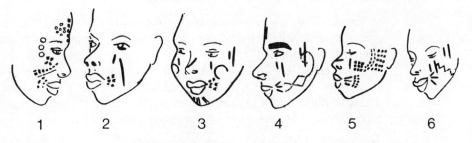

B. Scarifications of mixed types
From Paul Bohannan 1956

Fig. 14. Body scarification

temporary markings before incision decisions are finally made. It will be important, but admittedly difficult, to ascertain what the guiding principles of "fit" have been, that is, whether designs are placed "with," "against," or "across" the natural contours and planes. If the flat sketches of calabashes and walking sticks meant to be witnessed in the round are problematic, sketches of facial and body designs are impossible to use in making xenographic inferences about principles of fit. It would seem that ethnographic and xenographic judgments relating to a principle like discontinuity in scar designs would have to be undertaken simultaneously, since the subject matter can only be viewed, felt, in the flesh, in action, in context.

At the societal and symbolic level, however, the discontinuity function of scarification is perfectly clear, at least in the more traditional Tiv culture that Akiga and Bohannan are writing about.

> Akiga has, with high spirits, described the struggle between the "lumpy faces" and the "nail boys" which took place when scarification styles changed in the nineteen thirties. Although he has, in typical Tiv fashion, overstated his point in the interest of humour, it is true that young women's preference for young instead of old men is sometimes expressed in a fondness for new types of facial marking. There are four "generations" of scarification types to be found in Tivland today. [Paul Bohannan 1956, p. 118]

"Today" was circa 1950, and the four types were found by Bohannan to be overlapping from generation to generation.

> Tiv definitely associate these different types of scars with different ages of men. I have heard young men accused of putting scars of the older generation on their faces in order to make people think that they are older than they are. My informants in northern Tivland assured me that youngsters who are today four or five years old will undoubtedly think of or learn a new method of scarification by the time they are old enough to be interested in it. [Ibid.]

The spread of Western values has, of course, all but eliminated such obvious marks of "primitiveness" in the younger generation today, but it would not be surprising to find scarification of some fashion, or a near surrogate for it, revived in the future by the younger generation as the unmarked generation become elders. But let us listen to Akiga's story, for Bohannan, in typical Western fashion, may have understated the point in the interest of scholarship.

> This affair of the Nail is now doing a great deal of harm in Tiv country, owing to the fact that the women will have nothing to do

with those who have the old markings. For in as much as marriage by exchange has been replaced by the bride-price system, and a woman can no longer be given away in marriage forcibly, but only if she consents of her own free will, it goes badly nowadays with those who have the raised scars on their faces. A woman may have been married for a long time to a husband with raised marking, but leaves him on the ground that the white man has said that women must do as they wish, and she, for her part, does not wish to have a husband with a lumpy face. So the men who have raised scars do not know where to turn, and sometimes, in despair, a man who already has the lumps on his face will take a nail and make cuts on the top of them, thinking thereby to please the women; but this does not hit the mark either. So there is loud lamentation in Tivland. The younger Tiv are split into two factions, and there is bitter feeling between them. Those with the lumps make up mocking songs about the Nail Men, and the Nail Men about the Lump-faced. Those with the lumps are backed up by the old men, because the old men have these markings themselves, but the Nail Men have the women behind them, and for this reason they are getting the best of it. A man who has the raised marks can do little against a man who has the Nail, for amongst the Tiv the women have more influence than the elders. You may do something of which the elders do not approve, but if the women approve there is no more to be said. If, on the other hand, you do something which is praised by the elders, but meets with disapproval from the women, you are not satisfied.

The Nail Men have lately introduced another type of mark which they call "Ukari" after the town of Wukari, where they first saw it. This mark is not usually made high up, but is cut close under the eyes in a downward direction, as though a man were weeping, and a tear-drop were running down his face. It is quite short, made with a deep cut, and when it heals leaves a big black scar. This is a sure woman-killer. Women who see it never stop admiring it, declaring that the boy looked nice with his Nail markings, and now that he has had the Ukari done as well, it really suits him wonderfully! If the Lump-faced Men hear this, they start to quarrel with the women. Thus has the Nail shaken the country of Tiv. The men with the lumps on their faces shrink into their shells like the tortoise, but the Nail Men shoot forth their necks. [Akiga 1965, pp. 45, 46]

In the past and in the present (for lack of marks indicates the greatest generational divergence of all), scarification expresses a fundamental discontinuity in Tiv society.

The sexual component in the initial circles-and-angles hypotheses is not very clearly defined in the data at hand. As Bohannan puts it, "Scar-

228

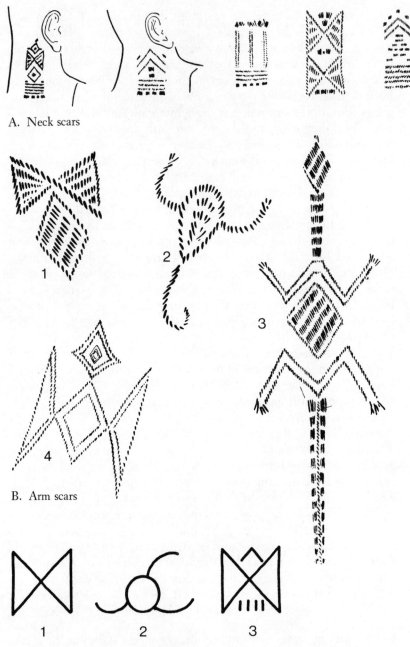

A. Neck scars

B. Arm scars

C. Swallow, scorpion, and fish patterns
   From Paul Bohannan 1956

Fig. 15. Body scarification

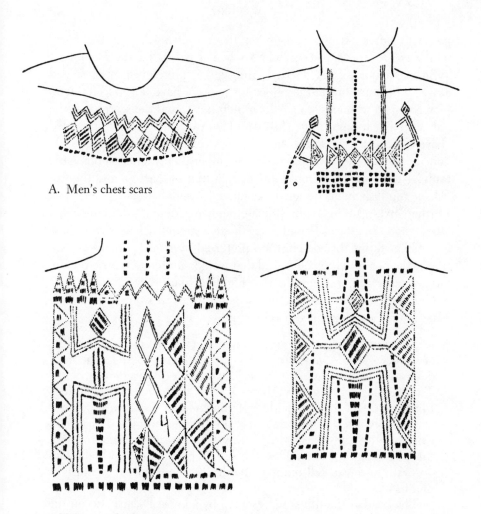

A. Men's chest scars

B. Women's back scars
From Paul Bohannan 1956

Fig. 16. Body scarification

ification designs are common to both sexes. They consist of geometrical designs or are representations of the swallow, the water monitor, the scorpion, the fish (*ishu*) or occasionally the chameleon." (See figure 15, B and C.)

Yet Bohannan notes a number of pattern preferences according to sex and location on the body. Women with full rounded calves are

230

prone to put a "fringe" design on them—" 'fringe' after the edges which are left on a piece of cloth when it comes off the loom. . . . Women have scars put on back and legs in preference to chest and arms," which are favored locations for men. "I have never seen a scorpion among a woman's scars," Bohannan states, and the scorpion is the only curvilinear motif (fig. 15B2 and C2) of the five basic types cited above. The *abaji,* or round face-lumps, were much more frequently done by men. There may be a correlation between women and aquatic forms—fish, water monitor (a favored pattern for backs), and the catfish or mudfish belly design (see plate 15 and figures 17 and 18). Further investigation might validate generalizations to the effect that while angular patterns heighten the body contours of both sexes, those curvilinear forms that do exist are preferred by men (perhaps as contrast to flat or angular planes), and that women prefer geometric presentations, especially of water life, that highlight their curves.

Certainly, the only curved lines that appear on women in Bohannan's figures are those of the belly scars.

> The most characteristic scars found on Tiv are those on the bellies of women (see *Akiga's Story* [1965], plate facing p. 43). The belly design is called a "catfish" (*ndiar*). Abraham (*A Dictionary of the Tiv Language,* 1940a) says that it is *idiar,* which means sexual lust. I have no doubt that Tiv told Captain Abraham that it was the same word—they often make puns on it. Unmarried women with particularly good scars are teased with this pun, and it is a favourite joke that the design of the tail of the fish is finished off with the clitoris. All, however, tell me that the design symbolizes the catfish or mudfish.
>
> The head of the fish is represented by a knot of scar between the breasts. It has a long neck, and fins which are represented by the wing-like extensions of the design on both sides of the navel. [Paul Bohannan 1956, p. 120]

At one point in my meditations on these scars I thought it might be a clever trick to superimpose a diagram of the Tiv expressive universe on one of them; the "arrows" of Bohannan (figure 17A here) suggesting a likely target. While this didn't work out very well, another of Bohannan's figures (fig. 17D here) lent itself very nicely to a self-administered projective test. Once a few symbols were assigned and others fell into place, a diagram emerged that (1) echoes the diagrams accompanying the featured story in chapter 2, "The Chief's Farm Bet"; (2) restates the climax of those tales in which a woman tries to trade

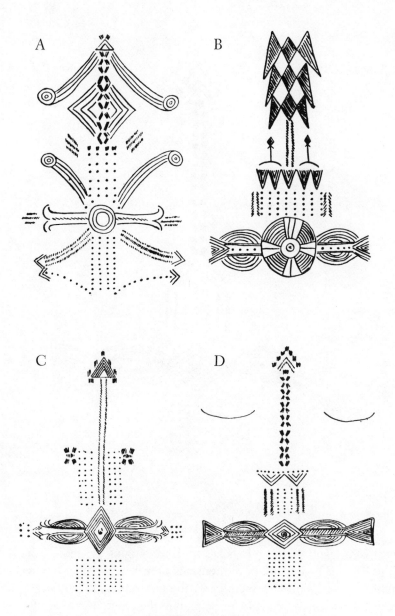

Fig. 17. Women's belly scars
From Paul Bohannan 1956

232

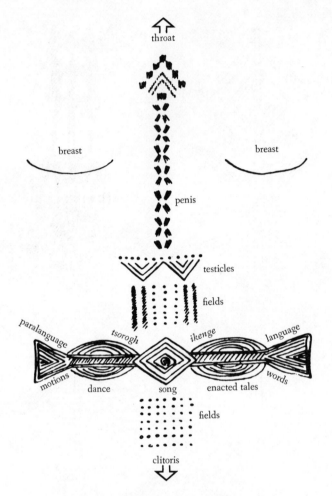

Fig. 18. Woman's belly scar: Mudfish design
From Paul Bohannan 1956

meat for a giant penis and chokes to death singing for more (chapter 2, p. 81); (3) summarizes the tensions between "words," "intensified speech," and *"ikenge"* principles on the one side and "motions," "disguised dance," and *"tsorogh"* principles on the other, discussed in chapter 4; and (4) proposes a model for seminal or fertile song as angles-around-the-navel or intervals-around-the-tonic, poised between symbolic male organs and real female ones, in the midst of cultivated fields, fed by and feeding into concentric dancing on one side and theater in the round on the other (fig. 18).

That this may be something more than an anthropologist's fantasy is attested to by the joke that "the design of the tail of the fish is finished off with the clitoris" and by the fact that these designs "are said to promote fertility." From xenographic and ethnographic perspectives these designs could be made more intensive, and rendered symmetrical, in two obvious ways: by adding the real female genitalia below; by inserting real male genitalia into the lower field. However, song's place at the center, the transformation of mudfish fins into "dance" and "enacted tales" does require a jump of confidence on the part of the reader, if not a leap of faith.[8]

> Mudfish scars on women's bellies are said to promote fertility, but if you ask Tiv in just what way this works, they say that the scars are tender for some years after they are cut, and are therefore erogenous, and that a woman who has them will demand more sexual attention than one without them, and hence is more likely to have children. Tiv are, as Frobenius put it, "ein sehr praktisch und unaberglaubliches Volk."
> The mudfish patterns are of two basic sorts: they are called the "okpoto fish," marked by a triangular motif [fig. 17B] and the "Tiv fish" which is more cursive in design [fig. 17C, D]. A "swallow" may be added many years after the fish design; this swallow is a different stylization from that used elsewhere on the body. It usually comprises long, swooping double or treble lines which more or less centre on the navel. Some women told me that these were put on after a child or two had been born in order to keep the skin of the belly firm [fig. 17A]. [Paul Bohannan 1956, p. 119]

Clearly all this has some bearing, even an overbearing, on the fourth hypothesis, that is, that friction between "angles" and "circles"—men

---

8. The rise of so many "phallic singers," such as the Afro-American James Brown or the Anglo-American Mick Jagger, and the popularity of a whole genre called "cock rock" in our culture may be the source of my projection. Or these phenomena could be taken as evidence for the universality of the Tiv sex-song nexus.
I may have imposed my schematic for Tiv expression on the "fins," or horizontal dimension, of this "mudfish," and "song" may have been arbitrarily placed in the pivot point of the vertical dimension as well, yet the whole sexus-nexus-perplex-us "feels right" when the head of the symbolic penis points toward the throat at one end, and the symbolic "tail of the mudfish" *is* a clitoris at the other end of the vertical. Are we being pointed back to "voice as female phallus" again? (See chap. 4.) It's still a puzzle I haven't been able to solve, but closer analysis of stories men tell of the giant penis that chokes those singing women, coupled with more knowledge of the songs that women sing as they weed, threatening men with castration, may clarify the picture.

234 and women, individual and society, discontinuity and intension—provides the energy for Tiv affecting forms. How far these erogenous, tactile, skin-tightening aspects extend beyond the belly to other areas of the female form, and whether or not they extend at all to men, are open questions. At a metaphorical rather than physical level, the friction between angles and circles, between scars and bodies, and between one marked man or woman and all the others, is generated in a field that is primarily visual. As persons move through space and time, both the roles and positions of observer and observed are constantly changing; stares, attentions, energies are forever being given and received, and pains are taken to assure a fair share plus a little bit extra—and that's the rub.

STANCE AND GESTURES

In this section we take a step back from the affecting continuum for a brief discussion of the body in everyday Tiv life to provide some context for a consideration of sculpture and, later, the dance.

Before going to Tivland, we went to visit the Bohannans with a set of preliminary drawings for a Tiv TAT study. After looking through our sketches, both Bohannans were troubled but couldn't pinpoint the source of their discomfort. As we looked through a set of their photographs of Tiv at work, at play, and in repose, someone exclaimed, "Elbows!" Indeed, all the drawings were too gentle in posture: shoulders sloped too much, arms hung listlessly at the sides, knees did not jut out far enough from squatting men, backs not sufficiently straight; in short, Tiv angularity was missing. It seemed a very interesting observation at the time. We asked the artist to revise the sketches accordingly, and once the error was pointed out, he had no trouble at all in making the corrections.

In retrospect, "the Tiv elbow" looms as a very much neglected pre–fieldwork insight. Once enchanted by a Birdwhistell lecture, impressed with the books of Edward Hall, I nevertheless failed to pursue kinesic and proxemic information in the field. My still photographs capture an abundance of elbow angles (see plates 2 and 7), but all the interesting processual questions about when and why elbows go out and at which angles, when and why they are retracted, remain unanswered. And what of knees? And those other juncture points—wrists and ankles, the waist, the neck? And how are gestures patterned by age and sex? No systematic observations made. No questions asked.

Plates 2 and 7 are merely snapshots; no one is posing, at least not for the photographer. In addition to showing a range of characteristic elbow configurations, the plates give us a sense of what "elbows-out" does to the rest of the body. While malnutrition and childbearing account for most of the stomach protrusion in children and women, respectively, the placement of hands on head or hips, or one hand on hip and the other on head, produces, with the resultant elbows-out pattern, a circles-and-angles presentation of self from front or back: the stomach protrudes even more in front; the shoulder blades angle out sharply in back. It is my impression that in everyday life the women and children are more likely to assume these elbows-and-bellies-out postures than men, perhaps because they feel a greater need to fill and define space. It is also my impression, formed by looking through dozens of photographs, that these stances are more likely to occur when there is space to fill and the person is relaxing. Children often group themselves tightly together when sitting on a log. Tightly packed crowds at a dance engage in the usual jostling, but there is no frantic elbowing for position.

I anticipate rereading the kinesics and proxemics studies and taking some film footage at Tiv markets and compounds so that these still very superficial perceptions can be deepened. Such work may be of some help in understanding certain sculptural conventions and will be indispensable to a thorough study of Tiv dance.

I have even less to offer and more to learn about hand gestures (see plates 9, 10, and 11). The big gap to be filled is defined on one side by the closed fist (a circle?) raised and shaken in greeting and friendship, and on the other by the stiff wide-open hand (angles?) thrust out, with or without the stated curse, "*tswar wou fong!*" literally "anus yours *fong,*" that is almost certain to provoke a fight. Everything in between is missing from my notes. Women dancing are usually open-handed (plates 21b, 22), while men often twist fingers, wrists, fists in various ways (plate 20); a storyteller before a sizeable audience presents a dazzling flow of postures and gestures; composers singing their songs use a variety of gestures for emphasis, which in some instances seem idiosyncratic, but the simplest inventory of conventional or conversational gestures on which to base judgments of the more stylized presentations has yet to be made.

SCULPTURE

Here we face a number of difficult problems, first and foremost of which is the rapid disappearance of specialists in adze work of any kind. I was able to find only one working sculptor in Tivland, a rather eccentric old man named Chiki, who had worked with wood all his life and would not give up in the face of a shrinking market for all his wares—hoe handles, pipes, "curiosity items"—the latter including a large replica of an airplane (wingspan about four feet); lifesize wooden shorts, complete with pocket holes; a long wooden snake swallowing a frog, carved from one branch of a tree; and last, perhaps least, sculpted figures. The one figure of his that I have (see plate 12) and a female figure that he showed me when I visited him were apparently not carved for any collective purpose.

The head of a compound where I was staying responded to my request for an *atsuku* figure—a small statue associated with one of the *akombo* (see Abraham 1940b, pp. 94, 136, 152 and plates)—by taking one of a few old figures he had stored away and revitalizing it. This consisted of going together to an abandoned hut, sacrificing a chicken, pouring the blood over the figure, recarving the face and neck slightly with a knife, and tying a string around its neck and another around its waist (see plate 13).

The household *adzov*, two posts that are not really figures when they are new and become completely featureless as food offerings are dripped on them daily, are still a fixture in most Tiv households. But sculpture of the kind pictured in the older ethnographies, the kinds of figures that Europeans like to collect and put in museums, has virtually disappeared from Tiv life within three generations of Western contact.

That this has happened in a culture renowned for its conservatism, a culture, moreover, in which other traditional crafts—song, dance, narrative—are flourishing, requires explanation. Most of the answer, I suspect, lies in a better understanding of that fourth dimension, time, that Fagg describes. Sculpture exists in space; it stands there, while life spins on around it. It's essential power resides in a sense of timelessness. It would seem that the minute clocks and historical calendars intrude upon "the changing same" of a traditional culture, these timeless forms begin to lose their energy, yielding it, perhaps, to the timelier modes of expression—narrative, song, dance.

A comparison with the Yoruba and a look at more recent developments in Armstrong's theory may be helpful here. While sculptural traditions have long been in decline among the Yoruba, they have certainly not disappeared, and this despite the fact that the Yoruba have been under acculturative pressure from Islam and have been coping with the interruptions of Western time for centuries, rather than decades. In *Wellspring: On the Myth and Source of Culture* (1975), Robert Armstrong elaborates the metaphor of "intensive continuity" in Yoruba forms along the lines indicated by the title with some supporting ideas about social structure integrated as well. Armstrong argues that Yoruba continuity in affecting works is interwoven with a hierarchical social structure tied down at one end by a belief in ancestors and at the other by a belief in reincarnation. Energies tapped are "cosmic," "infinite," "universal." Acts of creation, affective processes, are "additive," "incremental," "complimentary." The contrast with Tiv belief and social systems is sharp: no reincarnation; few ancestral ideas that bind; generational conflict; energies finite, human, hence competed for and particular; affective processes subtractive, incisive, contrasting.

Whereas Westernization, in the form of "indirect rule," reinforced the Yoruba hierarchy as it bent it to colonial purposes (Balandier 1966, p. 171), Westernization in Tivland, that is, the imposition of appointed chiefs, taxation, "witchcraft" investigations, and especially the abolition of exchange marriage in the late 1920s, exaccerbated the forces of individualism and the social discontinuities already present. Women were never easy to manage; now they pack and leave at will. Authority was always tentative; now it is further attenuated. The sculpted figures which embody continuity for the Yoruba persist. The Tiv figures, linked to big men, the central *akombo* (some of which must be passed on to sons of exchange marriages), and a Tiv sense of continuity as well, quickly lose their capacity to inspire awe and become symbols of the past rather than the affecting present.

It can be argued, I think, that all sculpture manifests some form of "intensive continuity" by virtue of its stability in the round and in space. Certainly many wooden figures from a variety of cultures throughout Africa manifest it, including Tiv and Fang (see below), where discontinuities can be pointed out only with the qualifier "relatively speaking." Relativity shades into uncertainty when one notes the dancing Shivas and Javanese puppets that Armstrong uses as examples of "extensive discontinuity"; not really sculpture at all.

As one reviewer put it:

One wonders why Armstrong has stacked the cards by contrasting cultures so clearly unrelated as those of Africa and Indonesia. . . . If Armstrong's argument is to hold, it must be demonstrated that his characterizations finely differentiate the "cultural metaphoric base" of the Yoruba from that of related African groups. . . . Short of a

more "controlled comparison" it is difficult to know what can be significantly compared. [Rosaldo 1973, p. 1461]

In the more recent Armstrong work the arguments are still elegant,
the comparisons still gross. This time the Yoruba are matched against
Western works of "intensive/extensive continuity"; "intensive/exten-
sive" as used by Armstrong covers the bipolar, extremes-meeting principle of so much Western art. The comparison of Yoruba and Western
tropes raises new and interesting questions for Tiv expression, for in
some respects the Tiv are more Western than Yoruba, indeed more
Western than West. If "intensive/extensive continuity" is the Western trope, might not a model of "intensive continuity/discontinuity"
produce a better reading of the Tiv forms? Until Armstrong and others
flesh out some of the missing paradigms ("extensive continuity," for
example), provide scales for measuring degrees of "extension" in space
and time, and so on, and apply this theory in more culturally contiguous field studies, we run the risk of playing with labels to our own delight and no one's edification. In the meantime, it is somewhat ironic
that the heavy focus on sculpture in Armstrong's theory, his Yoruba-
centrism, makes application to Tiv sculptural forms difficult.
   Let us look briefly at the spatial dimensions of the few Tiv figures
available.
   The statue in plate 12 was carved by Chiki and given to me by a
Tiv madman who called himself Gypsy Fullstop (among other titles)
and who claimed that the statue represented his former self, dead and
"cruciferous," before he was reborn as God Above. Whether he commissioned it or it served another function before he claimed it I do not
know. The overall form is generally columnar, hence continuous, and
there are no dramatic extensions of features, hence intensive, but one
basic Armstrong definition of discontinuity applies, "junctures of the
body are stressed at the expense of the long lines" (1971, p. 69)—that
is, sharp angles take the place of ankles (discontinuous); shortened
thick legs bent about forty-five degrees at the knees (discontinuous)
create a sense of vertical pressure up into the torso and down into the
base (intension); the hands are radically turned in at the wrist (discontinuous) and folded into the body (intension); elbows are quite
pointed, as might be expected, and would probably jut out more were
it not for the dictates of the log from which the figure was carved (repressed extension or discontinuity); the neck seems a columnar entity
unto itself (continuous), sharply demarcated from both head and torso

(discontinuous); head, torso, and particularly the thighs are well rounded (intension); small, precisely incised angles define eyes, mouth, and ears; the nose is a neat triangle, its edges only slightly smoothed off (discontinuous). Looked at from certain perspectives, as in plate 12, squatting legs and protruding elbows define various angles in space (intensive discontinuity).

The *atsuku* (plate 13) mentioned above is the only other Tiv figure I have before me, and aside from its unnaturally separated legs, it is the very model of intension. Two facial planes contain no eyes and angle to a point to form the nose. A single horizontal cut defines the bottom of the nose. A small angle makes a mouth. The arms are so in-folded as to be but a suggestion. The cross section of the lower torso is almost a perfect circle. Figural discontinuities at the waist and at the neck, where it joins the head, are heightened by the strings tied around them.

The ten *atsuku* figures illustrated in Abraham plates (1940b, plates 32 and 34, p. 88) are quite varied in style, some slender, some chunky; some with perfectly round eyes, others with angular slits. All but three have arms and hands well folded in. Neck juncture is a marked feature of most of them. But generalizations that cover all figures do not come easily. Intensive, yes, almost any panel of judges would agree on that, but sharper criteria will be needed to evaluate the continuous/discon-tinuous dimension. A basic problem here is that rigorous intension cre-ates a sense of the continuous, and vice versa. An even more basic problem may be that these ten figures were probably all done by dif-ferent carvers, and individuality of expression may have been just as much of an ideal for them as it is for composers of songs. In which case, a theory that uncovers cultural common denominators in Tiv sculpture will have to be very refined indeed.

Paul Bohannan's article "Artist and Critic in an African Society" contains a small photograph (Smith 1961, p. 102, plate 13 b; repro-duced here as plate 15) of two *twel* "fetish" statues that are a bad dream of intensive discontinuity come true! Tall, thin arms and hands pressed into sides, these poles give a feeling of intense vertical thrust, yet they are thoroughly disjointed. Rounded knobby knees seem to be holding calves and thighs together. The point of contact between the top of the legs and the bottom of the torso is so sharply articulated that it gives the illusion of two pieces glued together. Since the photograph is taken from the front, we'll probably never know, but a line midway in the arms suggest that angular elbows would be visible from the side and

240   rear. Breasts are large triangles and define an even larger triangle or cone between them that points, like a large arrow, to the head. Since the head hangs out over the neck somewhat, a shadow is created which gives the effect of a gap between head and torso. Even from such a small illustration, the faces glare out at us, deeply chiseled horizontals for mouth and nose, round eyes set beneath angled brows. If any sculpted figures embody the Tiv trope, these do. They also recall those stories (chapter 2) in which discrete body parts have roles to play.

The *twel* figures pictured in *Akiga's Story* (1965, plate 8a) also fit the theory, though not to such perfection. The male figure on the left is little more than a phallic post. While generally round in shape, the circumference is slightly faceted or angularized, a decagon perhaps. A head is indicated by a slight bulging at the top, and one horizontal line serves to suggest both nose and mouth. The full female figure shows discontinuity at ankles, knees, crotch, waist, and especially the neck. Small, almost perfectly rounded breast and navel "knobs" give the illusion of being pasted on. Arms, atypically, are free of the sides, elbows pulled back at an angle, and the hands are unusually large and blocked out. The neck is very elongated, a cylinder inserted between head and body. Two round eyes are set close together at the top of a triangular nose. Three rounded forms around the top of the head suggest stylized hair.

With the exception of a few small pieces in metal, this exhausts the sample of figures at hand for interpretation. It is encouraging that the presentation of intensive discontinuity is so clear in the largest and most traditional forms, the *twel* figures just described. Skepticism returns immediately, however, when one considers the range of expression in such a small Tiv sample or when one contemplates the statuary from other cultures, for example, the Fang pieces illustrated in the Fernandez article (Jopling 1971, pp. 364, 365), which are remarkably similar to some Tiv works, for example, plate 12 here. Fang noses are not as triangular; prominent lower lips tend to replace chins; concave faces are not the Tiv norm; breasts and elbows not quite as pointed; calves given greater weight; stricter symmetry perhaps; body parts flow into each other with more continuity than is found in most Tiv figures; but in general proportions, in the thick squatting legs especially, these could be pieces by another Tiv sculptor.

It is too easy for intensive discontinuity to be read into Tiv sculptures, or Fang pieces, since the rules or guides for reading from them have yet to be carefully worked out. One wonders if it is worth the trouble. These "beings" remain mute, and the analyst's points remain moot, for the most intensely discontinuous feature of Tiv sculpture is that Tiv have virtually discontinued doing it. We can perhaps afford to discontinue our studies of it as well, since there is so much happening in other fields of force that demand Tiv attentions and our own.

DRUMMING

The Drum of the Dance I clasp to my breast,
(Answer) Hie!
From the Drum of Death I draw aside, that it may pass by me, go down, and fall into the water.
(Answer) Hie!

Tiv drumming, more precisely *kwagh kuhan,* "thing beating," should be the subject of a book in itself. While the variety of percussion instruments and the techniques for each is great, from swinging a pair of children's rattles on a string to knocking out two-tone messages on the giant slit-log *indyer,* and while there are almost as many specific rhythmic patterns as there are drummers in Tivland (and every sizeable compound has at least one accomplished drummer), the basic principles involved are quite simple and can be described succinctly.

A two-tone, high-low, male-mother dialectic operates throughout *gbande* drumming and in most other percussion. At least 90 percent of the percussion sounds I heard in Tivland were produced on the *gbande* family—*ngou gbande,* "mother drum," and *nom gbande,* "male drum" (see plates 6, 7, and 8)—usually supported by the *kwen,* or "double bell." It is this ensemble that supports dancing and singing at millet beer halls in towns and major markets, and that is heard in numerous compounds on moonlit nights. Add a *gida,* "double-reed shawm," to the family and you have a *swange* band (plate 4), the delight of customers and prostitutes in the town nightclubs. *Ngou* and *nom gbande* are also used exclusively in the four or five most popular men's and women's dances and in most of the forty to fifty localized styles, where they are sometimes mixed with other drums, like *genga* or *ajo.* In these lineage-based dances (as opposed to the mixed town dances, like *swange*) the *ngou* and *nom gbande* are usually played as a pair by one man (plates 7 and 21a). Each of the four to eight drummers either sits on both drums or sits on a larger mother drum and

242

Sec. 1. Approximation of drumming for *Icough*

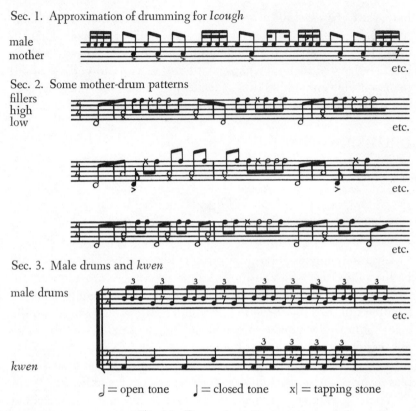

male
mother

etc.

Sec. 2. Some mother-drum patterns

fillers
high
low

etc.

etc.

etc.

Sec. 3. Male drums and *kwen*

male drums

etc.

kwen

♩ = open tone   ♩ = closed tone   x| = tapping stone

Fig. 19. Drumming patterns

cradles a male drum in his lap. Most beats are played on the higher pitched male drum, the mother drum supplying lower pitched accents (see fig. 19, sec. 1).

In the beer hall, market, and compound ensembles, however, one man plays the mother drum, using a round heavy stone held in his left hand to change the pitch from low to higher by pressing the stone onto the skin at a point just off the center, while the flat right hand hits an off-center point on the other side of the drum. Plate 6 shows a drummer about to hit a high tone, using this technique. When the stone is raised from the skin, the right-hand stroke produces a low tone. Occasional heavy accents are made with a glancing right-hand blow, fingers slightly open, stone usually off the head. A few mother drummers employ a third or higher tone in their variations by placing the stone at the very center of the drum. Tones lower and duller than normal are sometimes evoked by reaching back and placing the left or stone hand at or inside the open bottom of the drum. But essentially, mother drumming consists of high and low tones interspersed with what might be called "filler beats," made by the right hand striking the edge of the drum and also by barely audible taps of the stone. These filler beats can be open (bouncing strokes that let tones ring) or closed (pressed into the skin), usually the latter (see fig. 19, sec. 2).

A second player uses two male drums of different pitches, usually one between his legs, the other resting on his lap, to *tsorogh* the mother drum with repeated patterns and a few minor variations, as cued by the mother drum. If a *kwen* player is present, he simply goes back and forth between the high and low pitches of the double bell, usually in straight quarter notes or a "shuffle rhythm" (fig. 19, sec. 3).

One can superimpose the bar lines of section 3 over section 2 and gain a general sense of what the typical three-man drum ensemble sounds like, high and low pitches interpenetrating in a steady stream of "tripletized" or "shuffled" eighth notes, punctuated by the accented highs and lows of the mother drum.[9]

Where are circles-and-angles in all this? How is intensive discontinuity presented as a sequence of sounds in time? At the very simplest level, only men beat drums, and drums are round; male over mother is the basic symbolic message of Tiv drumming. At a step further along in the act of playing, hands move in and out, on and off the center of the drum; this technique, while not specifically Tiv, is not typically African either. Yorubas, Westerners, and—to the best of my knowledge —Javanese (to use Armstrong's points of comparison) do not drum this way. Furthermore, the round stone in the left hand, with the right hand doing virtually all the in-and-out-from-the-center tone production, is an intensified form of this general procedure, not reported elsewhere, still more specifically Tiv, if not uniquely theirs. But these interpretations only point toward the sounds and remain on the visual or spatial side of the space/time trope.

In the metaphorical sound sequence, the symbolic message, male over mother or angles into center, is reversed: the mother drum dominates or controls, plays the basic accents and variations, cues the male

9. I use the notion "tripletized eighth notes" to indicate an intangible, and as yet unmeasurable, quality of phrasing (Keil 1966a); that is, the triplets in section 3 and the eighth notes of section 2 should not be taken as a true three-against-two polymeter, though it is often suggested; rather, the beats of all three players fall somewhere in between eighth notes and "triplets with the middle note missing." While there is little polymetric drumming per se in Tivland, vocal melodic lines that are added to drumming are often in another meter.

drums for pauses, shifts in tempo, conclusions. To *tsorogh* is to "blend, counterpoint, support," and that is the role of the male drums and *kwen.* (If ethnographers were to assign as much importance to drumming as Tiv do, this metaphor might be the base for a revision of prevailing anthropological *and Tiv* conceptions of the patrilineage. Recent feminist analyses of women's roles in production and reproduction, plus the various residual-mother-right arguments offered by Rupert East in his annotations for *Akiga's Story,* suggest that these revisions might be extensive.) Working from the sounds back to the graphic image, one can say that each two-tone pattern in isolation (mother drum with left-hand stone, two male drums, double bell) defines a circle, three concentric circles. Yet the manner in which the highs and lows of the three players interpenetrate asserts angularity.

Intension is created by the steady stream of tripletized eighth notes and the constraints imposed by the limited range of the two-tone principle. Discontinuity is heard in the accents or "interruptions" of the mother drum and the less frequent variations of the male pair. The kinds of juncture phenomena, particularly stop-time, that Armstrong suggests as the key diagnostics for discontinuity in time are not a major feature of most Tiv drumming patterns, but occur much more frequently and dramatically in styles of more recent origin. In the preeminent modern style, *swange,* for example, stop-time, short mother drum breaks, and three or four abrupt shifts in tempo—two or three accellerations and a sudden return to the initial tempo—are basic features of any twenty to thirty minute performance segment. This stronger emphasis on the discontinuous aspect of the trope in recent styles echoes the arguments advanced with respect to social change and discontinuation of sculpture.

We must point again to the problem noted above, the intensive continuity of all sculpture, for if a "steady stream" of beats accounts for most of the intension in Tiv drumming, all African drumming could be described in terms of varieties of intension. It would probably not be too difficult, however, to develop a rating scale that would separate continuous/discontinuous percussion across the continent. Armstrong's characterization of Yoruba drumming as dense, atomistic, illustrating a type of pointilist continuity, seems a valid perception. Words fail, of course, but any Tiv drum ensemble sounds "choppier," "broken up," "back-and-forth" in comparison with a "fluid" Yoruba one. At some point it will be important to collect Tiv and Yoruba descriptions of each other's percussion, and the other media of expression too.

ENACTED NARRATIVE

Having described in some detail (in chapter 2) the enactment of Tiv tales, I need only summarize those elements so basic to the Tiv metaphoric base. In most cultures of the world, interruptions of a story being told are frowned upon, even tabooed and sanctioned; in Tiv they are the norm. The struggle is for the center of attention, is constant, and is perfectly overt.

> Sometimes it needed only the momentary inattention of part of the audience to embolden one of the other storytellers to jump into the center, even while another fable was being told. Then for a few moments we heard two tales, two songs at once. Soon people would take up only the one chorus and the other fable teller would sit down. [Bowen (Laura Bohannan) 1964, p. 287]

What clearer presentation of intensive discontinuity could one ask for?

The "opening shots" of Tiv tales, as we have seen, are targeted for the center of the expressive grid. Once there, the man of force exploits every angle to maintain the center—by shifting voices, introducing songs, or dancing different characters, or by making exclamations or asides, or by employing onomatopoetics. "*A ta urum*," "he shoots brightness"; one spark or shot or shift after another. Discontinuities create intension.

I once watched a storyteller hold an audience for over five minutes with a nonstory consisting almost entirely of double-talk and nonsense syllables. When his listeners caught on to the "plot," they laughed, and as it became progressively clearer and clearer that there never would be any plot, they laughed more and more until finally there was no more energy to be gained, and another storyteller burst into the center.

DANCE

In a book on Tiv song, the ultimate time-space spanner, dance, must take a penultimate position for the time being. Whether or not dancing is "the principal or central art" in West Africa, or in Africa as a whole, it most certainly is for Tiv. Quantitatively and qualitatively, by any measure I can devise, the amount of energy Tiv put into dancing must compare favorably with any culture anywhere.

If all the lineages of Tivland were surveyed, the list of dances known and named from past and present would total at least two hundred fifty, probably closer to five hundred. I have listed over one hundred. Of these, six or seven can be called traditional, or "dances of the fore-fathers"; these are or were embedded in rites of marriage (e.g., *Amar*), death (e.g., *Girnya*), and the acquisition of prestige by elders (e.g., *Ibiamegh*). Some of the traditional dances described by Akiga (1966, p. 15) and Abraham (1940b, pp. 60, 65) are falling into disuse or have stopped altogether. A few dances may be in the process of acquiring "traditional" status, perennial favorites that have enjoyed ten or more years of continuous performance. The rest have had widely varying degrees of popularity, diffusion, and longevity. Of the forty to fifty or more dances being performed in Tivland in any given season, the majority will have been in existence less than five years, and many of these will have disappeared in another five. Some are invented by one man or woman, are performed by one group for a season or two, do not diffuse, and are forgotten. Others represent current revivals of dances once discarded or the current phase of a long stylistic evolution. A man from one area may see the dance of another lineage, compose new songs for it, change the costumes somewhat, add a new twist or two, rename the "new" dance according to his fancy, and then organize his kinsmen to perform it.

How many of today's dances are products of transformation and diffusion of this sort, and how many are "independently invented" it is very difficult to say. A Tiv likes to list the dances of his area in sequence: "first there was *Kwaza*, then *Jiga*, then came *Inyon*, followed by *Ihinga*, *Iceghel*, and *Ingiogh*, then *Gbangi*, which became *Swange* that we are doing today." Though similarities between dances in the sequence are often pointed out, most Tiv insist that each dance is really a new dance, citing distinguishing features and perhaps a story of its origin to prove the point. Only a few people I have interviewed stress continuity rather than change, insisting that almost any "new" dance in question is but a revision of a predecessor. Further observations, comparisons, and polling of the experts may clarify this question, but in the meantime I make the usual ethnographic assumption that each dance name represents a distinctive style—in which case the variety of Tiv dances is astounding.

The most popular dances are performed by many groups. In September of 1966 it was possible to witness three different groups of women practicing *Atasa* within nine miles of each other along the road from Makurdi to Aliade. While these groups were part of a general *Atasa* revival, the competition between nearby minimal lineages and their elders is probably the primary reason for a burst of interest in a particular style in a particular area. "If so-and-so's women can do *Atasa*, we can do a bigger and better version," and "If the men of MbaJua are preparing *Gbercul,* we will do it so much better that they won't dare attend any market where we are performing." This lineage competition, coupled with the important functions of dances in courtship and the food, money, and prestige that accrue to any good dance group, insure that almost every large and well-established compound will be the nucleus for one or more dance groups.

These factors, of course, insure high quality as well as quantity. Tiv perfectionism culminates in the dance. It is claimed that some groups practice daily for six or seven months before the first performance; three months is probably the average preparation time. I was disappointed as often as not in my spot check visits to compounds where a dance practice at dusk was said to be part of the daily routine, but those few rehearsals I did witness were remarkable for the pains taken to achieve perfect synchrony within the line and between the dancers and drummers. In general, a new dance may be organized in April or May, practiced sporadically through June and July, intensively in August and September, first performed in October, and honed to perfection for the "Christmas season." As the rainy season approaches, the demands of agricultural labor increase and dance activity slackens. Formal lineage-based dancing seldom occurs during the peak cultivation months.

Tiv dances are usually very well organized. In fact, so far as I can determine, dance groups represent the highest degree of organizational complexity to be found in Tiv society. At any other Tiv event—for example, an *akombo* repair or a court case—there are usually no more than four or five roles to be filled, or parts to be played. But a performance of *Icough* (plates 21 and 22), a popular women's dance, usually requires: (1) a dance chief; (2) her assistant or coleader (both dance within or outside the circle, often opposite each other), (3) the leader of the line; (4) members of the line, (5) one or two smaller girls (also sometimes dancing as a pair within the circle), one of whom may be carried around the circle on the shoulders of a drummer at the end of the dance; (6) one or more "policemen" to keep the crowd from moving in on the dancers; (7) young men who press coins on the foreheads of their favorites; (8) senior women, mostly mothers of the girls, who mop the dancers' faces, hold coins, dust the dresses, ululate their support; (9) chief of the drummers, who may or may not have (10) an assistant chief, (11) drummers, (12) onlookers, and (13) a sponsor or sponsors; not to mention, of course, the compound head and usually other elders of the minimal lineage—at least a dozen roles and half as many concentric circles. This sort of role specialization and integration can not be found in any other Tiv activity, a matter of singular importance when we review the individualism, the personalization, that informs all the other affective presentations, a matter of even greater importance when we consider the imagined role specialization and nefarious cooperation of the *mbatsav* as they set about designating, killing, exhuming, reviving, dividing, distributing, and eating a victim in order to continue the vicious circle of flesh debts (Akiga 1965, pp. 235–95, esp. 250–51).

Why is dancing so important to the Tiv? Why a dozen new dances each year? What motivates the expenditure of time, money, energy? Why this exceptional cohesion and organizational complexity? Dance affirms life, negates death and the evil aspect of *tsav*, demonstrates the enduring solidarity of the lineage and the strength, the discipline, the power of its young men and women who, in marriage across lineage and clan lines, will procreate and perpetuate the Tiv people. These themes underlie all dances and are stated explicitly in many of the most popular styles.

The men's dances which are currently popular always display strength, speed, agility, and endurance, and often make a mockery of disease, witchcraft, and death. *Gbercul*, or "strike the forehead," is typical of those dynamically "hot" men's dances that are relatively uncostumed and stress agility. (See plate 16.) A long line moves swiftly through synchronized steps, and suddenly all heads dive at once, nearly touching the ground. In each of the seven or eight segments of this dance, somewhat different steps are punctuated by a variety of surprise unison dives.

Ingiogh (plates 19 and 20) parodies "dropsy," kwashiorkor, madness, muscular distrophy, and more; at a signal, a normal dance pattern is interrupted, and the dancers break from the line to distend their bellies grotesquely, take on idiotic grins, cross their eyes, and dangle or angle their arms, presenting a portrait gallery of total afflictions. At another signal, the situation returns abruptly to normal, the line moving in a circle. The dancers huddle around the inner drumming circle, and suddenly everyone is wandering around in a daze, holding up stuffed badgers and other rodent skins by the tail but acting as if they are unaware of what they hold. After some conventional circling, everyone gets the "staggers," and one dancer rolls over on his back, feet stiff in the air, dead. But he is quickly revived by his fellows. Now they dance their diseases in a line of bulging bellies, elbow thrusts, and shaking knees, facing out to the encircling audience (plate 19). One

dancer is able to touch his shoulder blades together, and no amount of
elbow jerking will get them unstuck. Again they wander aimlessly
(plate 20b), but suddenly paralysis sets in (plate 20a) and they hold
their stances until the laughter fades and the dance is resumed.

Some versions of *Agatu* feature a masked elephantiasis "victim," a
soccer ball slung beneath his loincloth. Onlookers come forward to kick
his inflated testicles and put money in his hand. In other versions, and
sometimes in the same dance, the climactic episode is a brief drama in
which a sorcerer slays a "doubting Thomas" with his "juju," shaking
two animal horns, with metal rings attached, until the skeptic keels
over. This victim is, of course, miraculously resurrected. All versions
of *Agatu* include sections (two or three of the eight to twelve) that
mimic the imagined movements of *amar a mbatsav*, "the dance of the
sorcerers." The dancers spin about wildly and then freeze in paired
positions (plate 18), almost touching each other. It is said that if sorcerers touch each other during their nocturnal dances, they will die
(Akiga 1965, p. 149).

These cryptic descriptions of a few features of three men's dances
(for a fourth, *Girnya*, see chapter 3) are, as it were, but the weak verbal
equivalents of some individual frames snipped from a hypothetical film
of many many hours duration. Given an infinite array of circles-and-
angles and intensive discontinuities in the many dances as performed
or as partially captured on film, the application of theory to hazy recol-
lections and still photographs seems ludicrous. Were the work of understanding the Tiv expressive universe to be done well, we would begin
with a long sound-synchronized film of dances and spin off a discussion of the other affecting forms from that.

Unfortunately, the one short film (*Tiv Women: The Icough Dance*)
that does exist is seriously flawed.

It is not an ethnographic or documentary film. The performances
have either been staged for or adjusted to the camera; costumes have
been changed (dresses covered with wrappers, pith-helmets and
shoes removed) to look more "native"; the usual audience of a few
hundred enthusiastic supporters pushing forward for a better look
or breaking into the dance to press coins on perspiring brows is altogether absent. A dance sequence of eight or more segments lasting
well over an hour has been reduced to interrupted portions of three
segments from two different groups. [Keil, 1969, p. 1234]

While the distortions noted were irritating at the time the review
was written, they seem more basic in the light of the theory of Tiv ex-

250 pression developed here. The removal of a surrounding audience, the absence of men breaking into the women's circle—both of these "adjustments" favor camera angles at the expense of Tiv angles and are at least understandable. But the wrapping of the dresses for the sake of some "authenticity" achieves the exact opposite of the effect intended. The dresses in the original dance, all flounced and starched out in circular hems around the knees, provided a moving circumference against which knee bends, elbow actions, and neck angles could counterpoint themselves. Similarly, the removal of pith helmets from the heads of the dance co-leaders seems a petty suppression to complain of until one realizes that two pivotal hubs that literally cap the presentation and balance the skirt circles are missing (plates 21 and 22). I can remember Peggy Harper in conversation describing the long and heated argument that preceded acceptance of her modifications, and at the time I accounted for it in terms of Tiv stubbornness. But more was at stake than I realized. Not only were the central symbols of a "rite of modernization" taken away or repressed, but the power of Tiv tradition to master those symbols, incorporate them into Tiv metaphor, was being denied.[10]

The best, the most authentic movement in the film occurs midway in the first segment as the double file of women makes its slow processional way to the dancing area, feet inching forward a step every few seconds, arms swinging freely in flowing patterns punctuated by flicks of the wrist that release a soft "shhhick" from the *icough* rattles held in the right hand. Suddenly one of the leaders backs onto the screen, head leaning back at an angle, dress unwrapped and jutting out nicely in front in response to her bent knees and arched back; her open hands are at either side of her face, palms out; her elbows are held out, as her forearms describe slow circles in the air. Then her hands flop to and past her sides (see background dancer, plate 21d), ruffling the dress, and she stands still for a second, head still tilted, before resuming the same pattern, this time moving forward and off the screen. It's only twenty seconds or so, but magnificent, glowing.

10. The modernization program continues apace in the newest fashion in women's dancing. As I was leaving Tivland in 1967, a dance called *Dasenda,* "policemen," was gaining popularity, in which, I was informed, semiuniformed young ladies with wooden rifles smoothed out some of the conventional drills to an accompaniment of exceptionally varied percussion. By contrast, a major men's dance that has emerged since I left is called *Kwagh Hil,* "folktale" or literally "thing miraculous"; it draws upon the characters and plots of tales for its dramatic action.

Although not strictly ethnographic, this *is* a dance film, and some remarkable moments of human grace are captured. The camera eye takes in the smooth, boneless mysteries of young Tiv ladies in motion, and the tape recorder very nearly synchronizes the steady, clipped segmentation of the continuum offered by the percussion. Labannotators and microanalysts beware; as well try to slice the Benue River with a machete. The drummers insist it can be done precisely. The unison flow of the women suggests acquiesence; indeed, their heads nod to the earth together and the barely audible swish of the rattles they hold in their hands links drummers and dancers. But where does a swish begin or a nod end? [Keil 1969, p. 1234]

Repeated viewings of the film have revealed a few interesting juncture points in the midst of the smooth, "cool," flow of forms that were not at first apparent, for example, a pronounced settling of shoulders and elbows (plate 21e) that concludes each "phrase" of the third segment, or the nodding heads in the second section (performed entirely from a kneeling position) which *do* touch the ground at specific instants. Eventually, I think, we will find that Tiv men and women share the same kind of limbs—both "in their muscular strength," *melea,* and "as moved by the joints," *guia,* (Snell, 1960, p. 5)—and use similar motions, the same circles and angles. It is only that the men exaggerate and break them apart, while the women fuse them together in slow motion.

Similarly, while the mocking of death and the miracle of rebirth are explicitly enacted in a number of men's dances, it is an implicit or subliminal theme in many women's styles. The kneeling section of the *Icough* could easily be a stylized version of women in mourning and could almost as easily be given a phallus-worship interpretation, since that symbol is at the very center of the bowing circle. Stories about the origins of particular dances begin with death. One dance is alleged to have begun when a woman who lost all her children was staggering in grief and anger, singing accusations at the suspected witch. Her distinct stagger and part of her song were picked up by another woman and elaborated into a dance. In another origin-tale a woman died, was duly buried, only to be exhumed and revived by the *mbatsav,* who took her to the forest of the dead and tied her to a tree. Night after night she watched the wizards dance until she made her escape and returned to perform the dance she had seen.

All observers agree that our category "religion" is diffused in Tiv be-

252   lief and practice: the linking, albeit tenuously, of the imagined powers of the *mbatsav* to once observable ceremonies of prestige acquisition and control of major *akombo;* the propitiations of minor *akombo* that shade into Tiv "medicine;" the divination practices that can point to *tsav* or *akombo* problems; those troublesome *adzov,* some of whom may be dead ancestors in disguise, others fit only for monster roles in tales, still others sent to trick the anthropologist into espousing theories of animism. It is all very murky and mostly negative, a series of bad dreams for Tiv and anthropologists alike. And so I would like to propose song and dance as the positive, brighter, human, and unimagined half of Tiv religion. More than the exhortations of the Introduction, the etymological speculations of chapter 1 and the assertion that dances function something like initiation rites is required to make this proposal persuasive. But it is my hope that anyone attempting an interpretation of Tiv religion or worldview or ideology in the future will at least evaluate the arguments which conclude the Introduction and the concise restatement of song-versus-*tsav* issues which follows. Not to include the experienced reality of song and dance life-forces is to picture the Tiv coping ineffectively with real and imagined evil, and this picture, in turn, can only serve to reinforce the murderous prejudices and practices of our Western world.

TSAV

The first citation from *Akiga's Story* adds an important moral dimension to "circles" (the rounded *tsav* of wisdom) and "angles" (the notched *tsav* of cannibalism), while the second gives a vivid picture of the final confrontation between "killers" and "musicians."

> According to the Tiv, *tsav* has actual material existence, and is a thing which can be seen and touched. The place where it is found is in a man's heart, and it can also sometimes be seen in animals, both domestic and wild. In appearance it is like the liver, but is not so broad or so thick. In man it is of two kinds. In some it is large and its edge is finely notched. This is the bad kind, the *tsav* of killing men and eating human flesh. In others, though it may be big, its edge is not notched, but rounded. This is the good kind, the kind of protecting the land; it is not the *tsav* of eating men, but the *tsav* of wisdom. As to its exact position, it is attached to the base of the heart. During youth it is quite short, but separates off when a boy grows up. In some cases it becomes detached while a child is still young.
> In the days before the white man came, if a man died the mem-

bers of his age-grade cut open his chest and examined his internal organs. If he had the serrated type of *tsav*, they said that he had brought about his own death, for with this kind of *tsav* he would not fail to be an eater of men. But if when they opened him up they found only the rounded type of *tsav*, they said that he had been killed out of malice, and that they would not let the matter rest. So they went to the diviner, and, having learnt who it was that had killed their age-mate, they called together all the members of their grade and subjected the man named to the *hoyo*. The knife which had been used in cutting open the body of the dead man was stuck into a tree by the side of a path along which many people would pass. Every one who saw it expressed his approval. "So-and-so belonged to a fine age-grade," they said. "His death is not being left to go un-avenged. His age-mates have cut him open to examine him, and though he is dead they are fighting his battles." [P. 241]

If the dead man was some one of great importance, he is not killed again at once. When they have brought him to life they first ask him many questions, and if he has any secret thing which he has been hiding from them he must declare (e.g., an *imborivungu* or ancestral relic . . .). If he was a composer in his lifetime, they tell him to com-pose a chorus for them to learn and sing by day; or if he sang solos, or played the pipe, or did anything else whatever, they force him to perform for them, before they kill him and hand him over to the *Haabuar* for cutting up. For the cutting up of human bodies only one knife is used throughout the whole group. The *Haabuar* shares out the meat, but gives the head to the man who provided them with the victim, because "The killer eats the head."

If a man has a very handsome child and is anxious always to take the lead at the nocturnal meetings, he will kill and flay the child, in order that he may wear the skin around his shoulders and so outshine all his companions. [P. 254]

SONG

Song is pulled out of (*dugh*) the chest or heart of particular individ-uals, a "quick subtraction after slow addition," and the verb *dugh* links the actualization of new songs metaphorically to catching fish, harvest-ing yams, collecting honey, withdrawing funds, deposing chiefs, filing down teeth, digging wells, marrying a non-Tiv wife, removing the dan-gers from an *akombo*, and exhuming a corpse by magical means, among other things. Like another verb, *gba*, "to create, to carve," *dugh* is mor-ally neutral, derived from an idea of motion, and indicates a tapping or transformation of more basic processes.

Song is "placed or fixed into" (*wa*) or "incised" (*gber*) into public consciousness. Other uses of these verbs suggest that singing may be like the processes of clothing or adorning oneself, making a bridge, tying a knot, and so forth (*wa* uses); wounding, scarifying, vaccinating, cutting a door in a wall, and so forth (*gber* uses); building (*wa*) and igniting (*gber*) a fire; placing (*wa*) or lifting (*gber*) a curse. One cannot cut down a tree (*gber kon*) without singing a song (*gber imo*).

A song created is like a yam harvested; a song sung is like a yam tip transplanted.

A praise song is like a roof raised over the person praised, a roof filled with social significance and some sexual symbolism.

Song is one kind of "voice" (*imo*) and is usually made of two parts (*icam*), individual calls and social responses.

Song begins, as does a tale, with a burst, a roar; it begins abruptly, like a shot or explosion; it is lifted up with force, like a roof frame.

Song responses are agreement, welcome, a joining in, catching something thrown, a seconding of the motion, or a blending.

Song is like a fluid—one can speak of brewing it like beer (staging a celebration), drinking it like medicine (learning to compose). Singers need a wet throat, while composers need a dry, clear system.

Song unites the "hot," high-loud-fast, and "cool," low-soft-slow, dynamics of men's and women's dancing.

Song, when it is good, is complete, clear, distinct, exact, detailed, thorough, accurate, purposeful, open, fluent, fearless, proud, dignified, crisp, precise, steady, vivid, perfectly clear and so clearly perfect (*tsembere*) that it glows (*wanger*), putting everything else in the dark.

Particular songs are not tied to particular emotions. Tiv are moved by songs but do not emote about them much.

Song and dance terminology indicate a basic male/female dialectic at work, the higher synthesis being a celebration of fertility or life.

Song is certainly sexual—phallic, seminal, vaginal, clitoral, coital. At least no character in a tale can perform intercourse without a song, and the call/response pattern is explicitly coital at times.

Song, to put it bluntly, fucks authority in the ass; kings never sing in tales. In life, songs seem to work exclusively to the advantage of the weaker party in a dispute. In recent politics, composers seem to have raised and lowered the status of party personalities significantly, to no great advantage for themselves.

Song, in the Tiv imagination, can distract an enemy, lead to masturbation, work wonders when sung on an "empty stomach," disguise spitting and substitute for farting, mask cannibalism or human sacrifice temporarily, and be a medium of energy exchange; and as noted above, those who sing are usually the energy gainers; those who don't, loosers.

Song is a mode of crying oppression and blaming those who caused it, begging for help and praising those who give it; a strategy for raising and lowering status, your own and others', in pursuit of drink, food, money, gifts, and women.

Song makers may earn pan-Tiv reputations, but their basic constituencies remain localized.

Songs are made, mostly by men, out of *ican*, poverty, mental anguish, physical affliction, and, some say, out of laziness.

Song-making can "cool your mind."

Tiv tend to see composers as gifted and the status as ascribable, while the composers usually stress desire, training, and achievement factors.

Composers are thought to be physically slow, mentally active, unusually stubborn, and prone to travel.

Song supply far exceeds demand, and composers often earn more fame than fortune.

Songs bring men together around the problem of women; while some women make songs, not enough is known about their motives, styles, and lyric content.

Songs are made in isolation, away from noise, away from women. The preferred position is lying on one's back, gazing up into the roof, and the preferred time is the night.

Songs are partially a product of unconscious or dream processes, at least for some composers.

While opinion varies markedly on the effectiveness of medicines for composing, those medicines that are used stress ingredients for (1) memorization, (2) clearing the system, (3) bird mimesis, (4) stimulation, endurance, and better voice qualities.

Opinion also varies on the relationship between words and melody, or *ikenge*, but it appears that most composers plug their lyrics into a preexistent melodic model which is reshaped by the parameter of phonemic tone. The other major parameter for song construction is motion as reflected in song meters, usually the motions of a particular dance.

Song reconciles discourse and dance, integrates words and motions, *ikenge* and *tsorogh* principles; speech is intensified, dance disguised, in song.

Songs tend to have a wide range that can be felt as extension or as discontinuity, since the high part of the range is loud or "hot," and the lower part soft or "cool."

Songs move downward in overall melodic shape, and usually in internal phrases as well. The striking use of wide descending intervals, for example, "interlocked fifths" (see figure 2), presents a drive toward base or ground, from high to low, from beginning to end, or from circumference to center along radii in the spatial model, from male to female in the sexual metaphor.

Song intervals in general and the high proportion of wide intervals in particular assert angularity, discontinuity, a mode of becoming.

The repetitive monotones, tonics, and sense of "double duration tones" provide the ground of being, the concentric circles, a sense of intension against which the intervals work in a friction of essential parts.

A preponderance of simple AB structures, the weighting of social responses as against individual calls, a lack of both overlapping call/response patterns and improvisation, tight unison singing, all contribute to the Tiv goal of perfect clarity and suggest, perhaps, an abiding respect for the individual song maker's achievement that is not often expressed without ambivalence as Tiv appraise the composing role verbally.

The expressive grid for Tiv song (figure 5) can be seen spatially in the roof, in the sawed cross-section of a tree, in the layout and sightlines of the compound (figure 6), in the conceptualization of lands (figure 8) and the world, in the patterns imprinted on pots (figure 9), in the common stool—two horizontal elements, seat and base (tonics), decorated with angles (narrow intervals) and joined together by three or four bent legs (wide intervals) (plate 14).

Every song, like every carved calabash and walking stick (figures 10–13), is a unique configuration of angles incised upon circles. While it is the round elements that contain or sustain in these two kinds of objects, the angles being mere surface decoration, in song the angles (intervals) move, dominate, and point to the sustaining elements (tonics).

Song is pain personally experienced, given form, and shared—individual scarifications in sound that can and will be borrowed as they fit.

Song is stance and gesture, the sound of "kinesics in context," elbows and bellies out (plates 2 and 7) in relaxation, attitudes that are further exaggerated when parodying the sorcerers (plates 17 and 18) or their victims (plates 19 and 20) in the dance.

If song is the dance disembodied, an echo of the fundamental space-time trope, a reflection in time alone of "the limbs in their muscular strength," then sculpture is the dance reembodied, frozen, mute, standing alone in space (plate 12). The inherent intension of sculpture and the equally fundamental discontinuity of singing are joined in the dance.

Drumming is midway between song and dance; while essentially a presentation in time more intensive than song, the physical action of drumming displays essential features of the spatial grid.

In tale-telling, as in singing, discontinuities create intension.

Song is incisive, another kind of knife—not the knife of the *mba-tsav*'s flesh divider, and not the knife of the age-grade's autopsy, though closer in spirit to the latter.

Song achieves measures of fame and immortality for its maker, not the other fame of the big man's *tsav*, and not the other immortality of the progenitor (though, of course, a man might be a chief and a father as well as a composer). Song is a child, but cannot be sacrificed;[11] song is flesh, but not negotiable for paying debts.

Song is sexual friction sublimated or transcended, and social conflict transformed.

Song is an energy, a power, a life force.

Song is.

I have been saying "song" rather than "Tiv song" in writing these definitions derived from specifically Tiv circumstances, because I believe that what song is for Tiv it was for us once upon a time and can be again. Song is an energy that can be generated by a variety of frictions and conflicts, but the deep and dialectical ones—individual vs. society, male vs. female, exploiters vs. exploited—work best. These conflicts and other oppositions only a little more abstract, such as the tension between language and dance as modes of communication, are seemingly inexhaustible resources for song energy in the West. To say that we share these oppositions with the Tiv people is not enough. Our failure to confront these dilemmas is destroying us. Song as a higher synthesis of these oppositions, song as a resolution of small problems in everyday life (Gari Kwaghbo shortchanged by the tailor; Kuji Iyum jilted by Dondoaor), and song as a counterforce to evil, disease, and death are all *imo* for Tiv and what you can *dugh* individually when *ican* has you down. Dance and enacted tales do the same thing more collectively, more dramatically, more powerfully, for Tiv. Whether the name or *logos* for all this activity in Tiv life is "intensive discontinuity"

11. See the conclusion of the discussion of songs in Appendix A for a further elaboration of this theme.

258

and whether the logogram or "logo" for it is "circles and angles" is much less important than the value we place on these forms of expression.

Tiv see and hear, know and understand the great value of song, drama, and dance in the struggle for justice and equality. But do we? Most of us no longer have these skills, sharpened by constant practice; and those who do have been very carefully trained to display their arts rather than apply them. We don't *dugh* anything when we feel cheated at the department store or supermarket. Gari Kwaghbo, where are you? Pathetically few of us sing out when the killers in charge say they want a new bomb that sacrifices people but saves property.

Compared to Tiv activity in the song and dance spheres (see Introduction, footnote 3), our passivity is very impressive. Over the past few generations we have been increasingly willing to let others make music for us. If we continue to tune into radio and television, if we keep consuming things called "singles" and "albums" and "tapes" by the billion rather than make songs for ourselves, we should not be surprised to find that these songs, and the tales and dances that are sold to us too, are designed to help us escape our reality. Certainly they don't help us to confront it. Fieldwork in Nigeria taught me that reality moves right along, with or without you; that trying to ignore or escape it is often fatal; and that—to answer Kuji Iyum's basic question—only madmen and specialists can face reality "in a completely confident state." In these times, even they have their troubles and worries.

So to survive we need to make songs of our own that are like Tiv songs, in both quantity and quality. We need to make songs like Auta Anwuna's that can frustrate the big men into bad health. We need songs like Anande Amende's that can persuade people to shift their political loyalties. We need song makers like Gari Kwaghbo to combat planned obsolescence. We will know that we have real protest songs again when their composers find themselves sitting not in plush homes counting their royalties, but in prisons counting the days. Even without elections, Tiv jails have their composers in residence, whose songs were too successful. We need songs with what the ancient Greeks called *ethos,* the power to define values, to shape character, and to challenge what only seems to be our fate. And we need to learn much more about song-making processes in those societies where songs still have this energy.

If you, the reader, can't pull out such a voice yourself just yet, keep up the slow addition of felt injustices, keep trying, and be ready to join in the chorus when you hear the call.

Epilogue

WHEN I think of all the things that should be in this book but are not, I want to cry, blame the British for the Nigerian army, praise the Bohannans, and beg for help. Obviously, more books, chapters, and verses need to be added to *Tiv Song*. A sociolinguist and kinesics-in-context person could move us well beyond the dry dictionary that is chapter 1 and the bits and pieces on stances and gestures in chapter 5 into the whole unexplored terrain of actual interaction and ongoing creative processes. Tiv tales have long deserved a volume of their own that might also put the theories of Freud, Jung, Propp, Lévi-Strauss, and Marx to the test. A more sophisticated musicologist could work wonders if the tentative hypotheses concerning song production offered here are even partially correct. Most important, women's songs and dances require intensive study.

Eventually, I hope to spend at least a few summer months in one or two large compounds, living with composers and observing dance groups in rehearsal. And I would, of course, like to spend four to six weeks in Tivland during the peak of the dancing season (December and January), filming dance groups and singers and everyday life with the best possible sound synchronized equipment. With or without these two short field trips, I hope to be able to expand some of the opening and closing arguments about art as my understanding of Marxist critical theory improves and as I hear from any readers who may find this work worth criticizing.

Song Transcriptions

The transcriptions included in this appendix are of eleven Tiv songs that are typical but not a representative sample. They are included here as supporting evidence for some of the generalizations made about intervals, tonics, and general structure in the concluding pages of chapters 4 and 5.

Structure

All of these songs follow the call and response pattern so commonly found in African songs. The calls and responses do not overlap consistently, however, and in some songs there is a slight pause between the leader's statement and the chorus's rejoinder. By structural criteria the eleven songs may easily be divided into two groups, simple and complex, though none of the truly complex genres, for example, *ibiamegh*, are represented here. Songs 4 through 8, as well as 1 and 11, have a single call and response pattern, AB, repeated throughout, although the calls in song 5 vary slightly, and in song 11 two variations of the same call alternate with each other, while the response remains constant. Calls are always of one phrase, while responses may be divided into two or three phrases. Excepting 2, 3, 10, and 11, all songs have more than one phrase in response. In songs 2, 3, 9, and 10 the structures may be viewed in terms of macrostructures (A's and B's) and microstructures, the clusters of calls and responses (c's and r's) which make up the larger units, as follows: song 2, A(cr)A(cr)B(c′r′)A(cr) B(c′r′)C(c″r″)C(c″r″)C(c″r″)C(c″r″); song 3, A(crcr)B(c′r′c′r′ c″r″)B′(c′r′c″r″)A(crcr)B′(c′r′c″r″)B(c′r′c′r′c″r″); song 9, A(cr) B(c′r′)A(cr)B(c′r′)B(c′r′)A(cr). Attempting to structure song 10 by grouping c's and r's in this fashion, one finds a macrostructure something like ABCDCA(?)EEEEECDCDA(?)B, or condensed to a still higher level by grouping the AB, CD, and E sections, ABCDBBA. The problem here is that while two responses alternate fairly regularly in the song, the calls vary a great deal and do not seem to fall into any regular matching pattern with responses. The only rule for matching c's and r's in this song is that, with one exception, c13, calls ending in a rising split fifth figure, ACE, are followed by a falling GD response, and calls ending in a r-f (rising-falling) ACA figure are followed by a rising GC response. This may be the one song in the set where the leader improvises.

Duration Tones and Subjective Tonics

The duration tone, the one sounded most often or with the greatest durations, stands out clearly in songs 1, 2, 4, 6, and 8, a single circle in the visual model. Song 8 is the only song, however, in which the duration tone dominates all other tones completely. In song 2 the duration tone differs from the subjective tonic (a hypothetical pedal or harmonizing tone felt to be underlying the melody). In song 4 it is a listener's choice whether C, the duration tone, or F is the subjective tonic. This listener's-choice situation prevails in all the other songs as well, and it is difficult, if not impossible, to select a single duration tone, for in some instances a single note in the duration count may separate one candidate for the status of duration tone from its nearest rival. In songs 5, 7, and 9 three tones are in competition for the preeminent position. Certainly in the Tiv context the subjective tonic well deserves its name, and most songs could be mapped with two or three concentric circles. Often one "tonic" or implicit pedal tone seems to be the foundation of the calls, while another fits the responses more appropriately. With the exception of song 5, the duration tone is either *do, re, sol,* or a combination of these, *re-sol* being the most common duality (songs 3, 7, 10, 11). In the latter songs the subjective tonic seems to coincide with *sol;* in others, again excluding song 5, it coincides with *do.* As one might infer from the high frequency of fourths and fifths (36 percent of all intervals; see table 2), Tiv like to explore the melodic possibilities of these intervals; any implicit or subliminal harmonic theory we care to construct for them would probably be built on these intervals as well. This would suggest that at some level or other the circles-and-angles (tonics-and-intervals) of chapter 5 are the same.

TABLE 1. INTERVAL PERCENTAGES   263

| Song No. | Percentages of Each Interval by Semitones—Ascending | | | | | | | | | | | | Number |
	1	2	3	4	5	6	7	8	9	10	11	12	
1	2	50	17	5	22	—	—	3	—	—	—	—	65
2	—	50	13	6	31	—	—	—	—	—	—	—	52
3	9	70	9	2	9	—	—	—	—	—	—	—	43
4	—	55	18	—	27	—	—	—	—	—	—	—	88
5	1	43	17	—	33	—	5	—	1	—	—	—	78
6	—	7	43	14	36	—	—	—	—	—	—	—	98
7	3	53	11	—	33	—	—	—	—	—	—	—	93
8	—	66	16	1	16	—	—	—	—	—	—	—	97
9	—	36	9	18	36	—	—	—	—	—	—	—	66
10	—	34	23	4	34	—	—	—	—	—	—	—	56
11	—	70	12	6	13	—	—	—	—	—	—	—	119
												Average	77

| Song No. | Percentages of Each Interval by Semitones—Descending | | | | | | | | | | | | Number |
	1	2	3	4	5	6	7	8	9	10	11	12	
1	—	18	6	8	55	—	—	2	6	5	—	—	62
2	—	46	11	5	16	—	22	—	—	—	—	—	37
3	10	48	—	2	20	—	10	—	—	10	—	—	40
4	—	—	—	10	25	—	56	—	—	9	—	—	71
5	—	—	—	14	57	—	11	—	12	12	—	—	49
6	—	22	—	—	22	—	11	45	—	—	—	—	63
7	—	14	13	19	37	—	17	—	—	—	—	—	78
8	—	37	—	—	11	—	14	25	13	—	—	—	63
9	5	60	—	—	20	—	5	—	—	—	—	10	60
10	—	24	14	2	34	—	26	—	—	—	—	—	50
11	—	14	—	36	25	—	25	—	—	—	—	—	89
												Average	60

Melodic Interval Patterns

In order of importance or frequency, the outstanding melodic patterns in Tiv song are repetitive monotones (interpreted as stabilizing or circular elements), pendular fourths, and interlocked fifths (the basic angles).

Song 1 has twenty-three triple monotones, on C at the beginning and end of each call and at the beginning of the second and third phrases of the response, on E at the beginning of the response, and on A at the end. The song is full of simple pendular fourths, CGC and

TABLE 2. PERCENTAGES OF EACH INTERVAL IN THE TOTAL SONG BODY

Semitones	1	2	3	4	5	6	7	8	9	10	11	12	Number
Ascending	1	49	18	5	26	—	.7	.2	.1	—	—	—	855
Descending	1	24	4	11	29	—	18	7	3	2	—	.5	662
All Intervals	1	38	12	7	28	—	8	2	1	1	—	.5	1,517

TABLE 3. PERCENTAGES OF NARROW, MEDIUM, AND WIDE INTERVALS

Tiv	Ascending	Descending	Both
Narrow	68	29	51
Medium	5	11	7
Wide	27	60	42

Other Bantu Speaking Groups	Bashi	Yovu	Tiv
Narrow	79.4	68.7	51
Medium	9.5	12.9	7
Wide	11.0	18.4	42
Total Descending	55.2	69.3	44
Total Ascending	44.8	30.7	56

GCG in the calls, GDG and DADA in the responses. The latter set forms part of an interesting descending pattern consisting of a half note E followed by the pendular fourths, then interlocked fourths, and finally a major sixth falling to the duration tone C and stepping up to D, that is, EDADACGACD.

In song 2 repetitive monotones again appear every other measure or so. Some responses consist simply of four quarter note C's in succession, and the two longer responses end in D repeated four times. Every call in the 4/4 section ends on a triple monotone, either G (before C responses) or A (before responses ending on the D monotone). Interlocked fifths, f (falling), are prominent in calls 3 and 6, and simple pendular fourths, f-r (falling-rising), occur in calls 7 and 9.

Song 3 has eighteen monotones sprinkled through its thirty-four measures—six triple, three quadruple, seven quintuple, and two sextuple. Almost every phrase begins with a series of D's, or, less frequently but more repetitively, G's. Half of the responses are built around interlocked fifths, f, DGCF, though a passing C tone follows the first D. A falling minor seventh occurs in the middle of the other responses.

Song 4 is so typically Tiv that it was used as an example in chapter 4 (figure 2).

Song 5 has a quadruple monotone in the middle of the first phrase of every response, preceded by a rather atypical descending series of seconds and thirds and followed by a simple pendular fourth, r-f EAE. The second phrase of the response has two additional sets of EA pendular fourths, the first r-f-r and the second a simple r-f pattern. The first call has a repetitive monotone on F, the second a simple pendular fourth, GCG r-f, and the sixth call a pendular fifth, r-f FCF.

Song 6 has fourteen triple monotones, one at the end of each call, C, and one at the end of the first phrase of each response, G. A triadic split fifth, r ACE, occurs twice in every call: a pattern of minor sixth, f, triadic split sixth, r EGC, occurs four times in each response with a pendular fourth, GCG r-f, linking the first pair of such patterns with the second pair.

Song 7 has five quadruple monotones, one at the beginning of each response. The first call has two simple pendular fourths, r-f DGD, but the other calls do not. There are three pendular fourths in each response, the first an inversion of those in the calls, the second and third matching the call pattern exactly; the latter, coming at the end of each response, also forms part of a set of interlocked fourths, f GDFC.

In song 8 a C triple monotone occurs at the beginning of both phrases in the response. The same pattern noted in song 6—a descending minor sixth, CE, followed by an ascending split minor sixth, EGC —occurs twice in each phrase.

Song 9 has no less than twenty-seven monotones. Neither pendular fourths nor interlocked fifths appear, but rising split sixth figures, all major, are in some calls and in all responses. In the calls a jump up from C to A is mediated by D and F. In the responses the rising major sixth, F to D, usually follows an octave drop, and the intervening notes are either GA or A.

All the responses in song 10 consist of a fourth drop and a triple monotone on D, alternating with a fourth jump up and a triple monotone on C. The calls are somewhat atypical, as no monotones are found and minor pendular thirds are sometimes encountered. One descending interlocked fifth and fourth pattern, GCDA, also appears in most calls, the fourth shifting to a fifth, EA, in two of them.

The eleventh song is completely without monotones and is unique in this respect. A pendular fourth response and a falling interlocked fifth pattern at the conclusion of odd-numbered calls are the only distinctive features.

The titles for these songs were supplied by Prof. Sowande on the original tape; each subtitle in parenthesis is a translation of the first line of the song.

Though an explication of Tiv song texts is a project in hermeneutics for the future, song 1 deserves a special note. It is by Bam Gindi, the outstanding Tiv composer of the mid twentieth-century period, and though brought forth approximately twenty-five years ago, it is still well known in Tivland today.

Leader: M mar wan shin ikyo   M dugh akuul
        (I begot a child in the forest   I take out claws

        eren er anyam u korun yo.
        like the leopard that seizes.)

Chorus: Ayaya Churbenga or a soom ga nan de.
        (Hey there, Churbenga, a person who doesn't like me
          should leave.)

        Mo iyol yam   kpa m soo nan ga
        (I myself   I don't like him either)

        Ayaya wuruu   Bam Gindi mar wan shin ikyo
        (Ayaya wuruu   Bam Gindi begot a child in the forest)

In addition to expressing Bam Gindi's joy at having fathered a child in the big city (Lagos or Ibadan), his eagerness to protect it, and his defiance of those who don't like him, it is also, I think, a song about a song.

The short call establishes (1) that song is a child, given birth to under adverse circumstances in the jungle of the city; (2) that song is incisive, brought out (*dugh*) like the claws of a leopard; (3) that it can seize the public imagination. The chorus, which in a sense has become all of Tivland, joins Bam Gindi and his friend Churbenga in affirming these claims, celebrating the composer's defiance of those who would demean a composer like Bam Gindi, a man, after all, who can describe in a dozen exceptionally well chosen and melodized words what it takes an anthropologist a few hundred pages to discover, minus, of course, any memorable melody.

Bam Gindi's call was my very first introduction to Tiv song fifteen years ago. My response has been a little slow in coming.

Song #1

"Love and Hate"
(I begot a child in the forest)

♩ =176

Leader

M mar   wan shin   i-kyo m du- gh a   kuur   er-en

Chorus

er an- yam u ko-run   yo- o   A   yaa(aya)   Chur- ben-

ga   or   a   so-   om   ga   nan   de   Mo   iyol   yan

kpam   soo   nan   ga   A   ya   ya   wu-ruu   Bam- gin-di mar

wan shin ikyo

268

Etc.

Song #2   "The Yam Spoiler"
                     (Kokoityo, pull away the yam vines)

♩=170

Leader

Ko-ko-ityo tu- le i- youv a- gar- o

Chorus

Me Ko- ko- ityo tu- le i- yol a- gar- o

tu- le tu- le

A ku- me yor-o kpa ya dzwa   na

tu- le tu- le

Ooo
To Coda
after D.S.

To Coda
after D.S.

yo o oo   oo   Ko- ko- ityo tu- le iyo- uv   tu- le tu- le

Song #3 "I'll Forget My Sufferings"
(I will tie up my sufferings and go to Ugondu)

♩=160

Leader

Me kan-ge ican too ya me yem sha Ugon-du

Chorus

Kan-ge ican too ya me yem sha Ugon-du

270

dzo-ho we   I   dzo-ho we   I-a   dzo-ho yo i son-gu

Ei   Ei

O o o o o   i-a   dzo-ho yo i son-gu

D.S. al 𝄐

D.S. al 𝄐

𝄐 Coda

𝄐 Coda

Song #4   "Women's Advice"
(That one you love, what does he give you?)

♩=152

Leader

A doo we   la-a nau nyi

Chorus

Ir or lo doon we

la-a na-u nyi   Mis-tah Nyi-nya do-o-m wan wam-aa

Ir or lo do-o-m wan wam

Etc.

Song #5

"I've Been Warning You"

(I warned you not to steal)

♩=152

Leader

Me ven-da   kwagh mba-iv a we

Chorus

Or ir wa-ma-o me ven-da

u gba ye-

kwagh mba-iv a we   U ung-wa ga   U gba ye-men sha tor ve

men sha tor ve

Etc.

Song #6   "The Wrongdoer Will Be Punished"

(He unsheathed his knife, see how he wounded "my child")

♩=144

Leader

Tsu-a (i)shom nen- ge er   vi-hi   wa-n iyol-o

Chorus

Or

ya tsu-a ishom nen-ge er   vihi wan iyol-o   Or   ya tsu-a ishom nen-ge er

vihi wan iyol-ooo

Etc.

274 **Song #7**   **"She Reaped What He Planted"**
(She ate pepper, but it was hot in my mouth)

♩=140

Leader

A ya mke-m   yu-wa ma- a-   aa- aa

Chorus

Ma u

ver-em gben-da, ma m yem A- ni- ca   ma m   dza kor wa-n won-du

Mba-ya-ga ya mke-m   yu-wa ma-a-   a- aa

Etc.

Song #8   **"Song of Comfort"**   275

(She should stop crying)

Song #9   **"Poor Amande"**

(He picked up and started pounding)

276

Ngu kaan er or kyer wam wu-a or ga

A-man-de shi nam i-shwa i or i-ker m ku-me

To Coda
after D.S.

Or i-ker ka wa- u- u am ku

To Coda
after D.S.

A-man-de too i-shwa ku-me sha iyol na ve

ga

A-man-de too- ma ag- bo u ikya A-man-de dzen-den faan shin

D.S. al Coda

D.S. al Coda

shi-maaa

D.S. al Fine

D.S. al Fine

Song #10   **"Beggar's Riches"**
(I told you before to bring a sack)

♩=144

278

Kwagh shen m kaa mer   va-   a i- bya ne- o

ung-wa

To kar ooo

va- a ta- kar- a- da

Song #11   **"Old Tiv War Song"**

(Weuoo . . . . a leopard has given birth)   ♩=168

Leader

O we- u- o   we- u- o   we- u- o anyam mar

Chorus

Oh-ooo anyam mar

We-u-u- o   we- u- o   o-o- o   anyam mar nyi-a-na

280

Etc.

Questionnaire

The following questionnaire was used as a guide by the five students whose reports are the basis for the second half of chapter 3 and portions of chapter 4.

During your vacation I would like you to gather as much information as possible about every composer (or *u dughun amo*) and all the dance groups in your area. For each dance group that you report on, you should try to answer the following questions in detail.

D1 What is the name of the dance?

D2 Who is the "*tor ishol*"? His name, age, fathers' names, "*ipaven*"?

D3 Where exactly is he located?

D4 What is the history of this dance?
(a) Where did it start? (b) When did it start? (c) Who started it? (d) Why did he (or she) start it? (e) How did the starter or originator get the idea for it? (f) If the dance didn't start in your area, who was the first to bring it there? (g) How many other groups are doing the same dance now? And where are they located? (h) What does the name of the dance mean exactly?

D5 How was the dance organized and practiced in your area? (Ask the dancers themselves for all the details.) When, where, who, how often, how long, did they practice the dance before bringing it to the public?

D6 If possible, try to list ALL the names and ages of the participants in the dance group and the job of each (for example: leader, assistant leader; members or "laborers" 1, 2, 3, 4, 5, etc.; leader of drumming; "policemen"; sponsors; and so forth).

D7 How often is the dance performed? How often in the wet season? In the dry season? During the Christmas holidays?

D8 What are the different parts (stages) of the dance? Number the stages (the dances I have seen usually have between eight to twelve parts) and describe each stage briefly. Do they follow any particular order? Can the order be changed? Can some parts (stages) be left out if necessary? What parts of the dance are most important? Why are they important? Is it ever declared that one person in the group is the "winner" or "champion" of the dance? How does the audience decide that one dancer or some dancers are better than the others? Which motions in this particular dance are most pleasing?

D9   What adjectives, adverbs, phrases do people use to describe the general style of this dance, and particularly those motions (steps, movements) that are pleasing. (Write these words or phrases in Tiv first and then in English translation.)

D10   What instruments are used to accompany the dance? How many of each?

D11   Who composed the songs for this dance?

D12   If the dancers receive a goat from their host, how is it divided? Who gets which parts and why?

When talking with a composer, ask him the following questions and add to your report any other information you may obtain concerning these questions as well.

C1   His full name, age, father's name, names of forefathers.

C2   His *ipaven*, largest to smallest.

C3   Name of *or ya* at his home or childhood compound.

C4   A brief biography, the story of his life; be sure to include information about his original family (father, mother, mother's co-wives, brothers, and sisters) and his own family (wives, children).

C5   What are the different types of songs that he knows how to compose? List these in Tiv with English translations. Which type of song has brought him the most fame and attention? Why is this so?

C6   If he is known for singing praising songs, take down the names and locations of the persons he has praised and what rewards he may have received from each person.

C7   During the time of politics did he ever compose songs for a particular party or of a political nature? If so, which party and what effect did his songs have? If no, why didn't he?

C8   Has he ever been abused by another composer? If so, explain fully. Has he ever been employed by one man to abuse another man? If so, please give all the details of the dispute—how it started, what happened, how it ended? What part did the composer (or composers) play in the dispute? Who "won"? (Or did everyone "lose"? [Note to Research Assistant: Many composers claim that they never sing abusing songs, but you should check up on this matter with other people in the area; if you hear of any dispute or argument between big men in which composers were taking part, please make a full report on it.]

C9   Who helps him with his composing and singing? Give the name of each helper and describe the way in which he helps.

C10   Does he ever compose songs for particular dances? If so, which dances? Where are they located? What did he receive for his compositions? When was he doing this? Is he still doing it?

C11 When did he start to make his own songs?

C12 Why did he decide to become a composer?

C13 How did he go about it? Did anyone teach him how to compose? If so, who? If not, how did he learn the work?

C14 Did he ever take any medicine to help him compose songs? If so, who gave it to him? What were the ingredients of the medicine and how does each ingredient help the work of composing? Are there different kinds of medicine that you can take for composing? Are there separate medicines for composing and other medicines for singing? Or will one medicine do for both? If he has never taken any medicine for composing (or singing), why didn't he do so? Did he inherit his composing ability? If so, from whom?

C15 What must a man do to become a successful composer? Try to make a list of the things a man must have or must do to become a great composer.

C16 How does he judge whether another singer is good or bad?

C17 How does he judge whether another composer is good or bad?

C18 Which other composers and singers does he admire? What does he like about them? What words does he use to describe good singing and good composing (in Tiv, with English translations)?

C19 Ask these questions (numbers 15, 16, 17, 18) of any knowledgable person (or u fan kwagh) in your area, not only composers and singers. I would like to have the opinions of any older people who have experience and have thoughts about such matters. You can ask anyone (yourself included): "What qualities do you like in a composer?" "What sort of singing pleases you?" "How should the voice sound?" Etc., etc. (Write answers in Tiv and English.) But please identify each person whose opinions you report.

C20 How does the composer actually make new songs? Describe the process of composing a new song, point by point, stage by stage. How does he begin, what next, what comes after that, how does he know it is finished? What is the hardest part of making a song? What is the easiest part of the work?

C21 If he hasn't already talked about the following questions when answering question 20, ask him which comes first, the melody or the words? How does he fit the words and melody together? If he took medicine, did it influence the shape of his melodies? How?

C22 Does he do any other work besides composing? What is it?

C23 What do other people in the area say about him? What do they say about his character? Temperament? His songs? Other activities?

Bibliography

Abraham, R. C. 1940a. *A dictionary of the Tiv language*. London: Crown Agents.

———. 1940b. *The Tiv people*. 2d ed. London: Crown Agents.

Akiga. 1965. *Akiga's story: The Tiv tribe as seen by one of its members*. Translated, annotated, and edited by Rupert East. 2d ed. London: Oxford University Press.

Ames, David W., and King, Anthony V. 1971. *Glossary of Hausa music and its social contexts*. Evanston: Northwestern University Press.

Anderson, Warren D. 1966. *Ethos and education in Greek music*. Cambridge, Mass.: Harvard University Press.

Armstrong, Robert P. 1971. *The affecting presence*. Urbana: University of Illinois Press.

———. 1975. *Wellspring: On the myth and source of culture*. Berkeley: University of California Press.

Arnott, David W. 1964. Downstep in the Tiv verbal system. *African Language Studies* 5: 34–51.

Balandier, G. 1966. *Ambiguous Africa*. New York: Pantheon.

Beidelman, Thomas O. 1961. Hyena and rabbit: A Kaguru representation of matrilineal relations. *Africa* 31, no. 1: 61–74.

Benedict, Ruth. 1934. *Patterns of culture*. Boston: Houghton Mifflin.

Blacking, John. 1967. *Venda children's songs*. Johannesburg: Witwatersrand University Press.

———. 1972. *How musical is man?* Seattle: University of Washington Press.

Bohannan, Laura. *See* Bowen, Elenore Smith.

Bohannan, Laura, and Bohannan, Paul. 1969. *The Tiv of central Nigeria*. 2d ed. London: International African Institute.

Bohannan, Paul. 1956. Beauty and scarification amongst the Tiv. *Man* 56, no. 129: 117–21.

286

————. 1957. *Justice and judgment among the Tiv.* London: Oxford University Press.

————, ed. 1967. *Law and warfare.* Garden City, N.Y.: Natural History Press.

Bohannan, Paul, and Bohannan, Laura. 1958. *Three sourcebooks in Tiv ethnography.* 3 vols. New Haven, Conn.: Human Relations Area Files.

————. 1968. *Tiv economy.* Evanston: Northwestern University Press.

————. 1969. *Five sourcebooks in Tiv religion.* New Haven, Conn.: Human Relations Area Files.

Bowen, Elenore Smith [Laura Bohannan]. 1964. *Return to laughter.* New York: Doubleday.

Bunker, H. A. 1934. The voice as a female phallus. *Psychoanalytic Quarterly* 3: 391–429.

Burke, Kenneth. 1969. *A grammar of motives.* Berkeley: University of California Press.

Canetti, Elias. 1963. *Crowds and power.* New York: Viking Press.

Chinweizu. 1975. *The West and the rest of us.* New York: Random House.

Clarke, Kenneth W. 1958. A motif-index of the folktales of culture-area V, West Africa. Ph. D. dissertation, Indiana University.

D'Azevedo, Warren L., ed. 1973. *The traditional artist in African societies.* Bloomington: Indiana University Press.

Dentan, Robert K. 1968. *The Semai: A non-violent people of Malaya.* New York: Holt, Rinehart and Winston.

Deren, Maya. 1953. *Divine horsemen: Voodoo gods of Haiti.* London: Thames and Hudson.

Devereux, George. 1961. Art and mythology: A general theory. In *Studying personality cross-culturally,* edited by Bert Kaplan. Evanston, Ill.: Row Peterson.

————. 1967. *From anxiety to method.* New York: Humanities Press.

Dewey, John. 1934. *Art as experience.* New York: Minton, Balch.

Diamond, Stanley. 1974. *In search of the primitive.* New Brunswick, N.J.: Transaction Books.

Dietherlen, Germaine. 1950. *Essai sur la religion bambara.* Paris.

Dundes, Alan. 1964. *The morphology of North American Indian folktales.* Folklore Fellows Communications, no. 195. Helsinki: Academia Scientiarum Fennica.

Fagg, William. 1963. *Nigerian images.* London: Lund Humphries.

Fallers, L. A. 1956. *Bantu bureaucracy*. Cambridge: Cambridge University Press.

Fernandez, James W. 1971. Principles of opposition and vitality in Fang aesthetics. In *Art and aesthetics in primitive societies*, edited by Carol Jopling. New York: E. P. Dutton.

Fischer, John L. 1961. Art styles as cultural cognitive maps. *American Anthropologist* 63, no. 1: 79–93.

Frobenius, Leo. 1924. *Die Muntschi: Ein Urwaldvolk in der Nachbarschaft der sudanischen Kulturvölker*. Part 3 of *Volksdichtungen aus Oberguinea*. Munich: Atlantis.

Geertz, Clifford. 1973. *The interpretation of cultures*. New York: Basic Books.

Griaule, Marcel. 1965. *Conversations with Ogotemmêli*. London: Oxford University Press.

Hall, E. T. 1973. Mental health research and out-of-awareness cultural systems. In *Cultural illness and health: Essays in human adaption*, edited by Laura Nader and Thomas W. Maretzki. Washington: American Anthropological Association.

Hornburg, Friedrich. 1948. Die Musik der Tiv. *Die Musik Forschung* 1: 47–59.

Jahn, Janheinz. 1961. *Muntu: An outline of the new African culture*. New York: Grove Press.

Jones, A. M. 1959. *Studies in African Music*. London: Oxford University Press.

Jones, Le Roi. 1970. *Black music*. New York: William Morrow.

Jopling, Carol F., ed. 1971. *Art and aesthetics in primitive societies*. New York: E. P. Dutton.

Kagame, Alexis. 1956. *La philosophie bantu-rwandaise de l'etre*. Brussels.

Keil, Charles. 1966a. Motion and feeling through music. *Journal of Aesthetics and Art Criticism*, spring.

————. 1966b. *Urban blues*. Chicago: University of Chicago Press.

————. 1969. Review of *Tiv women: The Icough dance*, a film by Francis Speed, Peggy Harper, and Akwe Doma. *American Anthropologist* 70: 1234.

Kennedy, E. L. 1972. The Waunan of the Siguirisua River: A study of individual autonomy and social responsibility with special reference to economic aspects. Ph. D. dissertation, Cambridge University.

Klipple, May Augusta. 1938. African folk tales with foreign analogues. Ph. D. dissertation, Indiana University.

288   Koestler, Arthur. 1964. *The act of creation*. New York: Macmillan.

Lambrecht, Winifred. 1968. A tale type index for central Africa. Ph. D. dissertation, University of California, Berkeley.

Lévi-Strauss, Claude. 1966. *The Savage Mind*. Chicago: University of Chicago Press.

————. 1969. *The raw and the cooked*. New York: Harper and Row.

Lomax, Alan. 1968. *Folk song style and culture*. American Association for the Advancement of Science, publication no. 88. Washington, D. C.

McAllester, David P. 1960. *The role of music in Western Apache culture*. Edited by Jon Anthony and F. C. Wallace. Selected papers of the Fifth International Congress of Anthropological and Ethnological Sciences.

Merriam, Alan P. 1964. *The anthropology of music*. Evanston: Northwestern University Press.

Mills, George. 1957. Art: An introduction to qualitative anthropology. *Journal of Aesthetics and Art Criticism* 16, no. 1: 1–17.

Murray, K. C. 1943. Tiv Pottery. *Nigerian Field* 2: 147–55.

————. 1951. The decoration of calabashes by Tiv (Benue Province). *Nigeria* 36: 469–74.

Otten, Charlotte M., ed. 1971. *Anthropology and art*. Garden City, N. Y.: Natural History Press.

Parsons, T., and Shils, E. A. 1951. *Toward a general theory of action*. Cambridge, Mass.: Harvard University Press.

Propp, Vladimir. 1968. *Morphology of the folktale*. Austin: University of Texas Press.

Roberts, John Storm. 1972. *Black music of two worlds*. New York: Praeger.

Rosaldo, Michelle Zimbalist. 1973. Review of *The affecting presence*, by Robert P. Armstrong. *American Anthropologist* 74: 1461.

Sieber, Roy. 1959. The aesthetic of traditional African art. In *Seven metals of Africa*, edited by Froelich Rainey. Philadelphia: University Museum.

Slater, Philip. 1974. *Earthwalk*. New York: Doubleday.

Smith, Marion W., ed. 1961. *The artist in tribal society*. London: Routledge and Kegan Paul.

Snell, Bruno. 1960. *The discovery of mind*. New York: Harper and Row.

Snyder, Gary. 1969. *Earth house hold*. New York: New Directions.

Tempels, Rev. Placide. 1959. *Bantu philosophy*. Paris: Presence Africaine.

Thompson, Robert F. 1971. *Black gods and kings*. Berkeley: University of California Press.

———. 1974. *African art in motion: Icon and act*. Berkeley: University of California Press.

Tutuola, Amos. 1952. *The palm-wine drinkard*. London: Faber and Faber.

———. 1954. *My life in the bush of ghosts*. London: Faber and Faber.

289

Index of Tiv Terms

abaji, 36, 224, 225 (fig. 14), 230
a bin dedadi, 181
abuku, 68
aco, 49
Adembelia, 66
adigue, 214
adzov, 18, 64, 66, 103, 124, 207, 236, 252. See also sing., *ijov*
Agatu, 249; plates 17, 18
agba, 36
agee agee, 41, 50
agegha, 205
agela, 203
ager ager, 50
Agigben, 149
Ahopue, 119
aie, 36
ajo, 241
akar, 36
akenge, 98, 172. See also sing., *ikenge*
akiki, 70, 165
akombo, 18, 31n, 43, 74–75, 114, 130, 148, 193, 204, 206, 236–37, 247, 252–53
akor, 36
akov, 36, 205
akuul, 266. See also sings., *ikuul*
akuve, 204
alo, 42
alom, 166
Alom, 65–66, 70, 91–92
aluibiam, 98, 122, 152
aman, 48–49, 51, 52n, 70, 108–9, 139, 148, 246, 249
amine, 36, 52
amo, 33, 38, 97, 159, 163, 181, 281. See also sing., *imo*
anger, 108, 117
Anjieke, 65, 92

anyam, 266
anyi, 31
aɔndo, 34–36
asange, 36
Atasa, 246
atemityo, 124
atoon atoon, 42
atsam. See sing., *icam*
atsuku, 236, 239; plate 13
ayem ayem, 41, 51
ayɔɔso, 29

Baja, 123–24
bank, 31
bar dam, 163
baver, 38, 45
Benki, 128
boon, 70
Budeli, 143
bume or, 78, 202
burukutu, 97–98, 104, 126

cagh, 49; plate 5
cia, 129
cien, 162
cov cov, 42

dang dang, 42, 50–51
Dasenda, 250n
dechi, 210 (fig. 7)
deda, 205–6
ding, 60
doo, 42, 46
dough dough, 41
due, 220–21
dugh, 31–33, 35–37, 45, 48, 52, 97, 159, 163, 181–82, 221, 253, 257–58, 266, 281
dzomon, 49–50

292

engem, 44, 76–77
enger, 73

fa, 193
fefa fefa, 41, 50–51
fele fe fele, 41, 50

gaadi, 35
gba, 33–37, 45, 52, 60, 182, 221, 253
gbagir, 125
gbande, 40, 47, 129–30, 142, 241, 242 (fig. 19); plates 6, 7, 8, 21
gbang gbang, 41
Gbangi, 173, 246
gbar gbar, 42, 51
gbedaa gbedaa, 50
gbedoo gbedoo, 50
gbegheleee, 50
gben gben, 42
gber, 34–38, 41–43, 45–46, 52, 182, 221, 254
Gbercul, 247–48; plate 16
Gbev, 65–66
gbor, 205
gbue gbe gbue, 51
gbwidye, 215
gede gede, 91
geen geen, 51
gende gende, 50
genga, 75, 108, 148, 241; plate 5
genger, 38, 41
ger, 38
gercam, 109, 173
gever, 38
gida, 47, 136, 142, 148, 241; plate 4
giegwe, 167
Girnya, 91, 130, 151, 246, 249

Haabuar, 253
Haakaa, 143–44
haav, 205
hambe, 40
hamber, 37
hen, 193
hii, 38
hiin hiin, 41
hom, 165, 167
horkula, 163
hough, 34
hoyo, 253
huer, 65
Hum, 65

hunda, 36
hwa, 70–71
hwange, 203
hwav, 203

ibiamegh, 49, 98, 109, 170, 173–74, 176, 188, 246, 261. See also aluibiam
icam, 29–31, 38, 40, 47–48, 117, 254
ican, 7, 99n, 128, 255; plate 10
icaregh, 114, 165
iceen iceen, 51
Iceghel, 246
ichor, 205
Icough, 247, 249–51; plates 21, 22
icul, 36
idiar, 230
iduwe. See dugh
idyua, 130
ifan, 36–37
ifough, 164
igba, 12–13, 15–16, 18, 66, 133, 149, 191, 193
igbe, 114
igber, 36
igberigbwe, 206
iginde hila, 205
Ihambe, 75, 146, 204
ihange, 205
Ihinga, 65, 79, 246
ihuran, 29
ihwa, 36
ijor, 31
ijov, 81, 143. See also pl., adzov
Ijua, 66
ikavel, 205
ikegh, 36
ikehegh, 164
ikenge (ikyenge), 46–47, 97, 109, 115, 117, 122, 132, 142, 162, 166, 168–70, 173, 175–77, 232, 255. See also pl., akenge
ikoho, 75
ikon, 34
ikov, 205
ikpi, 73
Ikpienger, 73
ikpine, 221
ikur, 66, 68, 206
ikuul, 206. See also pl., akuul
ikyo, 266
ikyuliko, 202–3, 205–6

ilu, 214
ilyu, 91
imar, 49, 70
imborivungu, 70, 93, 132, 166, 253
ime, 20, 36, 44
imo, 29–31, 33, 38 40–43, 46, 48,
   72, 129, 138, 146, 163–65, 182,
   254, 257. See also pl., *amo*
indyer, 47, 75, 91–94, 130, 214, 241
Ingiogh, 246, 248; plates 19, 20
ingol, 108
inja, 27–28, 31–32, 35, 42, 44, 49,
   51, 55, 142, 154
injar, 130n
Inyon, 246
iondo, 132
iov, 29
ipaven, 14–16, 281–82
ishav, 75
ishe, 35
ishima, 36, 193. See also *shima*
ishol, 31, 48–51, 69, 281
ìshól, 48
ishom, 49
ishongo, 108–9
ishor, 129. See also *ishol*
ishu, 31, 228 (fig. 15), 229
itiegh, 213 (fig. 9), 214–15
itseghen, 42
ityɔ, 74
ityɔ, 12–13, 15–16, 18, 74, 107, 109,
   115, 118–19, 141, 191, 193
ityosule, 74
ivaan, 34
ivambe, 36
Ivase, 143
ivav, 36
ivom, 109
ivungu, 70
iwenge, 50, 133
iwer, 215
iyav, 31
iye, 109n
iyiase, 91
iyol, 45–46, 266
Iyon, 135
Iyon man Ikya, 135
iyou, 31
iyouv kera, 31

jande jande, 41
jiagba, 164

Ji Agwai, 129n
Jiagwey, 128–30, 152
Jiga, 246
jighilii, 42
jijingi, 163
jimba jimba, 50
jime, 34
jine gba kpeng kpeng!, 60
Jongur, 66

kakaki, 129
kalangu, 136
kande kande, 41
kasua tugh, 44
kav, kaven, 36, 193
kelen mon, 50
kem, 137
kenda mku, 36–37
kende, 38
kever, 39
kile kile, 42
kimbi, 130n
koho, 75
kon, 34, 36, 254
kor, 37, 130, 266
kov, 205
kpa, 68
kpaam, 68
kpen kpen, 42
kpire, 70
kpo, 205
kpoo kpoo, 51
kpwen, 31n
kpwer, 214
kpwera, 214
kpwer u kumen itiegh, 213 (fig. 9)
ku, 34
kuca, 164
kuhan, 47, 241
kule kule, 50
kule m kule ngu la jo!, 61
Kulugh, 65
kume, 214
kundu kundu, 45
kung ge kung, 51
kure kure, 41
kusa, 216, 217 (figs. 10, 11), 218
   (fig. 12), 220
kusu kusu, 41
kuva, 203
kwagh, 28, 34, 36, 139
kwagh hil, 34, 59, 60, 250n

294

kwagh kuhan, 47, 241
kwase, 31
kwav, 138
Kwaza, 246
kwen, 129, 241, 242 (fig. 19), 243–44; plate 5

legh, 50
logu, 36, 52
luam, 36
lugh, 41, 50

ma, 40, 163–64
maa, 216, 217 (fig. 10, 11), 218 (fig. 12)
mar, 48–49, 70, 266
mbakur, 64, 66
mbakuv, 64, 66, 172, 207
mbatsav, 18, 31n, 34, 66, 70–71, 87, 89, 103, 143–44, 146, 162–63, 165, 172, 219, 248–49, 251–52, 257. See also *tsav*
mgerem mgerem, 36, 164
mil, 40, 138–39, 164
mimi je!, 60
mkali, 224, 225 (fig. 14)
mliam, 38
mmar, 49
mnyam, 162
msorom, 138n, 164
msuram, 163
mtsaan, 70
mtswan, 66

nambe, 130n
namegh, 133, 138
nande, 38
ndera, 39
ndiar, 230, 231 (fig. 17), 232 (fig. 18); plate 15
ndohor, 45
nduruku, 204–6
ngol, 39
ngou gbande, 142, 241, 242 (fig. 19); plates 6, 7, 8, 21
ngurum, 49–50
nombor, 33
nom gbande, 241, 242 (fig. 19); plates 7, 21
nom hur, 164
Nomwange, 206
nongo, 14

Nor, 65, 76, 88
Norkeghkegh, 168
nul a nul, 68
Nyambua, 144
Nyinya, 147, 152
Nyipa, 122
nzughur nzughur, 42

or kwav, 138
or u dughun amo, 33, 97, 159, 181, 281
or u fan kwagh, 202, 283
or u tsorogh gbande, 40
or ya, 12, 98, 282
or yese, 40, 129–30, 134

pati, 124
pav pav, 42
pera pera, 42
piama, 79
poro, 130
pungwa, 203

rumun, 39

saan, 46
seragba, 165
shagba, 11
shagba or, 91, 114, 148
sha mi, 42
shav, 49
sha won, 212
shima, 46, 163. See also *ishima*
shima i mom, 60
shindi, 213 (fig. 9), 214–15
shiva shiva, 129
shoon shoon, 41
sombon, 50
sor, 164
soya, 124
sule, 69, 210 (fig. 7)
swande, 215
Swange, 47, 101, 142, 153, 170, 173–74, 241, 244, 246; plates 3, 4, 5

ta, 39
takerada, 36
tar, 14, 20, 34–35, 44, 70, 74, 245. See also pl., *utar*
tashi, 104
taver taver, 41, 50
tegh tegh, 41, 50

telegh, 49–50

tembe, 208 (fig. 6), 209

ter, 39–40, 79–81, 98

teran, 205

tindi, 34

toho, 34

tom, 34, 43

tondo tondo, 42

tɔɔ, 39

tor, 31, 64–65, 77, 79–81, 93, 138, 281

tsa ishondo, 164

tsar, 35

tsav, 18–19, 21, 33, 89, 143, 162–63, 190, 193, 248, 252–53, 257. See also *mbatsav*

tsee tsee, 42

tsember tsember, 42–43, 50, 254

tsorogh, 40, 46, 52, 173, 175, 177, 232 (fig. 18), 243–44, 255

tsue, 49

tswar, 68

tswar wou fong!, 235

tugh, 34, 44

tugudu, 12

twel (twer), 204, 239–40; pl. 15

Udam, 111

Ukari, 227

ukase, 203

u kura iyol, 102n

ungwa, 34

urum, 20, 44, 245

usu, 36

utar, 16, 210, 211 (fig. 8). See also sing., *tar*

uwer, 213 (fig. 9), 214–15

vaan, 99n, 128

van, 34

vanger, 133

vighe vighe, 42

vihi, 46, 220

vine, vinen, 40, 49

wa, 20, 34–38, 40, 44, 52, 75, 254

wan, 266

wanger, 20, 43–45, 163, 224, 254

wanibiam. See also *aluibiam; ibiamegh*

Wantor, 64

war war, 42

wase, 70

Yar, 65

yese, 40, 52, 129–30, 134

yiagh, 11, 210 (fig. 7)

yiye, 164–65

yohor, 39

yuwa, 39

zamber, 99n

Zambia, 129–30

zelagba, 163

zever zever, 41

zwar, 106

Subject Index

Abende, Agwaza, 101–4
Abrahams, R.C., 9; *Dictionary of the Tiv Language, A,* 9, 33–35, 38–40, 60, 214–15; "Hare and the Leopard," 89; "The Imborivungu Pipe," 70; *The Tiv People,* 9, 39, 56–57, 67, 70–72, 89–90, 139, 204–6, 211–12, 239, 246
Abusive song, 98–99; of Aneke Tire, 141–42; of Auta Anwuna, 113–17; composers' union against, 122; and Anande Amende, 112–13; against sorcery, 144, 146; of women, 156–57
Adagi, Kuhe, 114–15
Adi, Ada, 140, 143–46, 152
Affecting Presence, The (Armstrong), 191, 194–97
Agi, Bashi, 113–16
Agigben, 149
Agriculture, 11; competition of, with dance and song, 74–75, 134. *See also* "Chief's Farm Bet, The"
Agure, Kundam, 153, 162, 164, 166, 169
Akiga's Story (Akiga), 9, 19, 70, 143, 226–27, 240, 244, 246, 252
Akpoo, Theodosius, 151, 161
Akume, Iorcagh, 105
Alom. *See* Hare
Ambi, 105
Amende, Anande, 101, 104–25, 155, 165, 173
Ames, David W., 26
Anchan, Akumba, 146–49, 152–53, 155
Anche, 173
Angularity: in calabash decoration, 215–20; in compounds, 209; in drumming, 243–44; in expressive universe of Tiv culture, 253–57; in posture, 234–35; in sculpture, 238–40; in stools, 207; in walking stick designs, 222. *See also* Circularity
Anjieke, the hare's wife, 81–82
Antelopes, 65
Anthropology: "action theory" in, 6; biases and flaws in, 25–27, 181–83, 197–99; and imperialism, 4–5; master scholars of, 55–56; and Tiv uniqueness, 181–202 passim
Armstrong, Robert P., 191, 194–99, 236–38, 244
Arnott, David W., 159
"Artist and Critic in an African Society" (Bohannon, P.), 216–18, 220–22, 239
"Art Styles as Cognitive Maps" (Fischer), 189–90
Auta, Anwuna, 113–17
Authority: humiliation of, in tales, 64, 78–81 (*see also* "Chief's Farm Bet, The"); power, 32–33; symbols of, 93. *See also* Politics
Aza, 145

Bantus, 10–11, 25
Basongye, 28–29
"Beauty and Scarification amongst the Tiv" (Bohannon, P.), 43, 223–26, 228–31
Bee, 76–77
Beer, and song, 97, 138n
Beidelman, Thomas, 89
Benki, 128
Bente, Adi, 131–35, 140, 152, 155, 165–66, 168

Bente, Zaria, 131, 133–35
Biafran conflict, 2–3
Blacking, John, 26, 170–72
Blau, Richard, 19n
Bodanyi, Naikor, 103
Body parts, 66. *See also* Genitalia
Bohannon, Laura: *Return to Laughter,* 8, 20, 57–58, 156–57
Bohannon, Paul: "Artist and Critic in an African Society," 216–18, 220–22, 239; "Beauty and Scarification amongst the Tiv," 43, 223–26, 228–31; *Justice and Judgement among the Tiv,* 8
Bohannon, Paul and Laura, 234, 259; *Five Sourcebooks in Tiv Religion,* 31n, 66, 107n; *Three Sourcebooks in Tiv Ethnography,* 202–6; *Tiv Economy,* 8, 11–12, 16, 208–11; *Tiv Farm and Settlement,* 8; *The Tiv of Central Nigeria,* 8, 12–14, 36–37, 66, 107n
Bowen, Elenore Smith. *See* Bohannon, Laura
Brown, James, 168n, 233n
Budeli, 143
Buffalo (animal), 65
Buffalo, New York, 17n
Buga, Iorlaha, 162, 164–65
Bunker, H.A., 160
Burke, Kenneth, 56

Calabash decoration, 215–20
Canetti, Elias, 183–86
Cannibalism, tales of, 89–91. *See also* Human sacrifice
Cantometrics, 188–89
Carney, Harry, 148
Carpenter, Edmund, 4
Charms, for composers, 114, 132, 135, 138, 141, 150, 163–67. *See also* Sorcery
Cherry, Don, 45
Chief: humiliation of, 64, 78–81 (*see also* "Chief's Farm Bet, The")
Chief's daughter, 64–65, 82
"Chief's Farm Bet, The" (tale), 66, 77–78, 94–95, 230, 232; version 1 of, 67–70; version 2 of, 72–73; version 3 of, 73–75; version 4 of, 75–76; version 5 of, 76–77; version 6 of, 77

"Chief's Grinding Stone, The" (tale), 82
Chiki, 236, 238
Circularity: in calabash decoration, 216–17; in compound layout, 13–16, 21, 209; in drumming, 243–44; of land possessions, 209–11; in posture, 235; in roof construction, 202–7; in scarification patterns, 223–30; in sculpture, 238–40; in walking stick design, 222. *See also* Angularity; Tiv culture, expressive grid of *and* expressive universe of
Coasters, 181
Competition: among composers, 120–22; in Tiv culture, 21; between Tiv dance groups, 246–47
Composers: assistants of, 133–35, 137, 142, 146, 149, 155; "charm medicine" for, 114, 132, 135, 138, 141, 150, 163–67; competition among, 120–22; court cases involving, 99; distinctive personalities of, 119–20; fathers of 101–2, 106–8; gifts to, 98, 129–30, 132–34, 136, 142–43, 151; identification of, 97; making of, 101–4; raisons d'être of, 152–55; union of, 106, 122; women as, 155–58; women, problems of, 131–32, 161. *See also names of specific composers*
Composition: general procedures of, 167–70; meter in, 172–75; need for isolation in, 159–61, 167; opportunities for, 97–100; role of meditation and dream in, 161–63; Tiv concept of, 31–35, 221–22, 253; and tonal quality, 177; wet/dry motif in, 164; words and melody in, 167–72
Compounds, 12–16, 21, 74, 209
Conductors, 183–85
Cosmetic arts. *See* Scarification
Creation, 34–35, 221–22, 253
Crowds and Power (Canetti), 185
Cuckoldry, 79–82

Dance: composers' opportunities in, 97–98; esthetics of, 45; *Girnya,* 130; *Jiagwey,* 128–30, 153; as life-affirming force, 20–21, 48–49; and melody, 175; metrics of, 172–75; organizational complexity in, 247–

298

Dance (*continued*)
48; seasonal impact on, 74–75; sexual differentiation in, 50–51; terminology of, 47–50; as the ultimate Tiv art, 245–52
D'Azedeo, Warren L., 26
"Decoration of Calabashes by Tiv, The" (Murray), 215–16
"Dog and the Leopard, The" (tale), 90–91
"Drumming the Scandal among Tiv" (Bohannon, P.), 99
Drums and drumming: *genga* set of, 108n; in tales, 74–75, 91–94; technique and intension in, 241–44
Dundes, Alan, 56
Durkheim, Emile, 191
Dwellings: compounds, 12–16, 21, 74, 209; huts, 202–7; roofs, 202–7

Earth House Hold (Snyder), 9n
Earthwalk (Slater), 9n
East, Rupert, 9, 159. See also *Akiga's Story*
Elephant: and anal creation tales, 88; in "The Chief's Farm Bet," 76–77; as stock character, 65
Emotion: in song responses, 45–46; Tiv metaphors for, 32–33
Esthetics, 192; Armstrong's theory of, 194–200; of fertility, 51–52; as glowing, 20, 43–45; Jahn's theory of, 25–26; of jazz, 45; Merriam's framework of, 187; of primitive cultures, 182, 186–87, 191–93; of Tiv song, 40–45, 253–57; of the West, 182–86
Ethnocentrism, 25–26, 182–86 passim, 197–99
Ethos, 56, 258

Fagg, William, 200
Famine, in Tiv tales, 63, 82–87
Fang, 191–93, 240
Fate, Ityavger, 100–101, 103, 153–54, 169
Female/male dialectic. See Opposition; Sexual differentiation; Yin and yang
Fernandez, James, 191–93, 240
Fertility/life force, 20–21, 48–49, 51–52, (tale) 86–87

Fischer, John L., 187, 189–90, 219
Flute, in Tiv tales, 55–56, 67–70
Folk Song Style and Culture (Lomax), 187–89
Framing: to determine word meanings, 30–40; in tales, 60–61
Freud, Sigmund, 55
Frobenius, Leo, 56–57, 67, 88
Fullstop, Gypsy, 2–3, 238

Geertz, Clifford, 6
Genitalia: as characters in Tiv tales, 66, 81, 94; in scar designs, 230–33
Gifts, to composers, 98, 129–30, 132–34, 136, 142–43, 151
Gindi, Bam, 104, 122, 132, 260, 266
Gindi, Hule, 104
Girnya, 130
Glossary of Hausa Music and Its Social Contexts (Ames and King), 26
Glowing, 43–45
Gorozo, Tarker No. 1, 101
Gyenku, Aku, 168

Haakaa, 143–44
Hall, Edward T., 14n, 234
Hare: in anal creation tale, 87–88; in the "Chief's Grinding Stone," 82–85; in food sharing tale, 81–82; in millet tales, 78–79; as stock tale character, 65–66. See also "Chief's Farm Bet, The" *and following entries*
"Hare and the Leopard" (Abraham), 89
"Hare's Indyer, The" (tale), 91–92
Hare's wife, 81–82
Harmony, 46
Heat and cold, 45
Hornburg, Friedrich, 159
Horses, 147–49
Huer, the Iguana, 65
Human sacrifice, in Tivland, 71–72; in Western culture, 186. See also Cannibalism
Hut construction, 202–7
"Hyena and Rabbit: A Kaguru Representation of Matrilineal Relations" (Beidelman), 89

Idealism, 6–7

Igbo, 2–3
Iguana, 65
Ihambe, 75–76, 110
Ihinga, the squirrel, 65, 79–81
Ijov, 143
Ikyo, Anyor, 146–47, 149
Imbor, Adura, 140–42, 144–45
"Imborivungu Pipe, The" (Abraham), 70
Ime, Frank, 131–40 passim
Imperialism, and anthropology, 4–5. *See also* Western civilization, impact of on Tivland
Indyar, Abur, 130
In Search of the Primitive (Diamond), 9n
Ivase, 143
Iyongo, Hura, 135–40, 163–64, 168
Iyum, Kuji, 153–55, 165, 167, 173, 181

Jagger, Mick, 233n
Ja'gusa, Tarwanger, 51n
Jahn, Janheinz, 25–26
Jakobson, 55
Jazz, 45, 148
Jiagwey, 128–30, 153
Jung, Carl, 55
Justice and Judgement among the Tiv (Bohannon, P.), 8

Kagame, Alexis, 25
Keil, Charles, 174n, 243n
Kinesics (posture), 234–35
King, Anthony V., 26
Kinship: and dance competitions, 246–47; general characteristics of, in Tivland, 12–16; impact of, on art, 190–91; and land possession, 210
Kirk, Roland, 148n
Kulugh, the tortoise, 65
Kwaghbo, Gari, 152, 154–55, 174
Kwande, Ikpamkor. *See* Amende, Anande

Land possession, 209–11
Leopard, 89–91
Lévi-Strauss, Claude, 55–56, 183
Lineage. *See* Kinship
Linguistics, 26–32
Lomax, Alan, 176n, 187–89

London, Ikpamkor. *See* Amende, Anande
Lullaby, 172

McAllester, David P., 26
Male/female dialectic. *See* Opposition; Sexual differentiation; Yin and yang
Marxism, 6–7
Materialism, 6–7
Medicine, for composers, 114, 132, 135, 138, 141, 150, 163–67
Melody: composition of, 168–72; and dance, 175; interval patterns in, 263–65; terminology for, 46–47
Merriam, Alan, 6, 28–29, 187
Meter, 172–75
Migration: of Tiv malcontents, 16; of Tiv myth, 17; of Tiv society, 10–11
Missions and missionaries, 100, 109–10
Mondo, Kaa, 149–52, 154–55, 161, 164–65, 168
Monkeys, 65
Munsterberger, Werner, 160
Muntu: An Outline of the New African Culture (Jahn), 25
Murray, Kenneth, 181, 212–16, 220
Music, absence of word for, 27–29

Narratives. *See* Tales; Taletelling
Nightjar, 65–66
Noise: in Basongye culture, 28–29; in Tivland, 29–30
Nomwhange, Maza, 153, 165–66
Nor. *See* Elephant
Northern People's Congress, 123
Nyambua, 144
Nyamikongo, Jato, 153

Oedipus complex, 160
Opposition, 45, 191–93, 257–58. *See also* Sexual differentiation; Yin and yang
Otten, Charlotte M., 186
"Orchestral Conductor, The" (Canetti), 183–85
Owl pipe, 70

Paths, 209–11
Percussion. *See* Drums and drumming

300

Perfectionism: in dance, 247; in song, 40–46, 51
Phallic: bees, 76–77; flutes, 67–70; pipes, 70–71; song, 168n, 233n; tales, 67–70, 73–77
Politics: compositional opportunities in, 99, 122–24; of disease, 19–20; power, 32–33; role of song in, 257–58; as source of divisiveness among composers, 122–124; "without rulers," 10, 17, 186. *See also* Authority; United Middle Belt Congress
Posture, 234–35
Pottery, 212–15
Power, 32–33
Praise singing, 37, 39, 98, 133. *See also* Abusive song; Song
"Principles of Opposition and Vitality in Fang Aesthetics" (Fernandez), 191–93
Propp, Vladimir, 55–56
Proxemics, 234–35

Raw and the Cooked, The (Lévi-Strauss), 183
Religion. *See* Tiv Culture, religion of
Residences. *See* Compounds
Return to Laughter (Bohannon, L.), 8–9, 20, 57–58, 156–57
Rhythm, 46–47
"Role of the Storyteller in Relation to the Esthetic, The" (Armstrong), 198
Roof construction, 202–7

Scarification, 43–44, 223–34
Schneider, David, 6
Scholarship, idealism and materialism in, 6–7
Sculpture, 192, 197, 236–37
Seasons: and dance performance, 247; and song, 134
Sememes, 30–40
Sex: and song, differentiated (tale), 78; in Tiv tales, 63, 78, 79–82. *See also* Genitalia; Sexual differentiation
Sexual differentiation: and artistic style, 190–91, 197; in dance 50–51, 248–49, 251–52; in drumming, 241–43; in roof construction, 204–5; and scarification, 226–27, 229–34; in status, 10

Sieber, Roy, 26
Slater, Philip, 9n
Snell, Bruno, 181
Snyder, Gary, 9n
Song: anal creation theme in, 87–89; attribution of, 97; and beer, 97, 138n; Christian uses of, 100; in collections of Tiv tales, 56–57; competition of, with agriculture, 134; devining powers of (tale), 81–82; dynamics of, 41; endings for, 181; expressive universe of, 253–57; lack of improvisation in, 177; as a life force, 20–21, (tale) 86–87; and lifestyle, 188–89; melodic interval patterns in, 263–65; and sex, differentiated (tale), 78; as solution to critical Tiv problems, 94–95, 257–58; structure of, 176, 261–62; technique in, 45–46; Tiv adverbs for, 40–46, 51; Tiv verbs for, 35–40; tonal quality of, 175–77, 262; words and melody of, 167–72. *See also* Abusive song; Composition; Praise singing
Sorcery, 89; campaign against, 143–44; and the imborivungu pipe, 70–71; powers of, 32–33. *See also* Composers, "charm medicine" for
Soul, 19, 252–53
Squirrel, 65, 79–81
Stools, 207

Tales: of famine or hunger, 63, 82–87, of sex, song, and food, 79–82; stock characters in, 64–66; themes of, 63–64. *See also names of specific tales and characters*
Taletelling, 245; as dramatic event, 57–59, 63; endings of, 61, 63; morals in, 61, 63; opening formats for, 60–61, 245; settings for, 59–60, 63; structure in, 61–62; by women, 59–60
Technique: in drumming, 241–44; in song, 45–46; in taletelling, 60–61
Tempels, Rev. Placide, 25
Terminology: of creation/composition, 34–35, 221–22, 253; of music, 25–30; of pottery making, 214–15; of song, 35–52
Thompson, Robert F., 26

Thompson, Stith, 55
Tire, Aneke, 140–43, 152, 167–69
Tiv culture: age-grades among, 139–40, 205; Bantu origins of, 10–11; communal art of, 220–22; and contemporary anthropological theory, 181–202 passim; expressive grid for, 200–202; expressive universe of, 253–57 (see also Angularity; Circularity); insecurity in, 190–91 (see also Song, as solution to critical Tiv problems); law in, 17; military reputation of, 10, 99; musicianship in, 17–18; myths in, 17, 186; paranoia in, 20–21; religion of, 18–20, 251–52; and the West, 10, 21–22, 143–44, 236–37. See also Composers; Composition; Dance; Politics; Song; Sorcery; Tales; Taletelling; and names of specific cultural products
Tiv Economy (Bohannons), 8, 11–12, 16, 208–11
Tiv Farm and Settlement (Bohannons), 8
Tiv of Central Nigeria, The (Bohannons), 8, 12–14, 36–37, 66, 107n
Tiv People, The (Abrahams), 9, 39, 56–57, 67, 70–72, 89–90, 139, 204–6, 211–12, 239, 246
Tiv Women: The Icough Dance (Harper), 249–51
Tor. See Chief
Tortoise, 65
Trees, 207
Tutuola, Amos, 62, 199

Ugye, Chen, 127–31, 152, 162, 164
Ukura, Jato, 169
United Middle Belt Congress, 123–24, 128
Utege, Agojo, 161, 168

"Voice as a Female Phallus, The" (Bunker), 160
Villages. See Compounds

Walking sticks, 220–22
Wanikya, Iorlumun, 101
Wantor (chief's daughter), 64–65, 82
Wasp, 75–76
Wellspring: On the Myth and Source of Culture (Armstrong), 237
Werna, Joseph, 159
Western civilization: concept of art and culture in, 181–87, 194n; impact of on Tivland, 10, 143–44, 236–37; and Tiv society, compared, 21–22, 258
Wildebeest, 65
Women: abusive songs of, 156–57; as characters in Tiv tales, 64–65; as composers, 155; taletelling by, 59–60. See also Sexual differentiation
World map (stooping man), 18, 211–12

Yakobu, Joe, 127, 129
Yaven, Aciv, 128
Yin and yang, 181. See also Opposition; Sexual differentiation
Yoruba, 194–200 passim, 236–37, 243